Thomas P. Ryan

DISCIPLINES
for Christian Living

Interfaith Perspectives

Paulist Press ◆ *New York/Mahwah, N.J.*

The Publisher gratefully acknowledges use of the following quotations, used with permission:

Quotations from, "Keeping Sunday," by Gertrude M. Nelson, *New Catholic World*, March/April, 1987, p. 58; "When You Fast. . . A Biblical and Patristical Survey," by Joseph F. Wimmer, OSA, *New Catholic World*, March/April, 1988, p. 65; Teresa of Avila, *The Interior Castle*, translated by Kieran Kavanaugh, O.C.D. and Otilio Rodriguez, O.C.D., pp. 96, 100, 101, 130, copyright © 1974, Paulist Press, Mahwah, New Jersey; "Confessions of a Former Sabbath Breaker," by Eugene Peterson, *Christianity Today*, 1988; "Family Life: A School for Holiness," by Thomas Ryan, CSP, *Our Family*, Vol. 36, No. 8, Sept. 1985, pp. 26–27; "Father Without Children," by Thomas Ryan, CSP, *Marriage and Family Living*, Vol. 69, No. 9, Sept. 1987, pp. 12–13; quotations from *Prayers for the Domestic Church*, copyright © 1979, Forest of Peace Books, Easton, Kansas, pp. 112–113; quotations from *Table Prayer*, by Gabe Huck, copyright © 1980, Liturgy Training Publications, Chicago, Illinois, p. 25; *Prayers for the Domestic Church: A Handbook for Worship in the Home*, by Edward Hays, copyright © 1979, Forest of Peace Books, Inc., Easton, Kansas 66020; reprinted with permission.

Library of Congress Cataloging-in-Publication Data

Ryan, Thomas P., 1946–
    Disciplines for Christian living : Interfaith perspectives /
Thomas P. Ryan.
        p.   cm.
    Includes bibliographical references.
    ISBN 0-8091-3380-6 (pbk.)
    1. Spiritual formation.   2. Spiritual life.   3. Christianity and
other religions.   I. Title.
BV4501.2.R89   1993
248.4–dc20   92-42596
                                                                    CIP

Published by Paulist Press
997 Macarthur Boulevard
Mahwah, New Jersey 07430

Printed and bound in the
United States of America

Contents

DEDICATION

To my brother and sisters
and their spouses
Mary Jane and Bill
Daniel and Mary Claire
Michael and Pamela
Kevin and Denise

Appreciations

I am deeply grateful to:

Ann Herbert and Eliane Massoud for their invaluable assistance in the preparation of this manuscript;

Pat O'Rourke, John Borelli, and Francis McKee for their helpful comments on particular chapters;

Sharon Smith for her meticulous proofreading and attention to detail;

my colleagues at the Canadian Centre for Ecumenism for their expressions of interest, encouragement and support at various stages in the writing process; and

Larry Boadt, CSP, for his editorial guidance.

Heartfelt thanks!

"Until one is committed, there is hesitancy, the chance to draw back, always ineffectiveness, concerning all acts of initiative (and creation). There is one elementary truth the ignorance of which kills countless ideas and splendid plans: that the moment one definitely commits oneself, then Providence moves too. All sorts of things occur to help one that would never otherwise have occurred. A whole stream of events issues from the decision, raising in one's favour all manner of unforeseen incidents and meetings and material assistance which no man could have dreamed would have come his way. Whatever you can do or dream you can, begin it. Boldness has genius, power and magic in it. Begin it now."

JOHANN WOLFGANG VON GOETHE

Foreword

Thomas Ryan has written a very broadminded, eminently practical and deeply personal book about the Christian life. The question that has guided him is not so much "What is the Christian life" but: "How to live the Christian life on a day to day basis?"

I am convinced that this book will be of great help and support to the many people who have a deep faith in Jesus but are at a loss when they look for ways to practice it in their busy and always changing lives. I have been often challenged by remarks such as: "What you say about God's love is beautiful, but tell me what I have to do to make it real for me!" or "I love your beautiful vision, but please give me some concrete guidelines to make it useful!" or "I really understand what you say about the death and resurrection of Jesus. But tell me how to make it more than something comforting to think about!" or "I know the 'what' and even the 'why,' but please tell me the 'how'."

There has been a certain hesitancy to deal with the "how" of the Christian life. There even has been a certain disdain for methods, techniques and strategies in the life of the Spirit, as if these concrete practical matters were too mundane and not truly spiritual. But for people with little free time, many demands for their attention, large circles of family and friends, and countless choices to make about what to do and where to go and with

1

whom to live and work, the Christian life cannot remain a vague ideal to strive for. It has to be as concrete, practical and useful as daily life itself.

When Thomas Ryan took a sabbatical and went to India to study the religions of the Hindus, the Buddhists and the Moslems, he was most struck by their practices. In India he came to realize that there was nothing wrong with the "How to do it?" question and that all the great Hindu, Buddhist and Moslem teachers taught their disciples very practical disciplines to transform their lives. He became deeply convinced that unless Christians offer similar disciplines, the Christian faith will never become a truly transforming faith, with concrete and specific implications for daily life.

Fr. Ryan offers in this book several disciplines that can help us very directly to put in practice what we believe. He speaks about friendship, marriage, sabbath, exercise, play, prayer, fasting and service in ways that teach the "how" of the Christian life.

What makes these disciplines so appealing is their universal as well as their personal quality. While deeply anchored in his own Christian tradition, the author shows a wonderful openness to the gifts of Buddhism, Hinduism and Moslem religion. He discovers their great wisdom for the spiritual life of the Christian and does not hesitate to bring that wisdom home. He also listens carefully to some of the great rabbinic teachers and rediscovers there the beauty of the Jewish sabbath traditions.

But more important still than the universal quality of the disciplines that Thomas Ryan proposes is their very personal quality. He does not speak about anything he has not tried to live himself. Tom's personal stories about his attempts to live a disciplined life make this such an attractive book. He is a credible witness since he is so clearly a man struggling with all the problems of the ambitious, hardworking, perfectionistic, somewhat compulsive western executive. He knows all too well what it means to be busy, to move often from place to place and to be always victimized by new urgencies and emergencies. His personal stories about successes and failures in living a disciplined life in today's world make this book much more than a guide to Christian living. It is the testimony of a Christian who takes his faith very seriously and who wants to live it here and now.

I have increasingly experienced discipline in the Christian life as a concentrated effort to create space for God. There is such a fear of emptiness in our inner lives as well as in our society that any vacancy is often filled up before we get there. How can we truly listen to God's voice and discern the movements of God's Spirit, when all our lives are filled up with busyness and worries? The disciplines that Thomas Ryan writes about are all ways to create some open spaces and to keep them open so that God can truly transform us and guide us to where the deepest desires of our hearts can be fulfilled.

Disciplines in the Christian life are not ways to do God's work or to mold ourselves into sanctity, nor are they methods to control our own destiny and accomplish our own goals. They are simply hedges around the garden where God can meet us and speak to us. When we object "But God does not need a special garden; God can meet me at any place," we have forgotten that without a special garden to spend special time with God, we might not be able to recognize God's presence at other, less prepared places. Jesus repeatedly says: "Be prepared, be ready, be awake and alert." Disciplines are the concrete ways to live a life with a prepared, ready, alert and awakened heart, so that we can hear the voice of love and fearlessly follow its call.

Fr. Ryan went to India to learn from spiritual traditions other than his own. He brought home many treasures and offers them to us in the book. Living in Toronto and seeing new Hindu and Buddhist temples and new mosques and synagogues being built all over the place, I realize that the east and the west are no longer so far away from each other as before. Even without a far journey we can become aware of the many treasures that different religions have to offer us. In this sense a wholly new, wider ecumenism is becoming possible, allowing us to grow always deeper in the Spirit of love. Its goal is not the unity being sought by Christian churches, but increased understanding and respect. Tom has made an important contribution to interfaith relations. Further, with the inspiration offered to him by various religious traditions, he has given us very practical, direct and concrete answers to the question, "Tell me, how do I live my Christian life today?"

Henri J.M. Nouwen

Introduction: Let's Get Practical

As I sat one afternoon in the Shankar cafe in Rishikesh, one of India's Hindu pilgrimage sites on the banks of the Ganges river, I overheard a conversation between two clean-cut westerners in their mid-thirties—one German, one English—which made me feel as though I were in a scene in a Woody Allen movie:

"Have you ever had an experience of your *kundalini* rising?"

"An enlightenment experience? Yes."

"So have I. I awoke one morning with a very heightened consciousness. Reading the German philosopher Friedrich Schleiermacher, I could see the fallacies in his arguments as if by some illuminating insight. I felt an intense call to enter onto a path of self-realization. Within a month I had sold my house and come to India."

When the German left, the Englishman engaged me in conversation.

"Do you believe in reincarnation? I feel it explains a lot," he volunteered, and provided several examples.

I listened and then, drawing upon Christian faith, offered other ways of interpreting the events presented in his examples. He seemed a complete stranger to Christian concepts.

"Who is your guru?" he wanted to know.

"Jesus."

"Ah, yes, he's a good one. I think he must have been born in India, too!" he said with a wry grin.

Several conversations of this nature, which occurred in the course of a sabbatical in India studying other world religions, served as a catalyst for this book. The guest rooms in Indian ashrams and Buddhist monasteries are populated, it seems, with more westerners than natives. The word seems to have gone out in the West that God is alive and well and living in India.

An ashram is a place where people engaged in relentless quest for God live together under the guidance of one experienced in "God-realization." It is a forest academy in the spiritual life, a place of prayer conceived according to the Indian tradition where people come to find that restful awareness and to realize God in the inner depths of their own being.

In my conversations with westerners of all stripes in these ashrams, a constant refrain emerged: "Christianity doesn't teach us techniques and methods that serve as sure supports for our path."

A similar response came from a Hindu swami to a question as to why so many people leave Western religions for those of the East. "Because Judaism and Christianity are not teaching them practically. I am teaching them practically. Love of God is being taught both in the Bible and the Bhagavad Gita. But today's religionists are not actually teaching how to love God. I am teaching how. That is the difference."

It is to such critiques of Christianity that this volume seeks to make a modest response. The number of young people turning to the East would seem to indicate that we have not done a very effective job in teaching *sadhanas* or spiritual disciplines proper to our own religious tradition. But there can be no doubt that we do have them.

In these pages my aim is to set forth several disciplines for the contemporary Christian which are drawn from the treasure chest of Christian spirituality and practice and with which I have personal experience. This line of development forms the mainstream current of these pages. Into this river, however, will flow streams and rivulets which take their origin in other religions. These supplementary flows represent currents which I have discovered in other religions and found to be life-giving. As this awareness has led me to appropriate them for my own spiritual journey, they are integrated into my treatment of various disciplines for Christian living. By so doing, I wish to give clear witness to the salutary benefits for Christian living of openness to whatever is good and true in the experience of other religions in our common quest for communion with God.

In 1962, Thomas Merton wrote: "The 'universality' and 'catholicity' which are essential to the Church necessarily imply an ability and a readiness to enter into dialogue with all that is pure, wise, profound and humane in every kind of culture. In this one sense at least a dialogue with Oriental wisdom becomes necessary. A Christian culture that is not capable of such a dialogue would show, by that very fact, that it lacked catholicity."[1] In the late sixties, he condemned narrow understandings of catholicity: "The 'Catholic' who is the aggressive specimen of a ghetto Catholic culture, limited, rigid, prejudiced, negative, is precisely a non-Catholic, at least in the cultural sense. Worse still, he may be anti-Catholic in the cultural sense and perhaps even, in some ways, religiously, without realizing it."[2]

In the twenty-five years since Merton wrote those lines, the dialogues among Christians and adherents of other world religions have become a significant religious phenomenon. As communications have turned the world into a global village, economic, political, ecological and military interdependencies have linked our futures and our fates. "There will be no peace among nations until there is peace among religions," Gandhi declared. People today interested in cross-cultural understanding have come to realize the truth of his words. Interreligious dialogue is no longer a hobby for the specialist but a requisite for the conscientious citizen of the human family.

Christians often speak about Christ as the final word, that in him we have the fullness. But the fullness of Christ is in the future, not in the past. It is something to be achieved, not something given, like a ready-made blueprint which only has to be played out. And it cannot be achieved without the co-creation in freedom and dialogue of the different living faiths with each other and in collaboration with the Spirit of God. If the Church really believes in the universality of the Mystery it witnesses to then it must dare to cross religious frontiers and share in the experience of other religions.[3]

Most books on world religions approach them through their *diversity*, examining them objectively and academically from the outside. Other books approach the religions looking for a certain *unity*, a common ground based upon what they all share. A third approach is that of *complementarity*; instead of trying to show what the religions have in common or how they differ from each other, it recognizes each one as unique. According to complementarity, the world religions illuminate one another, acquainting us with insights that have escaped us and that enhance and clarify our most basic spiritual commitments. In addition to these three approaches there is a fourth, the way of *awareness and appropriation*,[4] which most characterizes this book.

"Awareness" simply refers to the discovery of wisdom for the spiritual life in some religion other than our own. "Appropriation" implies a process of examination, reflection, and integration of this wisdom into our own quest for union with God. Those who have had the opportunity for personal, involved, existential exchanges with adherents of other religions learn a surprising truth: these encounters have the unexpected effect of making one take a renewed interest in one's own heritage. Our examination of how we might integrate this new-found wisdom into our own life situations and actions brings new insights into our spiritual lives. The approach of awareness and appropriation leads to enriched self-understanding and the discernment of the driving forces of our own religion. "The Christian life, and especially the contemplative life," Merton decided, "is a continual discovery of Christ in new and unexpected places."[5]

Our first step, however, will be in the direction of developing a positive sense of the meaning and place of discipline in the spiritual life. Only when one clearly sees the role of discipline in Christian living and becomes convinced of the necessity of faithful practice does it make any sense to consider particular means.

Jesus' life included regular periods of solitude, prayer, fasting, time with friends, as well as a freely embraced life-style of simplicity, contemplation in the midst of an active life and availability for service in love. As I participated in various programs of studies in Hindu ashrams, Buddhist monasteries, and at the Henry Martyn Institute for Islamic Studies, I came to the conclusion that one of our most serious failures in Christianity is that we have not provided effective practical guidance as to how to live the life of Jesus.

The experience of sitting in on teachings being given by the Hindu swamis or Buddhist lamas is one of being introduced to a science of life in the spirit, the knowledge of which has evolved slowly and passed through the scrutiny and personal experience of wise and dedicated people each step of its long development. They have studied the workings of the mind and the senses and the nature of consciousness in a scientific manner and have deduced methods and techniques in light of their learning to serve people's quest for a higher spiritual consciousness. Christians have similar teachers, called Church Fathers and Mothers or Doctors of the Church. We are in the midst of a popular revival and rediscovery of their teachings, but we need more reliable guides who have translated these teachings into their lives and who can provide counsel for other seekers.

While sitting in ashrams and monasteries and listening to very practical and concrete teachings relating to things like breathing, posture, and the use of a sacred word in meditation, I found myself reflecting on the minimal extent to which we, in the life of Christian communities, teach people how to pray, how to meditate, how to develop and cultivate awareness and appreciate its relationship to God-consciousness. Our inclination is more toward lessons to memorize, books to read—approaches which operate on an intellectual plane but which do not take the mind down into the heart. A "head trip" of mental assent to doctrine is quietly substituted for a rigorous practice of discipleship that would bring a true transformation of character.

Trappist Fr. Thomas Keating, who is one of the leaders in a North American renewal of contemplative spirituality, says he finds "most Catholics starving at a well-stocked table of Catholic tradition. It's like food with a cover on it. No one bothers taking off the cover so they start looking around other tables—like Hinduism and Buddhism—and the dishes are very good. People feel helped by them."[6]

This was the late Anthony de Mello's appeal in the West. He grew up in Hindu India with an appreciation for techniques to aid one's spiritual development. He benefited from the wisdom of the Bhagavad Gita and the Upanishads and the Dharma of the Buddha. He found their points of resonance with Christian faith and he brought Eastern methods and techniques to a Christian West hungry for practical assistance but with few gurus to teach. Not surprisingly, his most popular book *Sadhana* is a series of "spiritual exercises," of concrete methods and techniques.

The Christian religion needs to recover its own rich tradition, which is safe and sound and very nourishing. But it needs to address the contemporary context in which people presently live and be responsive to the positive concerns that characterize our culture. Spirituality for today must be holistic. Physical, emotional and mental health and well-being must be seen as directly related to one's spiritual growth and development. Some readers may be surprised to see friendship and family life, or exercise and play, treated in this book as disciplines of the spiritual life. But if we are not taking time to share life with those we love, or to tend to our physical and mental health, ours will not be a Christian, incarnational spirituality.

1

The Meaning of Discipline
for Christian Living

By discipline I mean that which disposes and liberates us to realize, through the working of the Holy Spirit, what is deepest and best in us. The spiritual journey is a process of liberation, of unfolding, much like the petals of a flower in the light of the morning sun. The human spirit is set free to discover union with God, at-one-ment with our true selves, with others and with nature. Living this truth requires discipline, hard work, the giving up of cherished illusions, comforting security, and false pride.[1] The rewards are great, however, and the freedom and union that result make it worth all the effort.

We need more transformed and transforming people. The latest representative figures about the various religious allegiances that the present five billion or so inhabitants of our planet display indicate that virtually one of every three people is accounted a Christian and that Christians are found in all 254 countries surveyed.[2]

Yet one does not get a sense of Christianity as a guide to life for the nations and for humanity. It has not been faithful to its own message and taken seriously human transformation—divinization, in the language of the Christian East—as a practical issue to be dealt with in real terms.

But by what realistic methods and means are we to realize this transformation? How can the ordinary individuals who make up our congregations enter into the fullness of the Christ-life, becoming like him in character, attitude and action? Why are not our local parish communities "academies in the spiritual life"?

We think of Christ's power entering our lives in various ways: through liturgical ritual and the preaching of the Word, through the presence of the Spirit in our daily lives, through personal prayer and reading. Unquestionably, all of these are beneficial. Why is it though that these ways do not reliably produce large numbers of people who really are like Christ in their attitudes and actions?

We evidently need to take a deeper look at our commitment to these and other disciplines which can guide us into a constant, daily interaction with the Spirit of God who leads us to meet and abide with our Creator and our Savior. Let us begin by taking a closer look at the meaning of discipline in the Christian tradition of spirituality by way of analogy.

My sister and her husband gave me a unique birthday present of a gift certificate entitling me to a one-hour massage. I set up the appointment and reported to the health clinic. The masseur directed me to the steam cabinet to get the circulation flowing to the surface of my skin. I then showered and lay down on the massage table, relaxed and ready to be acted upon.

Then the expert and knowledgeable fingers of the masseur began to probe and knead. His sensitive touch unerringly sought and found areas of tension and went to work unknotting them to allow the vitalizing flow of energy to freely pass through where circulation had moments ago been blocked. For days afterward, I felt a special aura of energy emanating from me. I felt more peaceful, centered, rooted. I was amazed at the secret reserves which those knowing hands had tapped and sent into service.

That's what the disciplines of Christian living do: they prepare us, dispose us to be acted upon by the Spirit of God whose probing, expert touch heals, unbinds, restores and releases new vitality for fuller living. The Spirit's specific role is to mold and shape us, and our role is to yield our embodied selves to the life-giving hands of the quickening Spirit.

The disciplines of the spiritual life are carefully-evolved ways of consciously assisting in the work of the Holy Spirit to remove the roadblocks and make straight the pathways to gospel living. They are activities undertaken to bring us into more effective cooperation with Christ.

Spiritual disciplines effect a shift in focus—from ourselves to God—which is the beginning of healing and change. Such change toward wholeness is God's work, not ours. We participate by making space for God to work; our role is one of active consent and collaboration.[3]

Teresa of Avila lived in 16th century Spain where, as a contemplative, teacher, poet, and reformer of the Carmelite order, she lived an extremely active life. In *The Interior Castle* she writes (under obedience) about the various dwelling places leading up to the highest union with Christ. She stresses that the practice of a spiritual discipline is particularly essential at the beginning of the spiritual journey as a means of developing the foundations of the contemplative dimension of life: dedication and devotion to God and service to others. Our daily practice should include a time where we dispose ourselves in receptivity to God. She uses a beautiful analogy "to help us see how, even though we can do nothing in this work done by the Lord, we can do much by disposing ourselves so that His Majesty may grant us this favor."

The soul does no more in this union than does the wax when another impresses a seal on it. The wax doesn't impress the seal upon itself; it is only disposed—I mean by being soft. And even in order to be disposed it doesn't soften itself but gives its consent. O Goodness

*of God. . . ! All you want is our will and that there be
no impediment in the wax.*[4]

REMOVING IMPEDIMENTS FROM THE WAX

The metaphors of massage and the shaping of wax provide
an insight into the basic meaning of the word asceticism, which
denotes the artful shaping of a material. It is derived from the
Greek verb *askein*, to practice, to exercise, to labor, or in a
secondary meaning, to provide, furnish or adorn. As a noun, it
refers to training, exercise, diet. In classical literature, the term is
used with reference to technical adornment and artistic effort, as
well as with reference to mental and spiritual endeavors. Its import is positive and affirming. Asceticism is a matter of working
with a suitable material or means to adapt it to a desired end.

In the spiritual life, one might be considered to be ascetic
because one is interested in the artful handling of creation, the
artful forming of one's life into something beautiful for God. The
material with which one toils is one's own embodied self, and
thus it is that the spiritual person takes the "wax" in hand and
works to remove the impediments so that the impress of God
might be more clearly discernible. This involves setting priorities
whereby we forego lesser values for greater, and making choices
which may involve sacrificing certain worthwhile things for the
sake of supreme worth.

But the spirit of these disciplines which classical Christian
spirituality has called ascetical is the longing and desire to be like
Jesus. This is what attracts us to them, and this is what prevents
them from becoming ends in themselves or a form of bondage.
The activities constituting these disciplines may have some limited
value in themselves, but if in the end what we have done or given
up has not made us more gentle, compassionate, generous and
loving, then it simply wasn't worth the time and energy, for it failed

to bring us to deeper communion with the mind and heart of God. The aim of the spiritual life is not a body cleansed by fasting or an ability to cite scriptural chapter and verse or to focus one's attention without distraction through meditation. The goal of our heart's quest is communion with God. For that were we made, and "our hearts are restless until they rest in God" (Augustine).

What this makes clear is that a discipline is undertaken to prepare us for some activity other than itself. The skater works out with roller blades, the tennis or baseball player hits back endless balls shot out of a machine, the gymnast is faithful to stretching exercises not because they aspire only to this but because these exercises prepare them for what they really want.

The spiritual life does not consist in mere individual betterment or assiduous attention to one's own soul, but in a free and unconditional response to the Spirit's pressure and call, whatever the cost may be. Any practice which focuses attention on ourselves, and puts us with our small ideas and projects in the foreground, misses the mark. The disciplines, perceived as disposing us for what God wants, deliver us from all fuss about ourselves and prevent us from feeling self-important about our own little spiritual adventures while at the same time making them worthwhile as part of the great and secret economy of God.

PARTICIPATION IN GOD?

The view of humanity prevailing among Eastern Orthodox Christians is based upon the notion of "participation" in God. The human person has not been created as an autonomous or self-sufficient being; one's very nature is truly itself only inasmuch as it exists "in God" or "in grace." The most important aspect of Greek patristic anthropology is the notion that we only realize our true humanity when we live "in God" and possess divine qualities.

The presence in us of divine qualities, of a grace which is part of our nature and which makes us fully human, neither destroys our freedom nor limits the necessity for us to realize our full potential by our own efforts. The presence in us of grace secures that cooperation or "synergy" between the divine will and human choice which makes possible our assimilation to the divine dignity for which we were created. We are called to share in the "deified" humanity of Christ. "God became human," as St. Athanasius put it, "so that humans might become God."

A spirituality which is an *imitation* of Christ has no great following in the Christian East. Christianity is life *in Christ*, a life that is not merely metaphorical. It is in Christ that a true communion with God is made possible. The idea of synergy represents the doctrine of Eastern Christians on the question of human transformation or communion with the divine. For the entire patristic and Byzantine tradition, knowledge of God implies "participation" in God, i.e., not only intellectual knowledge, but a state of the entire human being, transformed by grace and freely cooperating with it by efforts—disciplines—of mind, body, and will. "Participation" in God is our very nature, not its abolition.

> *His divine power has given us everything needed for life and godliness, through the knowledge of him who called us by his own glory and goodness. Thus he has given us, through these things, his precious and very great promises, so that through them you may escape from the corruption that is in the world and may become participants of the divine nature* (2 Peter 1:3–4).

". . . So that you . . . may become participants of the divine nature." Our sacred scriptures provide us with any number of such bold assertions. Are they to be taken realistically or only metaphorically? St. Paul says, "So if anyone is in Christ, there is a new creation: everything old has passed away; see, everything

has become new!" (2 Cor. 5:17) But what has become new?
What, in fact, is there to "see"? Is the power of the Holy Spirit for
real, does it actually change lives?

Evangelical pastor and writer Dallas Willard effectively
frames the question when he observes that, after many years of
ministerial efforts in a wide range of denominational settings, it
became clear to him that what Christians are normally told to do
was not advancing them spiritually. Go to church. Give generously in the collection. Pray. Read the scriptures. Do good to
others. Witness to your faith. All pleasing and doctrinally sound
schemes of Christian education and spiritual renewal led to the
disappointing admission that, with some beautiful exceptions,
these few necessary things did not lead people to lives filled with
and possessed by God. The church, he concluded, has become
an organization of well-meaning idealists, working for Christ but
far from his presence and power. By modest estimate, more than
a quarter of the population of the United States has professed an
evangelical conversion experience: "A pound of meat would
surely be affected by a quarter pound of salt. If this is real Christianity, the salt of the earth, where is the effect of which Jesus
spoke?"[5]

He rightly observes that this failure has nothing to do with
the usual divisions between Christians but is shared on all sides
due to a common failure to foster those behaviors of faith which
enable us to perceive all the little events that make up our lives as
contributing to the vitality of our life in Christ. We've relegated
God's life in us to special times and places and states of mind, to
special acts like going to church on Sunday. Our present state is
fittingly exemplified by a story of St. Thomas Aquinas walking
amongst the splendors of Rome with a friend who remarked, "We
Christians certainly have no longer to say to the world, 'Silver
and gold have we none'." To which Thomas replied: "But neither
can we say to the lame man, 'In the name of Jesus of Nazareth,
rise up and walk'."[6]

DOES IT CHANGE LIVES?

What we are essentially talking about is the appropriation of Christ's presence as a psychological reality in our day-to-day living. While we say that we have been baptized into Christ, do we have any experiential union with him? We say that we have died with him to sin, but in our conscious experience do we find that there is a new power and orientation operating in our natural impulses? The moment in which we become aware of this creative action of God is the moment in which our conscious spiritual life begins. In all the talk of spiritual progress, it is strange how very seldom we hear anything about this most momentous step forward that a human being can take. Large parts of the New Testament are concerned with the making of that step, but how widespread is the experiential knowledge of it among Christians? It is the step that takes us beyond self-absorption and egotism and sets up a direct intercourse with the Source of our life, with our true Self.

To distinguish in these pages between our deepest and truest Self which is rooted in God and guided by the Holy Spirit, from our false self, I will use the upper case "S" for the former. The false self is a monumental illusion, a load of habitual thinking and emotional patterns that are stored in the brain and nervous system like programs in a computer. Every time a particular life situation presses the appropriate key, the habituated pattern is activated. When we hear that someone has said something unkind about us, we may up the ante with another negatively critical response. When we're feeling strung out with work and in need of renewal and a friend says, "Let's go have a few drinks," we think, "Yeah, that'll make me feel better." When we've had enough to eat and the serving tray is put in front of us, we decide to have another helping.

To act spontaneously under the Spirit's influence rather than under the influence of the false self which seeks fulfillment in all the wrong places, the programming of the past has to be erased and replaced. How do we erase the old programs and write new ones based on the values of the Gospel? By the practice of Christian disciplines or virtuous actions which aim at dismantling the false self. This is the work which God seems to require of us as a proof of our sincerity.[7] Once we have gone through all the preliminary stages that bring one to the massage table, then God takes our liberation in hand, probing our deeply rooted blockage and points of spiritual tension, inviting us to relax and trust the divine touch. As Teresa of Avila said to her protégées: "If after God brings a soul here it makes the effort to advance, it will see great things."[8]

More often than not, faith fails to transform people in large numbers because it is usually unaccompanied by discipleship which involves an overall discipline of life. Consequently, when we face serious issues of war and injustice, what is called faith in Christ provides only comfort and the hope of an afterlife. Our faith is not radical enough to take us to the root of social order and disorder and to propose transformation of life and structures. We must at some point stop looking for stop-gap solutions to abolish war, hunger and oppression while allowing ourselves to continue to be and live as we are. Dallas Willard writes:

> *The debate about whether "the answer" lies in social or in individual change goes on and on only because both sides are thinking at a very superficial level. Establishing the rights of labor and of the various ethnic groups, shifting ownership or the means of production from private to public hands, outlawing various types of discrimination, governmental outlays for welfare and education and so on, will certainly make a difference—good or bad—but they will not eliminate greed, loneliness, resentment, sexual misery and harm, disappointment with one's lot in life, hunger for meaning and recognition, fear of sickness,*

pain, old age and death, or hatred of those of other cultures. They will not bring us to love and accept ourselves and our neighbors or enable us to enjoy our lives with peace of mind. But then neither will the vapid, mass produced experiences of repentance and faith—if we may indeed call them that—that now commonly are announced as entrance into a new and supernatural life.[9]

Counsellors and polls find little difference between the basic attitudes, actions, and afflictions of believers and unbelievers. Our world is hungry for genuinely changed people. But as Leo Tolstoy once observed, "Everybody thinks of changing humanity and nobody thinks of changing himself."

OUR CONTRIBUTION: WILLINGNESS

In taking up this or that discipline of the spiritual life, there are a few guidelines to keep in view. What opens us to continually new, unprojected, unforeseeable possibilities, to the willingness to live in the insecure security of faith, to the *willingness for whatever*[10] is valuable. What lures us to constantly reflect on our experience and construct a secure system is dangerous.

We can learn various methods of meditation and focused stillness, but we must not mistake these activities either for the growth process or for the grace which is invisibly at work. It takes a constant and delicate discernment to find and keep one's balance, to keep techniques from seducing us into the belief that we are powering ourselves forward on our own steam. A constant point of reference is the biblical notion of *kenosis*, of emptying oneself so that there may be room for something new to happen.

"Your attitude must be that of Christ: though he was in the form of God, he did not deem equality with God something to be grasped at. Rather, he emptied himself. . . ." (Philippians 2:2–

7). So the Incarnate Word of God participates in history, dwells in the ark, becomes an infant, laughs, cries, and is crucified, thus destroying death and our fear of it. It is in this process of emptying out that we see God's potency. As the image of God, we must learn that emptying out is our potency, too.

Like the ancient mariner who on his deathbed could not be sorry for his nights with "the dancing girls in Thailand" but who could only "want to want" (contrition), we may be able to contribute no more than to want to be willing. But that is enough. Our primary task is to seek willingness, willingness to be emptied. It is a task that costs not less than everything. God's love will do the rest, for even as we seek to be still, Love seeks to enter and transform. And as we are changed, we realize that our continuing rebirth itself demands further willingness, and finally a willingness for whatever.

Uncovering and surrendering anything which prevents our being "lived by God" represents an arduous process of radical transformation. How do we even dispose ourselves for the journey, how do we send the signal that we "want to want"?

We position ourselves on the massage table to be acted upon. That is to say, we engage in the practice of the disciplines for Christian living whose only function is to put us where God can work upon us and slowly remove the obstacles to fuller life. The disciplines of the spiritual life are God's means of grace, the means by which we are placed where God can bless us. It is not the activities we do which effect the change; they only put us in the place where change can occur. The inner transformation is God's work and not ours.[11]

This readiness to write God a blank check will, if we abide in it, shatter every idea we have about ourselves, about our interior growth and transformation, about the Christian life and about God. The degree to which a person is willing to be emptied out and thus filled with God is the degree to which new possibility is opened. Each of us is invited to radiate the divine glory. We are asked only to be willing, to trust that such is possible, and to know that with each person's willingness more than our own self is being transformed.

Every exercise of the spiritual life must somehow bring us to where our strength fails, to where we are confronted with our weakness. We are in fact guided in our choice of a particular discipline by the awareness of where we need help, of where we are floundering. To live out of our weakness is to live by grace. "When I am weak, then I am strong," St. Paul discovered. Grace inserts itself only in weakness. The only discipline possible for any follower of Christ is one that is embraced in the realization of one's own poverty and need to the point where one turns to God as the only hope.

THE CROSS OF CHRIST AS THE REVELATION OF GOD

In its own way the cross of Christ captures the paradox in life that those moments in which God seems most absent can be recognized as moments in which God is most present. The apparent silence of God at Calvary does not denote absence. Rather, it means that silence and signs, darkness and light, suffering and joy are now equally the location of God's creative presence and activity. In the cross, God is found to be active and present in the midst of extraordinary evil, suffering and death, drawing good out of evil, salvation out of suffering, and new life out of death. The message is clear: there is now no area of life that falls outside the presence and activity of God. The experiences of human failure, weakness, and tragedy are revealed to be within the scope of God's transforming action. Out of apparent confusion and failure comes a new kind of perception which is able to see strength *in* weakness and not just after weakness, light *in* darkness and not just after darkness, life *in* death and not just after death (2 Corinthians 12:10; 4:11, 6:9). The cross in the life of Jesus and in Christian existence is a creative moment on the way to newness of life.[12]

The experience of the cross in one form or another is a universal human experience with which all can identify. In fact we can only begin to talk about salvation in Christ after we have acknowledged the experience of being estranged from God. So if we are to talk about the resurrection, we must start with the experience of the cross. The former only becomes meaningful when it is grounded in our own experience of the latter. If it is not so grounded, the message of Christianity appears inflated and out of touch with human experience.

If the suffering and death of Jesus are passed over or played down in order to highlight the resurrection, then the identity of the risen Christ is destroyed. The risen Christ is always the crucified Christ. The union with God that we seek both now and in the full glory of the resurrection life will only come through an embrace in faith of the cross wherever we find it implanted in our lives.

The cross is central to the gospel understanding of God. The cross is not an accident in the life of Jesus. It is not as though he happened to be in Jerusalem at the wrong time, rubbed some people the wrong way, and was rashly executed. The cross is an essential aspect of Jesus revealing God. This is the symbol of God that Christianity celebrates and with which it signs itself. This is the only understanding of God that today many people can accept: a God of love who is revealed in suffering, who is with us in this suffering, and who transforms our dying into life.

The cross is also the tree of life to which we turn when, in touch with our weakness and frailty, we come to the realization that "I am not able to do this on my own." Here, liberation from the bondage of our sinfulness and guilt is offered. In the power flowing from Jesus' gift of himself in love upon the cross, we are set free. Here, our cell door opens outward to the union of love we seek with God. God alone can effect this union, but we must prepare ourselves. Our work is to clear away the obstacles.

Whatever activity of this type may be called for to dispose ourselves, we must undertake it. This is our part in the redemptive process. If I do not submit my life through the disciplines that fit my needs, God's readiness to work a wonder in me is blocked. John of the Cross illustrates this with an image. We are like windows: divine light—the natural presence of God—is there always beating on the panes, but the panes are dirty, so dirty that the light cannot penetrate. Our task is very simple. We do not have to make the sun shine, for God, like the sun, is already above us ready to fill us with life-giving light. All we have to do is let the sun in by cleaning the windows, that is, by letting go of our sense of self-possession and personal achievement. The more we rely on our own selves, on what we can attain, the less we resign ourselves into the only hands capable of making us translucent with the light.[13]

We apply our minds and hearts, we do what we can, but as always our part, though essential, does not "do" it. It does, however, enable God to "do" it. God needs our contribution as sticks are needed for a fire. Sticks are not fire and never create fire. Yet fire has to have something to set ablaze. Our freedom is God's respect for us. God only moves forward with a redemptive plan through people who are prepared to receive freely and cooperate in the next step. That requires diligence and willingness on our part, a readiness to give everything that we can in body and mind.

The mind part we understand easily enough; it is the body part which usually snags us. But biblical scholarship rejects out of hand the idea of a purely "spiritual" immortality even where the life to come is concerned. Christian faith insists upon a *bodily* resurrection. Thus, the massage metaphor again obtains: the disciplines require specific acts and dispositions of our bodies. They cannot be carried out except as our bodies, as well as our minds and hearts, are surrendered in precise ways and definite actions to God. The New Testament holds no witness to a purely mental faith. Rather, faith arises from a Life Force, a pressure acting upon our interior being; then it exercises a determining influence upon all aspects of our existence: physical, social, political. Faith has to do with life, and can only be expressed in the actions and dispositions of our embodied existence.

Most religions have their own set of sacred gestures and other bodily actions. In Christianity some of them are kneeling, bowing, prostrating, genuflecting, making the sign of the cross, raising the hands. All these can dispose the mind and heart. In other religions, yogis, Zen Buddhists, Sufis each have their own procedures. They are essentially consciousness-altering techniques where physiology is put to the service of mystical experience. The surrender of ourselves to God necessarily involves our bodies as part of the offering so that it can serve as a common abode: "Do you not know that your bodies are members of Christ? Do you not know that your body is a temple of the Holy Spirit within you, which you have from God, and that you are not your own. For you were bought with a price; therefore glorify God in your body" (1 Cor. 6:15,19,20).

The vitality and power of Christianity is lost when we fail to integrate our bodies into our faith practice with conscious intent. The unmistakably embodied nature of the disciplines—fasting, exercise, sabbath rest, worship, work or service—leave no room for waffling on this point.

NEW GENERATIONS DISCOVERING ANCIENT TREASURE

Today one finds a general failure in all the Christian confessional traditions to effectively implement the wonderful, positive functions of the traditional disciplines as having a valuable role to play in the full, applied redemption of the human personality.

The Eastern Orthodox Christians have never lost sight of certain traditional disciplines; their struggle is to convoke a Pan-Orthodox Synod in which these monastically-inspired exercises can be realistically adapted to the contemporary lay person with a job and family.

The Roman Catholic Church had its Council (1962–65) and in its renewal effort saw the faithful let go of some age-old practices like regular fasting, though this was never what was intended. Catholics are now in the process of slowly sifting through their treasure chest and bringing forth neglected riches for reevaluation.

Among North American Protestants, certain disciplines are enjoying an unprecedented popularity and attention in books, seminars, lectures and articles. Having once fallen victim to a false opposition of grace vs. works caused by a mistaken association of "works" with "merit," these practices are increasingly regarded as reliable means of growth toward maturity in Christ. Historically, the Protestant principle that we are saved by grace through faith, and not by works or merit, led to the exclusion of the disciplines in mainstream Protestantism. What could possibly be the point of such disciplines, if not the *earning* of merit or possibly forgiveness? Ironically, the Protestant Reformation may have done more than all the Catholic internal reform attempts to perpetuate ascetical practices in Catholicism by attacking them from the outside and causing those assailed to close ranks and reassert their vision of truth even more strongly in the Council of Trent.

Under the influence of John Calvin's writing and preaching, the notion of discipline came to be largely associated in the Reformed branches of Protestantism with efforts to keep the faithful in line. In Methodism, John Wesley's writings admirably spell out any number of Christian disciplines and invite his followers to their godly exercise as a sure route to spiritual maturity. But how much of it is a living reality in current practice today? Luther's emphasis on the teaching and preaching of the gospel, along with the administration of the sacraments, as the essentials for spiritual development resulted in only marginal treatment of many traditional practices in the spiritual life. The various Baptist and Pentecostal groups followed this orientation, but subtracted the sacraments from the "essentials."[14]

The ecumenical movement, come to full flowering in the last half of this century, is one of the clearest signs of the Holy Spirit's work to facilitate an exchange of gifts among the churches and to stir up new life through the sharing of spiritual wisdom and experience. The Protestants have taught the Catholics how to make the scriptures a daily food and drink. The Catholics, with their rich tradition of monasticism and contemplative prayer, have opened the doors of their retreat houses to all comers who feel a thirst for placing themselves regularly before the Lord in silence and solitude. The Orthodox and Anglicans call those who have given up on corporate worship's ability to inspire to look again. The Free churches, like the Society of Friends, testify to the impact a small number of committed believers can exert in work to establish the reign of justice and peace. The Eastern religions have provided the Western with valuable instruction in meditation and yoga. Judaism continues to twig the Christian conscience with its faithful observance of the sabbath. If anyone needed further witness of the unprecedented cross-fertilization taking place between Christians in the area of prayer and spirituality, the 1991 World Council of Churches' General Assembly in Canberra, Australia provided a glimpse of it when Protestant and Orthodox representatives from every confession and country stood in line with Catholics to receive ashes on Ash Wednesday and joined together in a day of fasting.

TECHNIQUES HAVE THEIR PLACE

Perhaps the most difficult of moments occurs in a preacher's or teacher's life when someone steps up and says, "What you're saying makes a lot of sense to me. Now what do I do, practically speaking? Tell me how to go about it."

That is the import of the chapters that follow. For each of several disciplines I will provide theological underpinnings for its practice and make some concrete suggestions of a "how to" nature. The justification for speaking about methods and techniques is the need to dispose ourselves for a more conscious experience of God.[15] We are incarnate beings, and our enfleshed existence is the place of our encounter with the divine. Methods, as suitable means for achieving goals, have long been a standard part of various traditions of spirituality.

When one studies the lives of holy people in the different religious traditions, one discovers there the imprint of the disciplines for the spiritual life. This is the common way to that fully alive humanity which gives glory to God. What leads us to believe that we might be an exception to this path? Why do we think that, where others have needed reliable helps for their journey, we do not? Christians can also benefit from the wise employment of certain techniques originally developed in the context of other living faiths, integrating them into their own Christian practice.[16] Examples of this drawn from my own experience will be brought into play where appropriate.

Methods in the spiritual life, however, are never akin to the points in an instruction manual. A proper method is more like a language. When we learn the grammar and usage of a language, discipline and attention is required. It necessarily involves a method or technique. But for true communication one must eventually go beyond rules and logic and grammar. We go along with them until our conscious use of them becomes instinctive; then we go beyond the methods and techniques into spontaneous exercise. So it is with their use in the spiritual life. Particularly in the beginning one needs the discipline of a method which gives guidance, calls forth the depth of the spirit, creates an environment for its flowering, and brings one to the brink where one will be challenged to transcend the method into the freedom of the Spirit. A true method has the dialectics of self-transcendence in it and eventually leads one beyond the method. [17]

The particular disciplines one embraces should relate to the various dimensions of our lives which may require attention. The disciple is one who, intent upon expressing willingness, systematically and progressively rearranges one's priorities and affairs to that end. By such actions, one passes from discipline to discipleship and comes to the awareness that the spiritual life is simply a life in which all that we do comes from the center where we are anchored in God. It is a life soaked through and through by a sense of God's reality and claim upon us. The demand of the Spirit, however inconvenient, comes first and is first. Our spiritual life is the Spirit's affair, produced by the Spirit's attraction and dependent upon our readiness to respond and move with it. It consists in being drawn, at God's pace and in God's way, to the place where God wants us to be—not the place we fancied for ourselves. [18]

2

Friendship and Family Life

When I left India, I headed for Australia where I had accepted to give some talks on my way back to Canada. I arrived in Western Australia on May 17 at 2 a.m. and was met at the Perth airport by my hosts. We arrived at their home about 3 a.m. and when they showed me to my room, there was a package which had arrived in the mail for me sitting on the bed. I decided to open it later in the morning after getting some sleep; the last two nights had been spent on a train in India and a plane from Madras to Singapore. Three nights in a row with minimal sleep made a normal bed the biggest gift of all.

When I awoke several hours later and had showered, shaved and opened the curtains to a fresh, blue-green morning, the package presented itself again. This time, I felt able to give it a just response and sat down at the desk to undo the wrapping. There were several pieces inside, each individually wrapped. I reached for the largest, an oblong object wrapped in foam padding. It was an elegant glass goblet. Next came a red vigil light, with candle inside. Then a small bottle of wine . . . unleavened bread . . . a table cloth with a floral pattern of roses around its border . . . a stiff paper offering plate, also decorated with roses . . . a post card featuring a display of roses with the words written on the back: "Happy anniversary of your ordination!" And on the very bottom, the scripture readings and mass prayers for

May 17. I noticed that certain of the verses were underlined in the gospel reading and took a closer look at it. The passage was John (21:1–19), one of Jesus' post-resurrection appearances to his disciples. Each of the three times that Jesus asked Peter, "Do you love me?" was underlined, as well as Jesus' final words to him: "Follow me."

I sat back and looked at all the pieces set before me on the table, quite overwhelmed by the thoughtfulness of a friend who had taken the time to assemble, wrap and send overseas this care package. I noticed a little note stuck on the base of the goblet: "For the celebration of the eucharist." Then, in a reference to the Jewish marriage custom of smashing the wine glass, it read: "After—to celebrate Jesus' fidelity to you—throw against Australian rocks!"

This is what friends do for us: make us feel special, challenge us to give ever fuller expression to what is deepest and best in us, support us in our commitments, celebrate our red-letter days with us, divide our burden on the blue ones, and keep a touch of craziness in our lives. Over the years I have come to the conclusion that the intimacy of friendship, whether of spouses or others, is one of life's blue ribbon experiences.

I
THE STRUGGLE FOR QUALITY TIME AND SPACE IN EACH OTHER'S LIVES

One of the things we priests have a difficult time being honest about with ourselves is our intimacy needs. Ours is one of the few professions in which men are encouraged—required even—to develop their empathetic, affective, nurturing selves. A lot of our intimacy needs get met through the caring, confidential, supportive ways in which we are constantly relating to people.

Yet, in most of these interactions, we are in a giving mode.

We seldom allow others to give to us. This reciprocity is for me what makes friendship both special and necessary. It is important for me to allow myself to be appreciated and cared for. When Jesus went to Mary, Martha and Lazarus' house, I'm sure it was because he also received from them in ways that nurtured him.

When I made the move from campus ministry to ecumenical work, the whole style of my ministry changed. On campus, many hours were filled each week sharing with people, few in reading and writing. At the Ecumenical Centre, the opposite became true. In campus ministry, there is a constant turnover in the campus population, but you usually have at least three to four years to grow in friendship before graduation. People in parish work look at the campus setting and say, "There's no stability. Everyone is always coming and going." But my work out of a national educational resource center for the promotion of Christian unity and inter-faith understanding makes even a campus ministry situation appear glacier-like in its stability. The people on campus do come and go, but a lot more slowly than in my present ministry. My encounters now with people in different parts of the country range anywhere from two hours in a short session to five days in a long one.

While engaging in this ministry of reconciliation, I have had to closely monitor my intimacy-needs barometer. While the work at the Ecumenical Centre brings its own real enrichment and challenge, now largely lost to me are the many opportunities for heart-to-heart talks with students and community members, for mutual affirmation, for handshakes and hugs, for counselling and shared prayer. And with them is lost the rich, cumulative level of intimacy with others which contributes to our ability to live happy and fulfilled lives. When I began work at the Ecumenical Centre, I realized that if the opportunity for heart-to-heart sharing wasn't going to be there for me as it had in the past, I would have to put time and energy into going after it by developing new opportunities.

My first move after three years of campus ministry at Ohio State University to Montreal had impressed this upon me. Each of us needs two or three people in our lives who accept us as we are and with whom no performance is required, a few friends who can be dropped in on spontaneously or called at six in the morning. When one or the other party moves, there will always be a special feeling for one another, but we can no longer *be there* for each other in good times and bad to share life. That means when we find ourselves in a new place, the relationships we had in the old place are no longer adequate. We'll have to work at cultivating new relationships in which the confidence and trust can grow and a community of meaning be established between ourselves. We have a basic human need to be connected to other human beings. Each of us has the responsibility to live our life in such a way that we are connected to others. This has to do with basic human intimacy needs. All we really need for this is to permit ourselves to be known *and* to have that received by another in a nonjudgmental way. If we feel the other judging us, then we pull back and withhold ourselves, thereby blocking the formation of intimacy. In permitting ourselves to be known, we risk the rejection, ridicule and negative reaction of the other, thus placing ourselves in a vulnerable position. But encountering the other's nonjudgmental acceptance permits the intimacy to flower and provides a fertile ground for real friendship.

There is an interesting paradox that plays itself out in the early phases of most relationships. When we have the courage to be self-disclosing, to show who we really are, warts and all, then the other person feels safer to show who he or she really is, too. The result is a new level of intimacy rather than an experience of isolation or rejection. During my training in graduate school as a group counsellor I observed that the critical therapeutic moment often occurred when one person exposed a "dangerous" feeling and found that it did not lead to catastrophic rejection or derision. We do not of course relate to everyone on this level, but if there are none with whom we feel we can really be ourselves, then it is ultimately isolating, stressful, and damaging to our human growth and development.

Medical Research on the Effect of Social Isolation

Every age has its particular challenges and difficulties, whether they be wars, famines, plagues, or economic depressions. The chronic stress in our contemporary Western world derives not only from the increased pace of modern life but also from the isolation, loneliness, lack of love and support that so many people experience. In his book *Reversing Heart Disease,*[1] Dr. Dean Ornish presents a series of study results indicating that anything which promotes a sense of isolation leads to chronic stress and, often, to illness. Conversely, anything that leads to real intimacy and feelings of connection can be healing in the deep sense of the word. Some examples of medical findings:

— People who live alone have more heart disease than those who live with someone or even something, e.g., a pet.
— The quality of social support is more important than the number of people involved who provide support.
— Among people with an illness such as cancer, those who participated in weekly support group meetings had twice the survival rate of those who didn't.
— Patients who scored above the average in loneliness had significantly poorer immune functioning.

One report stated that it is the ten to twenty percent of people who say they have nobody with whom they can share their private feelings, or who have close contact with others less than once a week, who are most at risk. The report indicated that social isolation is as significant to mortality rates as smoking, high blood pressure, high cholesterol, obesity, and lack of physical exercise.

The ability to be intimate has long been seen as a key to emotional health; what the medical evidence is indicating is that it is also key to the health of our hearts *physically* as well as figuratively. An impressive number of studies say that isolation from others can lead to illness, whereas feeling more connected and intimate with others can enhance health, well-being, and even survival.

Seek and You Shall Find

We may find the kind of connectedness and friendship we need and seek only to have the circumstances of life change the equation that made it possible. When such happens, as it surely will, *friendship as a discipline of the spiritual life requires us to begin again.*

When I moved to Montreal, on about my second evening there I was transporting some things from the adjoining residence to my new office at the McGill Newman Centre. There was a light on in another office and I stuck my head in to say hello. His name was Gerry; he was the treasurer for the Board of Directors and was bringing some bookkeeping up to date. I stood and chatted with him awhile, feeling an immediate and easy rapport. We quickly discovered some common interests, and when I was about to go, he said "My wife and I will have you over for dinner sometime."

"Fine," I replied, "When?" He's teased me about it on different occasions since. "I was just being polite," he laughs. "I didn't expect you to come back so quickly and take me up on it!" But I knew that when a new kid moves in on the block, he can't expect the others to have been waiting for him. Their calendars are full. If the new kid wants a corner on it, he'll have to speak up; the others won't come looking for him.

Gerry, and his wife, Cathy, became close friends. Their two subsequent children, Allison and Colin, grew up with me around the house and at their table and came to relate to me as an uncle. Healthy, mutually supportive friendships with other people whose lives are functioning well is an important component of our on-going, balanced spiritual growth because it is essential for our healthy human development. I have drawn something very special from families in particular.

Family Life as a School for Holiness[2]

In my years of ministry as a priest, I have been inspired and evangelized by the radical lives of Christian service being lived by my married friends. Both married and single people share the same fundamental goal of the Christian life: availability for service in love. But the closer I get to the experience of family life through my brothers and sisters and friends, the more convinced I am that married life has not received its just due as a school for holiness, a discipline in its own right, in the history of Christian spirituality.

In Jewish tradition the home, not the synagogue, is the center of religious life. By the fourth century writers like St. John Chrysostom were recognizing the family as the first form of the church on earth. It was this tradition that Vatican II drew upon in calling the family "the domestic church." Whatever else the following words of Jesus describe, they clearly apply to people who publicly profess their love and its fruits in children as a sign of God's covenant with us: "For where two or three meet in my name, I shall be there with them" (Matt. 18:20).

The discipline of availability for service in love that I see being lived out in family life evangelizes me because it asks me if my own availability is anywhere as radical. A pastor can be available for hours of counselling, home visitations, and sacramental ministry, but after a long day can retire to the quiet peace of a private room, take a day off, or go to a retreat house for a day away to regain equilibrium.

A young woman, the mother of three children, confessed to me, "Sometimes it is difficult to get a free moment to even go to the bathroom. As soon as I disappear from the room, one of the little ones is calling 'Mommy! Mommy!' and opening all the doors to find out where I went." And many are the mommies and daddies who, after working a full day, face dinner preparation, helping the children with their homework, bathing them, and being available to them as they get ready for bed. "I have a deep desire for some time to myself," one father confided, "but the day is filled with so many demands that I no longer seem to belong to myself, only to the others in my life."

"Unless a grain of wheat falls on the ground and dies, it remains only a single grain," said Jesus, "but if it dies, it yields a rich harvest" (John 12:24). This "dying" to one's own preferences, to one's personal wants and desires, takes many forms in married and family life. When Colin was born, Gerry could no longer meet me on the corner in the early morning to go jogging together. He certainly enjoyed the exercise and the opportunity to visit, but family life was demanding increased availability. Here is an exercise of the spiritual life that finds a person living as Jesus did: with constant attention and availability to the needs of others. There is a built-in asceticism in these situations which peels away the layers of self-centeredness and reconstructs one's life, orienting it towards others rather than self. No selected discipline evokes humility and poverty of spirit more effectively than the natural process of raising children.

My consistent observation is that children are at least as effective a test of character and vocation as are years of postulancy and novitiate. During my novitiate year, the master of novices and his assistant repeatedly zeroed in on me, trying to test my spirit of generosity and patience—but never with the relentlessness that children unerringly bring to bear upon their parents.

"Before I was married and had a family," my sister recounted, "I considered myself educated, poised, articulate, rational, and mature. In the last five years of raising children, I feel as if I have been retrogressing from a personal growth point of view. The kids have an uncanny way of ferreting out your weaknesses and playing upon them. I used to pride myself on how patient I was: then the kids showed me what a short supply I really have."

The objective of any Christian discipline is to put us in touch with our true self and to enable us to align more and more of our lives with what we discover there. Family life demands that a person find his or her worth in God's free gift of love and acceptance rather than in achievements which might feed our self-esteem. Many of the indicators of self-worth that one would like to pride oneself in are stripped away by the unerring honesty of the family unit. We tend to build our self-concept on what we can achieve or earn. But most parents at home with young ones find it difficult to achieve anything. They get to the end of the day having accomplished only a small portion of what they set out to do. This is the discipline of dealing with constant interruptions which continually bring one back to the heart of it all: being available for service in love.

Holiness is not what we often think it is. Sometimes what most fashions the image and attitude of Christ in us is what most strips us of our own preferences and conveniences. Once while on a retreat I sent a postcard to a family saying I felt as though I was getting things in perspective and getting my life to go in the direction I wanted it to go. The mother confessed to me sometime later, "I hated you for sending that card! I used to be able to say noble things like that, but now I don't feel as if I am in control of anything." The truth God was working in her (of not being in control) through the demands of family life was more on target than the illusion (of being in control) that I was enjoying on retreat.

Family life guarantees that self-absorption and self-illusion will not happen. When it comes to vacation time, for example, or even a free evening, a single person can say, "What do I want to do?" But a married person's response is often along the lines of: "I would really like to do that, but my spouse may not be free and even then it will all depend on whether we can get a sitter." This constant call to think "we" instead of just "I" is no small discipline of the spiritual life.

And then there is the question of detachment. Whereas on the face of it, families are much freer to acquire whatever possessions they wish, the vagaries of family life call for a profound sense of detachment from those possessions. Joey can come along with his dump truck and with one swing that beautiful polished piano has a gouge in it that will be there forever. I know a couple who saw their priceless collection of Hummels massacred on the shelf by a ball thrown across the living room. Detachment from material things is not much a part of the rhetoric of family life, but it can be very much a part of its spirituality if the parents see the circumstances of their life together as the matrix for their own formation in gospel values.

The discipline of family living involves a poverty of time, an obedience to the needs of the other family members, and the constant work of deepening the love which enticed you to link your futures to one another and to embark on this adventure. Did you really understand what you were saying when you committed yourselves "for better or for worse?" Did you appreciate at that moment that the "worse" comes to be as least as important—and eventually even as precious—as the "better"? Both are necessary to love. In the better times, we learn the joy of loving. In the worse times, we learn (and there is no other way we could learn) to love unselfishly. It is the "worst" which leads us from the kind of enlightened self-interest which often passes for love ("I like to be with her because I like how she makes me feel"), to truly loving, i.e., to selflessly desiring and serving the good of the other.

Living Ordinary Lives in an Extraordinary Way

Family life is a vocation to live ordinary lives in an extraordinary way. Love, humor, flexibility, patience, forgiveness, and a radical availability are virtues which are in constant demand.

All the members of our family, reunited for Christmas, had just sat down to mother's elegant dinner when one of the children said, "Poo-poo, Daddy."

"Do you have to go to the bathroom, Honey?" my brother asked his two-year-old daughter. "Do you want to try to go by yourself or do you want me to help you?"

"I want to try myself," she giggled as she scurried from the table.

We lifted our wine-filled goblets in a candle-light toast, and above the music of tinkling crystal came the next joyful noise from down the hallway: "I did it, Daddy! Do you wanna come and see?" Spontaneous laughter erupted from the four sets of young parents gathered around the table.

For me, the opportunity to share the reality of parenting is always a marvellous grace which enables me to see the light and shadows of the life I live as a priest. The routines and demands of an average family often appear to be a human obstacle course and an environmental disaster area. There is never enough time or money or closet space; there are always at least two people who want the same bathroom, car, chair, or phone. In such crowded quarters, someone is always stepping on somebody else's toe or psyche or sensitivity.

Though family members may complain and wish for more ideal conditions, this is the way it should be because this is how the family setting polishes rough diamonds. The chiselling and the sanding represented by constant give-and-take are often emotionally unpleasant, but this is the only way we human beings develop facets that sparkle. What's more, the rubbing doesn't just take place from adults to children. When my brother starts to razz his wife about being a little too compulsive with the vacuum cleaner, he gets immediate feedback: "Listen! You have your interests, and I have mine. I respect yours so get off my case!" And when I take a bite out of my sandwich at the lunch counter, I find my niece's big brown eyes fixed on me: "Did you give thanks yet, Uncle Tom?"

Frankly, I don't get much of this in religious community, and I suspect that's the case with most rectories. We haven't promised to live with each other "for better or for worse," and so we don't have the safety net with each other which family commitment provides. When we discover conflict, we tend to note it and avoid the occasion in the future rather than do the hard work of talking it through to some mutually acceptable resolution. If things get too tense, one can always put in for a transfer and hope the next assignment is better. I find that clergy and religious usually treat each other with kid gloves and the politeness of social contact. What families teach me is that human beings are not so fragile; it is better to occasionally take the gloves off and be real with each other. Families leave me with the sense that though our lives as celibate clergy may be more conflict-free in the long run, they may also by that same token be less conducive to growth. Dealing with conflict demands a certain readiness to examine and to change one's behavior. Families challenge me to be more emotionally honest, to develop a thicker skin to criticism, and to be as available in my celibacy to serve others as they are in their family lives.

There are also ways that priests, brothers and sisters challenge families to, for example, resist seduction by our consumer society, to protect time for prayer, reading and for their own holistic health and growth. We remind parents that silence and solitude need to find expression in their lives, too, and that a regular retreat or spiritual director is for *every* Christian interested in following what God is doing in his or her life and heart. Our choice to forego spouse and family is a reminder that there is

Another present to us all, speaking to our hearts, inviting us to a relationship of love. Our ministry to the wider community witnesses to our common responsibility for awareness of and solidarity with the needs of those in the extended community of the parish and beyond.[3]

But the orientation of my reflection here is not towards a comparison of the gifts offered in the community of the church. It is, rather, toward the conditions in family living which accomplish certain objectives of the Christian disciplines: to shape people who are less selfish and more sensitive to the needs of others, to foster the inner attitudes of poverty of spirit, surrender, abandonment, dependence upon God, flexibility, and humor.

My reflections on family life as an exacting discipline in its own right for Christian living are only possible as a result of spending time with parents and children. In short, they made room for me in their already busy lives. They were willing to enter into friendship. There are various elements at work in our North American way of life which conspire against our taking time for one another, be they family members or friends or both. I will touch upon but two of them here. Each one results in a situation where something as natural as spending time with friends becomes the object of a carefully made decision. The first was described in a *Time* magazine article[4] which charted North America's loss of time.

The Time Famine

Time that once seemed free and elastic has grown tight and elusive. Correspondingly, our measure of its worth has dramatically changed. It is now the most precious commodity in the land. Time is to the 1990s what money was to the 1980s.

According to a Harris survey, the amount of leisure time enjoyed by the average American has shrunk thirty-seven percent since 1973. Over the same period, the average work week, including commuting, has jumped from under forty-one hours a week to nearly forty-seven hours. In some professions like law, finance, and medicine, the demands often stretch to eighty-plus hours a week. Vacations have shortened to the point where they are frequently no more than long weekends.[5] This is the cultural context that has turned the sabbath into a day needed for shopping.

Everyone is looking for short-cuts, and these short-cuts are changing the way families function, the time they have for one another and for their friends.

The family unit behaves quite differently today, spending less time together than in the past. Meals are less likely to be eaten at home as a shared family experience. Vacations are shorter and less likely to include all members of the household. The average home now has multiple television sets, enabling children and adults to watch different programming in separate rooms. The teenagers are now more mobile and self-sufficient than ever, with one-third who have reached the driving age *owning* a car. Children who live with both their parents report that they spend less than thirty minutes per week in meaningful conversation with their mothers, and less than fifteen with their fathers.[6]

The arduous rat race is reflected in Hallmark cards which now market special ones for parents to tuck under the Corn Flakes box in the morning ("Have a super day at school!") or under the pillow at night ("I wish I were here to tuck you in"). Parents who like their jobs and love their kids find that the pressure to do justice to both creates a squeeze that puts family time and meal time out of reach. Twenty years ago sociologists were projecting a twenty-two hour work week and preparing us for the big challenge of enjoying all that newly-created leisure. The reality is that people feel more harried than ever by their life-styles.

In my travels to Africa and Latin America and India I have been struck by the way people have time for other people. They have none of the labor-saving gadgetry that enables us to prepare, serve and clean up after a meal in less time than it takes to boil an egg. It takes them hours just to procure water from the river or well for cooking and wood from the forest for fuel. Yet it is we, with our microwaves zapping and cuisinarts whizzing, who are out of breath and without time to sit down and talk to one another. It is ironic that in a culture so committed to saving time we feel increasingly deprived of the very thing we value. There never seems to be enough time to fit in all the things one feels "have to be done."

Therein lies the key to the quandary: our schedules are more ambitious than ever. As soon as one module of time is freed up by a time-saving technological device, there are two or three new attractions for which culture and advertising have us reaching. So all the new toys actually end up making us work harder or play harder. There are phones in the car, laptops in the den, and the humming fax machine eliminates that once satisfactory and celebratory lull between completing a document and delivering it. Whatever sense of patience and waiting existed, the fax has erased it. People now call you to tell you, with a certain upset in their voice, that your fax line is busy!

Doing more things seduces us into believing that our lives are fuller. But by what standard? If the intimate moments of sharing between family members or friends are life's blue ribbon experience, then technology is a diversion from true fullness of life. It may remove us from each other, transfix and isolate us. The new homes today have what are called entertainment centers or media rooms offering big-screen Nintendo or compact disc sound. Whatever happened to the kitchen table as a gathering place where people looked at and listened to *each other?*

Entertainment centers are so alluring that we end up taking little or no time for reflection. The risk is that the unexamined life becomes self-sustaining and increasingly lived at the level of surface stimulations and satisfactions. Climbing to the mountain-top takes time and effort. Preserving quality time in which as family members and friends we continue to share with one another who we're becoming is a discipline requiring the constant effort to hold in focus the particular priority of people over things. Speeded-up schedules not only strangle reflective and contemplative urges but have an insidious effect on the psyche. We find ourselves growing impatient and restless and it seems harder to think logically about a problem. If two hours miraculously open up one evening, our impulse is to immediately fill them with going out to a movie or watching TV. The impulse is towards "going" and "doing." "Are you having fun?" a father asked his son who was constantly on the run. The son looked at the father uncomprehendingly, and then tossed back as he went out the door, "I don't know. But excuse me—I gotta go!"

For many exhausted families, the premium placed on free time is effecting subtle and sweeping changes. In some cases it means a new division of labor between husband and wife, parents and kids, or a search for a more flexible work schedule. In other cases it's an outright rebellion against the rat race which expresses itself in climbing down the corporate ladder, trading in a big salary for a lower-level job with more vacation time or more flexible hours. The increasing rarity of the full-time homemaker has done more to eat away everyone's leisure time than any other factor. If both mother and father are working outside the home to make ends meet, as is the case in nearly two-thirds of U.S. families, someone still has to find the time to prepare lunches, shop, cook, mow the lawn, fix the faucet, wash clothes and take the children to their piano lessons or ball games.

On the surface, many families are coping by enrolling the children in day care, hiring nannies, sending out laundry and ordering in pizza—in short, contracting out family care. But there's a limit beyond which contracting out leaves one with something more closely resembling an enterprise than a family. And of course in the midst of all this spending time in order to buy time, there's no time in which to just hang around with the children. "I'm not so naive to say that money doesn't matter," said one dad who gave up a big salary to work on commission for a life insurance company, "but I want my children to know me as something besides their provider." Or as one mother said when asked what she would like people to say at her funeral when she died: "I don't want my children to say, 'My mother was a wonderful businesswoman.' " These are the words of people who are seeing the best years of their lives slip into the corporate black hole to support the life style they've bought into.

The premium placed on free time is resulting in the development of a sociological strata of "new hermits." They're the ones who beg off from invitations to dinner with apologies. It's not that they aren't interested in you. They may like you very much, it's just that, like their historical predecessors, they have fled the social whirl. Unlike the hermits of old who retreated for religious purposes, however, this new breed is motivated either by a sense of fatigue or the feeling that there is no room in their lives for any more "input." And rather than head for the forest and caves, the new hermits retreat into the realm of family and work. They are cutting away all the extraneous relationships that encroach on family time and work time. They have decided they can only fit so many people into their lives at one time. As one mother said, "With my work, my husband, and my three children, I just don't have very much left to give."

Many dual career families are making a move inward in an effort to gain some control over their lives. They're used to feeling in control, but gradually they have more to do than time to do it in and feel that their lives are getting away from them. They deal with it by cutting things back down to a manageable size. Some things have to be sacrificed, like having a few friends in for dinner. The cooking, cleaning, entertaining, and cleaning up again consumes most of the weekend. They've decided the price is too high—not in dollars, but in time and energy.

There is, of course, a downside to the hermit existence. A

certain sadness about the drying up of the relationships one doesn't have time for. Insularity to the point of isolation. Kids who don't have the opportunity to see their parents' involvement with other people, nor to see how much adults need other adults. Kids whose own world goes unexpanded by extra-family relationships. It's a difficult balance to strike. No combination of innovations, inventions or timely hints will restore the North American household to its imagined bygone tranquility; only a dramatic change in both attitudes and economics would represent a genuine respite. But at some point individuals must find the mental space to consider the toll on the spirit and on the quality of one's relationships exacted by the time famine.

Despite our seemingly difficult experiences with marriage and family, survey after survey reports that people's greatest source of happiness in life is family. A somewhat less publicized fact is that several surveys have also found that the greatest source of frustration and disappointment in people's lives is dealing with family problems. The family, as the basic component of society, has historically provided stability in times of great change and uncertainty. Our time has witnessed the gradual diminishing of the comfort zone traditionally provided by the family. The Church will likely be the last major institution in society to champion the conventional family model. It has a significant role to play in the 1990s for providing active support for permanent monogamy and cohesive family relationships. Part of its approach should be to celebrate those families and marriages that are making it, publicly lifting them up and treasuring them. Events that do this will serve as encouragement and support to other families in the rocky phases.[7]

Mobility

The second pattern in our contemporary lives which makes spending time with friends a discipline for Christian living is mobility. Several years ago I read a statistic from the U.S. Bureau of Labor which indicated that the average American moves fourteen times in his or her lifetime. That kind of transiency makes it very difficult to maintain close relationships. The constant investment of time and energy required by friendship, and then the repeated emotional uprooting when one or the other moves, brings many people to a point of saying "the pain outweighs the gain" or "I just don't have the emotional resilience to continue doing this."

Religious communities tend to move their personnel around on an average of every four to five years. The people we serve complain that this kind of transiency constantly undermines the positive effects of Christian friendship. Just as people are establishing a community of meaning and coming into a high level of comfort and trust with one another, the assignment process intervenes and sends the religious off to another part of the country.

Religious communities, of course, are not the only organizations to move their people around with little regard for the cost in relationship disruption. Large corporations have gotten more and more soulless in this respect, and where management has brought some sensitivity to this domain, the employee will oftentimes trigger a move by signalling interest in the career advancement a move entails.

I have been in the same city for the past fourteen years. That's unusual for a member of a religious community. In my case it's explained by the fact that I have had two different assignments in the same city, the second one requiring a longer placement by virtue of the specialized nature of the work. During my first assignment to the Newman Centre at McGill University, I formed a group of young professionals all of whom were beginning to raise their families. We met regularly for life-sharing, prayer, and play. Deep friendships were born and grew. But it wasn't long before the procession began out of Montreal to Ottawa, Toronto, Vancouver and other cities. When I left on my sabbatical this past year, Gerry and Cathy were the only couple remaining from our original group. I spent the last evening with them and their children before departing on my sabbatical study-leave. Their daughter Allison kept a steady flow of clippings from the sports pages coming to my thatched roof hut at an ashran in rural India to keep me fully abreast of the progress of the Montreal Canadiens toward the Stanley Cup. But one day, shortly after I had completed an intensive Buddhist meditation retreat in northern India, a letter came to me with her dad's handwriting on the envelope. The letter bore the news that he had been offered a new position in Toronto and, after much agonizing, he and Cathy had decided to accept it and leave Montreal. By the time I got back, their house would be empty and a "For Sale" sign standing in the front yard.

Gerry's letter effectively served as a sign of the times. Friendships are going to be harder to come by than ever as the 1990s progress. Even if we struggle valiantly against the limitations of transiency, fragmented schedules, and the prevailing unwillingness to make commitments, there will be new obstacles to add to the mix. The major new barrier will be reduced opportunities to meet people of like backgrounds and goals. With employment becoming more decentralized due to technological advances leading to more people working from their homes, we will lack the face-to-face encounters with people at work. The 1990s will also be a time when women assume greater roles of responsibility in the workplace, thus increasing their commitment to career rather than to personal interactions.[8]

These situations set the stage for the discipline required: *to make time on a regular basis to share life with one another.* The discipline is to continue investing in such friendships even when those with whom we have enjoyed this rich gift move away and we're tempted to simply become more wrapped up in ourselves in their absence. The discipline is to commit ourselves to doing this and to even develop, if need be, some form of periodic check upon ourselves to see if we're carrying through as intended. It may be a calendar on the back of one's bedroom door whereupon we write in each week the name(s) of the one(s) with whom we took some time, permitting us to literally see if the weeks are flitting by and we're not connecting. The particular form of the supportive device itself is not important. What does matter is that we open our hearts and share life regularly with a few good friends (this, of course, includes spouse) who will provide us with inspiration, support, perspective, and challenge.

Appropriate to this Christian discipline, therefore, is conscious involvement in activities that enable us to build a number of solid personal relationships. Once again, the Church has a vital role to play. As more and more adults search for opportunities to meet other people, particularly in demand are events which allow people who share common interests and goals to come together on a regular basis. Perhaps more than any other institution, the local church is poised to address people's need for more and deeper relationships. Parishes are particularly well situated to sponsor community events which provide people with the opportunity to celebrate some R & R: roots and relationships.

II
LIVING GAINS AND LOSSES
WITH EVENNESS OF SOUL

We could stop here, content with some reflections on the richness of family life and the importance of finding time for life sharing with friends, content with some sociological observations concerning paucity of time and the movement of friends from one city to another, and finally, content with a few reflections on what role the Church might play in all this. There is more, however, for the taking. There is a deeper, overarching discipline of the spiritual life called for in these situations of family stress and mobility. *On the one hand, it is the capacity to fully delight in the pleasant reality that is given without clinging to it, without attaching our happiness to it; and on the other hand, it is the capacity to live the unpleasant realities with equanimity, knowing that they are not forever.*

The Christian spiritual tradition offers a deep wisdom to serve as a compass for us in these matters of family and friendship and in other domains as well. That wisdom, I discovered, has a certain congruency with the core teachings of Buddhism. Both Buddhism and Christianity speak of this overarching discipline in the language of detachment (nonclinging) and equanimity. Delving however briefly and summarily into the counsel of both religions requires shifting the plane of reflection from the sociological to the psychological and theological. It is precisely because these teachings can be applied to so many other realms of our experience, in addition to the immediate themes dealt with thus far in this chapter, that it is worthwhile to go farther. At this point the themes of friendship and family life become a springboard for further, far-reaching reflection which, while including them, is not limited to them.

The springboard issue is impermanence: the fleeting nature not only of relationships, but of time, relationships, and all human experience. The impermanence of our jobs, family relationships and of the proximity of friends brings us face to face with a pervasive truth of our existence: everything changes. It is instructive to see how much in common the counsel of Buddhism has with Christianity for keeping one's balance in the cross currents of time pressure, personal and professional instability.

The occasion for my own tandem reflection on the appropriate Buddhist and Christian teachings was the reception of Gerry's letter shortly after finishing a course on Buddhist doctrine and meditation. Several points made by Buddhist teaching played an appreciated supporting role to my Christian points of reference and served as so much confirmation of the way forward. God uses all the circumstances of our lives—like an overseas letter from a friend received in a Buddhist monastery—to bring us to greater awareness of the activity of the Holy Spirit throughout the whole inhabited earth to bring us to kingdom living. From the Spirit's activity emerges an essential wisdom to guide our lives.

A Buddhist Perspective

Siddhartha Gautama (563–483) B.C.E., was the son of a king who ruled the lands at the foot of the Himalayas, along what is today the border between India and Nepal. Leaving home at age twenty-nine, he gave up his princely life and became a wandering ascetic, seeking the answer to the question of why people suffer. He attained enlightenment by turning his meditation inward, achieving the realization of ultimate reality and becoming "the Buddha," the awakened one. He never claimed to be divine or divinely inspired. He did not teach any religion or philosophy or system of belief. He called his teaching *Dharma*, which is variously interpreted as the law, the way, the path, the practice, the teachings, the truth, reality.

The Buddha did not give meaning to the word *dharma*; such meaning was already there in the Indian context. The word had a history in India. *Dharma* meant the Truth which is the basis of all truth and the guide for religious living. *Dharma* is the teaching of the truth which never changes. No one teaches a "new" *dharma*. The Buddha claimed that he had discerned the dharma, which opened up the secret of life and liberation.

Gautama had no interest in idle speculation or dogma. Instead he offered a practical solution for the universal problem of human suffering. He taught only what he had experienced by direct knowledge, and he encouraged others to develop such knowledge themselves. He wished to make the law of nature known plainly and widely so that as many people as possible might benefit from it.

One of the vehicles for his teachings today is *vipassana* meditation.[9] *Vipassana* means "insight" in the ancient Pali language of India. *Passana* denotes "seeing," the ordinary sort of vision that we have with open eyes. *Vipassana* means a special kind of vision: observation of the reality within oneself. The technique is the systematic and dispassionate observation of physical sensations, mental and emotional states within oneself. One becomes aware of the "dominant" event occurring in one's body-mind process, and names it with a concise mental "note." Then one observes what happens within the process until it ends.

In *vipassana* meditation, one simply observes bodily sensations objectively and as they normally occur—heat, cold, itching, throbbing, pressure, tingling, pulsation, etc. One observes them with the same detachment as a scientist looking through a microscope in a laboratory. One soon comes to realize that all our sensations are constantly changing. Everything inside oneself, mental and physical, just as in the world outside, is changing every moment. This is the reality of mind and matter: it is impermanent. Previously, we may have known this intellectually; now we experience it directly within the framework of the body, and it begins to speak to us about the nature of life and relationships. From the realization that every particle of the body, every process of the mind is in a state of constant flux comes the recognition that there is nothing to which one can cling or call "mine," for nothing is exempt from the law of impermanence.

In Tibetan Buddhism this is the lesson of the painstaking creation and deliberate destruction of a mandala: an exquisite drawing with colored sand. Several monks spend ten days making a circular design of spiritual images almost grain by grain, then in a few moments, sweep it away to signify the law of impermanence. In watching the monks slice through the magnificent creation and quickly sweep the multi-colored grains of sand into a great pile, a corollary reality becomes clear. Any effort to hold on to something, to keep it just as it is, is bound to make one unhappy, because sooner or later it changes and passes away. In other words, attachment to what is impermanent, transitory, and beyond one's control leads to suffering.

Seeing life as a constantly changing process, one begins to accept pleasure and pain, fear and joy, without clinging or anxiety; one begins to live with increasing equanimity and balance. Once the Buddha was asked to explain real happiness. After enumerating various actions that contribute to the welfare of others, he said: "When faced with all the ups and downs of life, and still the mind remains unshaken, not lamenting, not generating defilements, always feeling secure: this is the greatest happiness."[10]

The blessing of equanimity is in demand when friends move away, children run away, or a spouse walks away. It is equally in demand when friends are stable, the children stellar, and one's spouse serene. The Japanese samurai warriors had a notion of "emotional chastity": a low spirit is weak and an elevated spirit is weak. Success and depression are equally dangerous. Both tend to make one lose sight of the continuously changing flow of events. The challenge is to respond with equanimity no matter what arises, whether within the microcosm of one's own mind and body or in the world outside. Acceptance of the fleeting—and by that token, ultimately unsatisfactory—nature of things invites one to respond in every situation, pleasant or unpleasant, with equanimity.

Congruent Spiritual Paths: The Christian Witness

The teaching of keeping a balanced mind and a peaceful heart in the face of all life's circumstances comes to shining expression in Christianity as well. The reference points for this wisdom, however, are quite different. Siddhartha Gautama seems to have been a human being who thought that he had found the key to right living. His teaching goes forward on the basis of empirical psychology. On observing the barb of suffering stuck deep into human flesh, he set out to find a way to alleviate misery. He found what he felt was a satisfactory answer short of explicit talk about God: all life is suffering, in the sense that everything disappoints because nothing stays the same. When we cling to anything—a friend, a present phase in family life—we cause ourselves suffering. The answer is to learn to relate with joy and gratitude to whoever or whatever is given, but without clinging. We thereby maintain a peaceful heart and a tranquil mind. The Buddhist ideal of living with equanimity is effectively demonstrated by the following story.

A girl in a fishing village became an unwed mother and after several beatings finally revealed who the father of the child was: the Zen master living on the outskirts of the village. The villagers trooped into the master's house, rudely disturbed his meditation, denounced him as a hypocrite, and told him to keep the baby. All the master said was, "Very well. Very well."

He picked the baby up and made arrangements for a woman from the village to feed and clothe and look after it at his expense. The master's name was ruined and his disciples all abandoned him.

When this had gone on for a year, the girl who had borne the child could stand it no longer and finally confessed she had lied. The father of the child was the boy next door. The villagers were most contrite. They prostrated themselves at the feet of the master to beg his pardon and to ask for the child back. The master returned the child. All he said was, "Very well. Very well."[11]

In Christianity, Jesus himself is the first to sound the note of keeping one's heart peaceful and of enjoying all created things without clinging to them. St. Paul, St. John of the Cross, and Meister Eckhart are among those who most clearly echo the theme in rich variations. For all of them, however, the basis from which they proceed is not observation of human experience but

faith in the providential love of God and in the One whom God
has sent who is our peace: Jesus of Nazareth. His words are rich
and provocative:

> *Do not worry about your life, what you will eat, or*
> *about your body, what you will wear. For life is more*
> *than food, and the body more than clothing. Consider*
> *the ravens: they neither sow nor reap, they have neither*
> *storehouse nor barn, and yet God feeds them. Of how*
> *much more value are you than the birds! And can any of*
> *you by worrying add a single hour to your span of life? If*
> *then you are not able to do so small a thing as that, why*
> *do you worry about the rest? Consider the lilies, how*
> *they grow: they neither toil nor spin; yet I tell you, even*
> *Solomon in all his glory was not clothed like one of*
> *these. But if God so clothes the grass of the field, which*
> *is alive today and tomorrow is thrown into the oven,*
> *how much more will he clothe you—you of little faith!*
> *And do not keep striving for what you are to eat and*
> *what you are to drink, and do not keep worrying. For it*
> *is the nations of the world that strive after all these*
> *things, and your Father knows that you need them.*
> *Instead, strive for his kingdom, and these things will be*
> *given to you as well* (Luke 12:22–31).

Paul, the apostle to the Gentiles, faced more than his fair
share of trials and tribulations in serving the advance of God's
reign. He was afflicted in every way, but not crushed; perplexed,
but not driven to despair; persecuted, but not forsaken; struck
down, but not destroyed, always carrying in his body the death of
Jesus so that the life of Jesus too might be made visible (2 Corinthians 4:8–11). In his letter to the Philippians he shares the great
secret of his steadiness:

I have learned to be content with whatever I have. I know what it is to have little, and I know what it is to have plenty. In any and all circumstances I have learned the secret of being well-fed and of going hungry, of having plenty and of being in need. I can do all things through him who strengthens me (4:11–13).

While equanimity may look the same to the external observer in both the Buddhist and the Christian, Paul would leave no doubt as to the source of his comportment. "We have this treasure in clay jars, so that it may be made clear that this extraordinary power belongs to God and does not come from us" (2 Corinthians 4:7).

Another voice in Christian tradition which has clearly sounded this note belongs to John of the Cross, a sixteenth century Spanish Carmelite who played a major role in the Teresian reform of Carmelite spirituality. He is one of the greatest mystics in Western Christianity. His four major works, *The Ascent of Mount Carmel, The Dark Night, The Spiritual Canticle* and *The Living Flame of Love*, communicate the rich spiritual teachings of the saint.

John sees the same thing as Gautama: attachments are kill-joys. We are to find delight in everything but to cling to nothing. John himself loved others dearly and had many friends. He enjoyed music and stars and nature immensely. But in his relationships he, too, discovered that his capacity for deep, calm, enduring delight in each friend or family member heightened as he let go of his self-centered clinging. John's basic rationale for detachment or non-clinging relates to the harm that selfish attachments introduce into the soul's pursuit of the Lord.

In *The Dark Night*, John describes how, even in the greatest afflictions of all kinds, filled with yearning for God, it is possible to come to perfect equanimity. And in *The Spiritual Canticle* he writes "True love receives all things that come from the Beloved—prosperity, adversity, even chastisement—with the same evenness of soul, since they are (God's) will."[12]

Siddhartha Gautama would likely have had no difficulty in signing his name to these lines from John of the Cross:

> To reach satisfaction in all, desire its possession in nothing.
> To come to possess all, desire the possession of nothing.
> To arrive at being all, desire to be nothing. . . .
> For to go from all to the all, you must deny yourself of all
>   in all.
> And when you come to the possession of the all, you must
>   possess it without wanting anything. . . .
> In this nakedness the spirit finds its quietude and rest.
> For in coveting nothing, nothing raises it up and nothing
>   weights it down.[13]

Meister Eckhart was a fourteenth century Dominican master of theology and high official in his order, but he was far from being a conventional scholastic thinker. Since his rediscovery in the early nineteenth century, he has inspired and influenced thousands, both famous theologians and humble, holy seekers of God. Perhaps no Western mystic has appealed so strongly or offered so fruitful a conversation to the great mystical traditions of Asia.[14] His teachings contribute as well to contemporary Western world activists who are valiantly trying, amidst time, famine and uprooting mobility, to keep their ambitions in line with their deepest priorities.

Our true Self, according to Eckhart, has no ambitions or goals apart from union with God. It is simply free, open and receptive to the reality of the present moment and whatever there is of God in it. This detached openness and receptivity, this refusal to cling to anything, is one of its most God-like characteristics. Eckhart speaks of detachment as taking things at their true value, a value which is real but not absolute. Family members leave home; our children ignore us; friends move; loved ones die or walk away. With true detachment, the spirit stands as immovable in all the assaults of joy and sorrow, honor, shame or disgrace because these are only fleeting, transient, temporal, albeit lovable and cherished realities. Still, they are not God.

Yet detachment is not meant to be a cold and unfeeling thing; there is fire and passion behind it, the insatiable desire for God which reaches out to its goal and will not be bought off by anything else. Where God is concerned, one can be fiery and passionate. Detachment means being alert to the demands of the present moment, seeking God in all that one does, discerning what God asks of us in a given situation. What matters is the surrender of what we cling to, of selfish desire, and the ready response to God's will as it presents itself here and now.

> Whatever the circumstances may be in which we find ourselves, we will not be dominated or swallowed up by them so that we forget God. We will not become drunk on joy or depressed by sorrow, but will look beyond all these essentially changing and impermanent circumstances to the unchanging God who underlies them. Whatever experiences we may have recently undergone . . . will not overwhelm us now or qualify our total freedom, lightness and readiness to respond to the will of God as it presents itself in the present moment.[15]

Our task is to concentrate on the present moment and on its demands because it is here, and here alone that time intersects with eternity.

The Buddhist and Christian teachings on detachment and equanimity offer wisdom for Christian living. It can be applied to the changing patterns in family life or to the changing locations of friends. It can also be applied to the processes of aging one observes within oneself or to one's struggle to relate with greater detachment to cherished possessions. The complementary counsel from both religions is *to remain free from the desire which entangles us in regret or nostalgia for the past, and free from the anxiety which fills us with preoccupation about the future.* Both religions sound a similar call to the overarching discipline of keeping our minds focused on the present and of making ourselves available for service in compassion and love here and now.

As I stood in the bright sunlight outside the Buddhist retreat center with Gerry's letter in my hands, this was no theoretical counsel. It meant being grateful for the fourteen years we had been given where dropping by to share life was a valued gift frequently exchanged. It meant recognizing my feelings of sorrow and knowing that their present sharpness would, like everything, eventually pass. It meant trusting without anxiety that into this space in my life would come forth others, either more strongly if already there, or for the first time. It meant recognizing that there were those with me right there, at that retreat, who represented the apocalypse of the present moment of God's revelation in my life now and whose own worthy presence bid me not to be caught napping and miss God's visitation.

We struggle with the whole concept of detachment. When the word is used in a secular context the meaning is generally akin to "I don't really care." This is not the essential meaning of "detachment" as it is used in the Christian spiritual tradition. Detachment has nothing to do with indifference (to something), or with forgetting or not caring (about someone). It is not withdrawal from love, but the *expansion of love* beyond the kind of desire which entangles us in nostalgia for the past and preoccupation with the future. It is the ability to relate caringly and appreciatively to people and things without our happiness depending upon them. It is being able to say, "You enrich my life and are a source of joy and consolation to me. But if I lose you, I will not, I must not, spend the rest of my life in unhappiness."

An important distinction is made between *preferences*, which are normal and necessary, and *attachments*. A preference says: "I prefer this, but I'm not going to be unhappy if I don't get it or if it's taken away." Attachment says, "I cannot do without this (or you)." Thus attachment induces craving, clinging, anxiety, fear of losing. Subsequently, peace of soul is lost. The most peaceful person is the one whose happiness does not depend on what is/is not at his or her disposal.

Happiness is enoughness. In the words of St. Paul: "I have learned to be satisfied with what I have. I have the strength to face all conditions by the power Christ gives me."

In Christian faith, the reason one can let go of the past and not worry about the future, trusting in the ultimate graciousness of reality, is God. God's love for us and commitment to us is revealed in Jesus who sets us free from our fears. Free to serve God, and those whom God's providence has entrusted to us, in joy and gratitude all our days. Free to *enjoy* persons or things without *clinging* to any created good for our own happiness. The way to enjoy everything and everyone is to cling to nothing and no one.

III

THE IMPRINT OF THE PASCHAL MYSTERY
ON OUR LIVES

In friendship and family life, there is a constant call upon us to let go, to refrain from clinging. The time famine is continually squeezing out things we wanted to do, people we wanted to see, letters we wanted to write. The mobility factor gives us more practice than we need at saying goodbye. I have come to relate to all of these experiences of letting go as little "deaths" and to see in them the imprint of what my Christian faith calls the Paschal Mystery.[16]

The Paschal Mystery of Jesus Christ lies at the very center of Christian faith and discipleship. The word "paschal" comes from the Greek term, *pascha*, which goes back to the Hebrew, *pesach*, which refers to the annual commemoration by the Israelites of their liberating passover from slavery in Egypt. The Paschal Mystery is intended to pick up for Christians this rich Hebrew background and to locate the historical death and resurrection of Jesus as the establishment of a new, liberating passover. The followers of Jesus are invited to experience the effects of this new paschal reality in their own lives.

We first of all need, however, a basic sense of what it looked like in the life of Jesus himself so as to know what we're looking for in our own lives. What we discover when we look at the historical life and death of Jesus is that it is lived out of love for others. When we probe this life of love, we discover that it is animated by the presence of a powerful paradox—the paradox of finding life through death and of losing one's life to save one's life. The spirit of this paradox is captured in the saying of Jesus that "those who want to save their life will lose it, and those who lose their life for my sake will find it" (Matt. 16:25). This and other sayings of Jesus ("Unless a grain of wheat . . .") point to the paradox that out of death comes life and that living fruitfully requires a kind of dying.

This striking paradox which permeates his preaching comes to a particular climax in his historical death and resurrection. It now becomes clear that death after all does indeed give rise to new life and that the way to glory is the way of the cross. It is through the death of Jesus on the cross that the fullness of new life in the resurrection comes.

Whenever we are faced in any way, then, with a form of "dying" or letting go, the Paschal Mystery of Christ is there to shape our perception of what is happening and to give an affirming stamp to our hope that out of this "death" will come new life and growth. The Paschal Mystery represents a particular vision of life, a special way of responding to life's developments and the rhythm of our relationships in family life and friendship. It is this peculiar pattern of dying to live, of passing over, of letting go, that is at the heart of the Paschal Mystery of Christ. Being a disciple of Christ involves living out of this paradox and allowing it to serve as a special pair of lenses which enable us to see into the nature of all reality. The pattern of death and resurrection in Jesus' life is being reproduced in our own through many little "dyings" and "risings" until one day, one of these "letting go's" *is* our death and the new life *is* our resurrection.

In relationships of friendship and love, people do "die" for the sake of each other. Spouses give themselves in costly love and parents sacrifice themselves out of love for their children. Friends make themselves available to serve each other's good in sometimes heroic ways. From a purely human point of view, love that does not suffer is something less than love. It was this kind of love, one that suffers out of love, that was revealed in the passion and death of Jesus on the cross. In it we see a God who suffers in the world and on the cross of Christ out of an abundance of love for the world. To be a disciple of Christ inevitably involves sharing in that experience of willingly embracing suffering out of an abundance of love. In this experience which we might refer to as "the law of the cross" in human life, we see the cross in the life of Jesus and in Christian existence as a creative moment on the way to newness of life.

Joseph Campbell, the world renowned expert on cultural and religious mythologies, said in a televised interview something rather astonishing to secular ears: "By contemplating the cross, you are contemplating the nature of life. For the suffering involved in loving is the burning point of life, the experience of being truly alive." Could anything better explain the Christian conviction about Jesus on the cross? Campbell put his finger on an essential truth of Christian faith: when we, like Jesus, are available for service in love at the cost of personal sacrifice, the very act of living is a share in the dying-rising of Christ.

We are engaged in daily rehearsals for our grand finale. Death and resurrection are not separate from life. They are not just future. They are present. To look upon the resurrection as a narrow escape from death is to miss the full meaning of human life, to miss the death and resurrection that are present in every moment. It is reflected in the coming and going of the seasons, in the rhythm of our relationships, in the phases of our personal and familial growth.

Death and resurrection are not to be pushed out of life, are not to be seen as ultimate events but as immediate experiences. They are not final events but daily choices. They are every step of the journey, the inner exodus from the old self to the new. "I die daily," said St. Paul. But he also rose daily. And in this life we rise to new life only by dying, by ceaselessly dying. Dying to what? Basically, to sin and the false self. Dying to sinful patterns of behavior is never ended, for dying to sin is not merely turning from evil, but turning to Christ ever more fully in a process of constant, life-long conversion.

Dying to our false self is also a struggle we face daily. One illustration of it is seen in our struggle to let go of yesterday, of the past. Not forget it, just let it go. Whether it's turning twenty-one, forty, or sixty-five. Whether it's losing our health or our hair, our money or our memory, a person we love or a possession we prize. "Dying to self" is letting go of where our security once lay. Whether it's family or friends. Whether it's being retired, divorced or disabled. Whether it's a change of life or a change of pace. We must not cling to what once was but is no more.

Wherever or whatever or with whomever we've been, we dare not cling. We have to move on. And all moving on is a dying, a letting go. It's the imprint of the Paschal Mystery on our lives. Only by dying will we rise to fresh life. Only by letting go of yesterday will we open ourselves to tomorrow, where the seeds of fresh life await us.

Conclusion

The time famine and the mobility factor are two contemporary facts of life. Do we let these pressures control us or will we control them through building some structures of support into our lives which liberate us to realize the values in life which we consider deepest and best?

In the domain of friendship and family life, one strategy to prevent these pressures from tyrannizing us is the discipline of preserving quality time in which as friends or family members we continue to share with one another what we're living and who we're becoming through those experiences. An integral part of this discipline is the use of a method (like noting on a calendar the time actually taken and reviewing it weekly or monthly) which enables us to monitor how faithfully we are realizing our intentions in this regard.

If circumstances, such as changing one's city of residence, make that kind of sharing impossible on a regular basis with those with whom we have been fortunate to enjoy it, the importance of such for our spiritual, emotional, and physical health requires us to give this discipline another expression: the investment of time and energy in cultivating new relationships in which this kind of sharing can take place.

A third expression of this discipline is detachment and equanimity. Its role is, on the one hand, to enable us to delight in the gift of good friends who may be given to us for a time, but without clinging to them or attaching happiness to their physical presence and immediate availability. And on the other hand, its role is to help us live with equanimity the unpleasant realities of intervening geographical distance and the effort involved in starting over. Equanimity enables us to live in the midst of the sea of change that is life without being swept away. It enables us to embrace relationships in the secure knowledge that God is known and loved through them, all the while recognizing that they are not God. It enables us to look beyond all the impermanent circumstances of our changing lives to the unchanging God who underlies them.

Detachment and equanimity enable us to remain free from regret or nostalgia for the past, and free from the anxiety which fills us with preoccupation for the future. The source of such equanimity in Christian life is faith in God's love for us and commitment to us, revealed in Jesus, who sets us free from all our fears.

In the time that has passed since Gerry and Cathy's move to another city and my return to Montreal, I have gone to visit them and they have come to Montreal. We also stay in touch by phone. The friendship continues to be honored. At the same time, we are developing new or deepening existing friendships, each in our respective places. The struggle is constant to maintain priority of people over things. Work and projects are always ready to fill up time once reserved for the sharing of life with friends or family; that temptation must be stubbornly resisted.

The Paschal Mystery of our Christian faith summons us to go forward in the firm conviction that every "death," be it little or great, holds within it the seeds of fresh life. And the impermanence of every relationship reminds us that nothing is permanent save the love of God for us. The call is to accept that reality of life with equanimity and faith that this God, whose love is more clearly revealed to us through ours for one another, will not fail to send us new messengers of that saving grace.

3

Living with a Sabbath Rhythm

Some time ago I came to realize that I was regularly breaking one of God's commandments: "Keep holy the Lord's day." I began attending the local Jewish synagogue's sabbath service on Friday evenings to relearn the art of sabbath living. The response of Christians to the synagogue service is usually characterized by surprise. One feels quite at home with the ritual lighting of the sabbath candle. When the cantor begins to sing in hauntingly beautiful melodies, the response is: "I know those songs—those are the same psalms we sing in church on Sunday between our readings!" When the Torah is brought forth with reverence from the sanctuary and carried into the midst of the people who touch it with their fingers and then move their fingers to their lips, one is reminded of the liturgical gesture of signing one's forehead, lips and heart at the reading of the Gospel: "May the Word of God be in my thoughts, upon my lips, and in my heart."

The rabbi steps into the pulpit to read from the Torah scroll, and one notices that he wears a stole around his shoulders over a floor-length vestment. And when he proclaims from the Torah, there is again the shock of recognition: "I know that reading—it's from Genesis (or Exodus, Numbers, Leviticus, Deuteronomy)!" Even the architectural space seems familiar (Christian churches are basically fashioned according to the plan of the temple in

Jerusalem: sanctuary, place where the faithful gathered, and court-yard or vestibule for non-Jews).

"You, a wild olive shoot, were grafted in their place to share the rich root of the olive tree," St. Paul wrote to the Christians in Rome, reminding them of their debt of gratitude to Judaism. "Remember that it is not you that support the root, but the root that supports you" (11:17–18). A Christian who has never stepped into a synagogue service and experienced that glint of recognition of oneself is like a child who has never met her grandparents. She has only a partial knowledge of who she is. The older I get, the more people remark how my features resemble those of my grand-father Ryan. It's a reference I appreciate, because I grew up next door to him and knew him with a warm affection. And every now and then when I needed it, he was the purveyor of some ancient wisdom about life to me. With just such affection and recogni-tion of who I am as a Christian did I turn to Judaism when it became clear to me that I was a sabbath-breaker.

I began to see reflected in my own life the same deleterious rhythm of driven achievement time and compensatory escape time which I critiqued in the society around me. The conception that the meaning and value of leisure comes from its relationship to work leads to three contemporary ailments: 1) work addiction; 2) the exodus complex (the compulsive pursuit of freedom from everyday routine, the compulsive need to keep moving, to be always going somewhere—anywhere—to get away from it all); and 3) justifiable suicide (or, in other words, "I earned it, and I'm going to enjoy it even if it kills me"—and sometimes it does!). Ours is the only society in the history of civilization which offers us the choice of working ourselves to death or consuming our-selves to death, or both.[1]

I

SABBATH KEEPERS: AN ENDANGERED SPECIES

The perpetual activism inherent in striving, competitive, production-oriented North American individualism has made the sabbath keeper an endangered species. Sunday is often marked by the same hectic pace as the other days, but with diversionary activity from the normal work week. This might come in the form of complex entertainments that require large investments of time, planning, energy and money to support them. The correlation between simple, uncrowded activities and savored sabbath time lies buried beneath an agenda ambitious enough to fill twice the amount of time available. Our inclination is decidedly in the direction of trying to do it all and to have it all.

As leisure endeavors have taken on a more important role in our lives, we have also begun to reshape the nature of our leisure pursuits. We are slowly moving away from devotion to mindless, time-filler forms of relaxation toward an engagement with active, purposeful activities. With society becoming increasingly complex, demanding and stress-inducing, North Americans are relying upon their free time to make life worthwhile. Toward that end, we are striving to have a variety of experiences, each delivering top quality, and remaining conveniently accessible. To satisfy our hunger for multiple experiences, we allocate shorter blocks of time for any single leisure activity. We believe that the more different experiences we have, the more likely we will be to find fulfillment. Our desire to jam as many experiences into as short a period as possible is even impacting the way we schedule vacations.

Rather than taking the traditional two-week vacation at a single time, the trend is toward shorter vacations—two and three days plus a weekend.[2]

This underlying presumption that the more different experiences we have the more likely we will be to find fulfillment has created an environment around us and within us that is finally as poisonous and deadly as anything the corporate polluters may be adding to our air, water or land. Our machine-like, programmed busyness leaves us at the end of the day harried, more prey to anxiety and greed, and more susceptible to being controlled and to controlling others. In addition, the religious pluralism of our society has led us down the path of seeing days off in increasingly private terms. The labor laws which used to protect us from the debasement of uninterrupted labor, buying and selling have been washed out in city after city by the pressure to open stores for business on Sunday. The "in" of the Christian attempt to be "in but not of" the world tends to collapse into the "of" until one day we look into the reflective pool of our society's way of life and see that we are not in the role of the evangelizer but the evangelized. We have been sucked in. We are no different in our response to "keep holy the Lord's day" than non-believers—with the exception perhaps of an hour of church, which alone falls far short of the spirit of the commandment.

The Weekend: A Lost Art in Living

"Thank God it's Friday!" has become a universal, undifferentiated groan, sounding as relieved out of Christian mouths as any other. "There must be something more to life than this endless grind," we moan. The promises of work, even meaningful work, are limited. Way down deep, we want a "something more" which is as elusive as it is deeply felt. And to the weekend falls the burden of our hope and longing. It approaches like a chipper puppy, only to be itself worn out by too many sticks and balls thrown in unpatterned directions.

"This is going to be a great weekend!" we think, heading into it.

"No office phones to answer, no one coming in and laying another project on my desk, no deadlines." But by Saturday morning the guilt is already beginning to set in. We really ought to tackle the lawn, clean the garage, run some errands, do the laundry, replenish the refrigerator. And we're off to the races, card-carrying citizens of a culture that can do almost anything in and with space, but is fidgety, nervous and spastic with time.

Sunday will befall a similar fate. We know how to work masterfully with computers and fax machines and modular telephones, but when presented with an unplanned or undefined hour or day, we are suddenly overtaken with Saint Vitus' dance. Can't stand still. Can't be still. What was it we wanted from the weekend, anyway?

Lack of clarity in our expectations and of realism in our approach becloud us by Sunday afternoon and leave us with a sense of remorse, emptiness and betrayal at what might have been. We have lost the art, the liberating discipline of living with a sabbath rhythm.

It is immensely difficult for us to give ourselves permission to use time for being still, for being silent, for seeking nothing, for "wasting time with God"—and with regularity, not just when our backs are to the wall and we are too worn out to work at keeping control. The "common democratic religion" that Alexis de Tocqueville discerned in his visit to America is, in short, a religion characterized by a belief in the ultimate perfectibility of human society and by a devotion to work as the means of achieving that perfection. Fewer and fewer are the Christians who could say with Eric, the Olympic sprinter in the film "Chariots of Fire," who declined to run in his event when it was scheduled on Sunday: "God made countries; God made kings and the rules by which they govern. His law is that the sabbath is his, and I for one intend to keep it that way."

If there is something to be done we cannot rest until it is finished. When one project is over there is always another to be tackled, and Sunday is the day that catches the overflow of what we didn't get done on the other six days. Always and everywhere we are project-oriented, seeing the world as something to be changed, dividing it into what is useful and not-so-useful, holding everything and everyone slightly apart from ourselves in order to move them according to our purpose.

Naming the Demons of Compulsion

The moments when we feel we can stop are few and far between. Why do we work so much? Why do we never seem to have time to be with others? Why do we not have time to relax or play? We say we work incessantly because we have to, because we like to, because we are expected to, because we are devoted, because there doesn't seem to be anyone else to do it, because we are competent. Indeed, when something needs to be done, it is not to the incompetent that people turn. The kind of person sought is the one who immediately recognizes what needs to be done and who can do it better and more efficiently than many others. So it is not long before the talented person is asked to do more than is humanly possible.

But competency alone is not the culprit. It is when competency exists side by side with unfulfilled needs that problems arise. If we have unusually strong needs to please others, to appear generous or self-sacrificing or if we are pushed to excel or to be in charge—and at the same time are talented—we are particularly vulnerable to overwork. There is almost no way to avoid it. We want to be helpful and we can do many things well. The difficulty is that it is not long before we lose our vibrancy in the midst of too much to do.[3]

The result is burnout, a phenomenon which has become particularly familiar to people in roles of church ministry. The desire to serve others, to care compassionately, makes it all the more difficult to claim non-productive time. Without a clear sense of personal limit, a minister or helper easily succumbs to a kind of "promiscuous" ministry—the need to respond to every hurt and problem that arises in whatever form in the community, and at the eventual expense of the minister's fidelity to and effectiveness in that specific ministry to which he or she is preeminently called.

Such a person, assuming responsibility for the salvation of the world, becomes agitated, distracted and eventually exhausted, not just by responding to but by worrying about all that "has to be done."[4]

A related compulsion arises from the belief that the good we do makes us more worthy in the sight of God, even perhaps earning our salvation. If we are compelled to "earn our way" with God, to repeatedly prove our worth by what we achieve, then the time of non-achievement will appear a waste and be avoided. Periods of illness (flu) or recovery (a broken bone) strike fear into our hearts with all their dependency, reflection and passive experience of time. An uneasiness with such empty spaces suggests that, deep down, we need to be doing, achieving, earning our way. The grace of an illness or vacation is that it can reveal this compulsiveness, this unholy need to prove my worth to God and myself.[5]

Whatever the form of a person's compulsions, they are forces that make us unfree and unbalanced in our use of time. Christian spirituality is concerned with the exorcism of these compulsions or demons and the liberating of our time. An asceticism of time management begins in taking the time to reflect on how we structure our days and our weeks. It will include an effort to turn the world and its salvation back to God. With a less heroic sense of our own mission, we begin to have a better chance of helping others according to our gifts and limits. It will also include a recovery of space in our day for "useless" activities such as recreational time with loved ones and quiet time with God. An "asceticism of time" means taking responsibility for the decisions that shape the time of our lives. It is a response to grace, to the invitation to become less scattered and less self-centered, and more aware of a Presence already within. The delicate balance is between becoming strong, responsible agents of our own lives and simultaneously remaining responsive to a Presence that disrupts our plans. Christian history is, in part, the story of our continuing struggle to maintain the balance between greater dependence on God and greater personal responsibility in actively constructing a holier, more aware, just and caring world.[6]

Christian reflection on time has been influenced by the distinction in classical Greek thought between two kinds of time: *chronos* and *kairos*. *Chronos* translates the experience of time as duration, as chronological progression and continuity. When someone stops you on the street corner and asks "What time is it?" you respond in *chronos* time.

Kairos refers to time as opportunity or occasion, a time which has a special significance or potential—the "right time," a favorable moment, or critical period. When a couple who have been thinking about having another child look at each other and say "This is the time," they're operating in *kairos* time.

One way of looking at *chronos* and *kairos* in our lives is to distinguish three modes of experiencing time: dissipation, compulsion, and concentration. When experienced as dissipated, time is emptied of focus and presence and so of the awareness of God. When experienced compulsively time is a hostile and unholy medium through which a person is obsessively driven. These modes are *chronos*: the first, because time is felt as pointless and is "lost"; the second, because it is unfree, possessed by the demon of compulsion which distorts our awareness. But *kairos* time is experienced as graceful. It is the same time, but now concentrated, becoming a medium in which we love and work with special attention. It brings into focus what was always there—a God who sanctifies our time while inviting us to a future time.[7]

The intent of an asceticism of time is not an escape from time, but the *saving* of time, the transformation and salvation of it as the medium through and in which we encounter God and other loved ones who transform us. When by grace and effort we rescue ourselves from dissipated and compulsive time, we participate in its salvation and sanctify it. An exploration of our roots in Judaism offers a rich harvest with regard to sanctified and saving time.

II
THE MULTI-LAYERED SPIRITUALITY
OF THE SABBATH

We know what to do with space, but not what to do about time except to make it subservient to space. Time is like PacMan on our computer screens, a ravenous little monster that gobbles up everything in its path. In his wonderful book *The Sabbath*,[8] Abraham Heschel develops a beautiful meditation on the nature and celebration of the Seventh Day. Its thesis is that Judaism is a religion of time, not space, and the sabbath symbolizes the sanctification of time so that the sabbaths are our great cathedrals. They represent a day of separation from space and the material things that fill it, a day of devotion to time and the eternity that fills it. A synthesis of Heschel's reflections is a fitting place to start in an effort to reconstruct the discipline of keeping holy the Lord's day.

Holiness in space, in nature, was common in other religions, but in Judaism the idea of holiness gradually shifted from space to time, from the realm of nature to the realm of history, from things to events. There were no naturally sacred plants or animals any more. No longer was it *things* which lent significance to moments, but *moments* which lent significance to things. The higher goal of spiritual living does not consist therefore in amassing a wealth of material possessions or even information, but in participating in sacred moments.

When one sees how the Bible pays more attention to generations, events, and history than to countries, things and geography, one begins to appreciate that time has a significance and sovereignty of its own, a meaning for life which is at least equal to that of space. To be sure, space is not disparaged; to do so would be to disparage creation. Time and space are interrelated. A heightened appreciation for time counterbalances our tendencies to become enslaved to things.

To Israel the unique events of historic time were spiritually more significant than the repetitive processes in the cycle of nature, even though the people depended upon the latter for their survival. The deities of other people were associated with places or things, but the God of Israel was the God of events, the Redeemer from slavery, the Revealer of the Torah.

Christianity is a branch grafted onto the trunk of an olive tree, Judaism, which is dedicated to the sanctification of time. Judaism is a religion whose Holy of Holies is a shrine that neither the Romans nor the Germans were able to burn: the Day of Atonement. Jewish ritual may be characterized as the architecture of time. Most of its observances depend on a certain hour of the day or season of the year: the sabbath, the new moon, the festivals, the sabbatical and the jubilee year.

One of the most distinguished words in the Hebrew scriptures is *qadosh*, holy, a word which more than any other is representative of the mystery and majesty of the divine. What provided the first occasion for its use—a mountain, an altar? Time. "And God blessed the seventh day and made it holy" (Genesis 2:3). Accustomed religious thinking would expect that after heaven and earth have been established, God would create a holy place, a mountain or spring whereupon a sanctuary should be erected. But what comes first is the seventh day, the sabbath, holiness in time.

To the philosopher, the idea of the good is the most exalted idea. But to the Bible the good is the base of the mountain; the holy is the summit. Things created in six days God considered good. The seventh day God made holy. The meaning of the sabbath then is to celebrate time rather than space. Six days a week we live under the tyranny of things of space; on the sabbath we try to become attuned to holiness in time, to what is eternal in time, and to turn from the *results* of creation to the *mystery* of creation.

Heschel relates a legend which conveys that the sabbath and eternity are of the same essence. At the time when God was giving the Torah to Israel, God said to them: "My children, if you accept the Torah and observe my law, I will give you for all eternity a thing most precious that I have in my possession."

"And what," asked Israel, "is that precious thing which You will give us if we obey Your Torah?"

"The world to come."

"Show us in the world an example of the world to come."

"The sabbath is an example of the world to come."[9]

According to the Talmud, the sabbath is somewhat like eternity or the world to come. The idea that a seventh part of our lives could be experienced as a paradise came as a revelation to the Jews and a scandal to others. The sabbath is spirit in the form of time. With our bodies we belong to space, but our spirits aspire to be holy and soar to eternity. Every seventh day a miracle comes to pass, the resurrection of the human soul.

Judaism tries to foster the vision of life as a pilgrimage to the seventh day. The longing for the sabbath through all the days of the week is a form of longing for the eternal sabbath all the days of our lives. The thought and appreciation for what this day is, already now though not yet fully, provides a melodious counterpoint to the vicissitudes of living.

Judaism, however, did not inherit this sabbath theology in one rich lump.

Historical Evolution of the Sabbath's Meaning

From the earliest times, as far as can be discerned, the sabbath was marked by religious observance among the Israelites.

But its meaning rolled like a snowball down the hill and, over the centuries, accumulated many layers. At its earliest traceable stage, the principal component of the sabbath was *cessation from work*. Moses called the leaders of the people and told them that the seventh day was to be a day of solemn rest; this is what the Lord commands. He counselled them to gather twice as much food as normal on the sixth day, to put part of it aside for the next day and to stay out of the fields on that day. "Each of you stay where you are; do not leave your place on the seventh day. So the people rested on the seventh day" (Exodus 16:22–30).

As their appreciation for sabbath living grew, they wrote the notion of a day of rest and relaxation into the codes which described their covenant with God. Now the accent was not upon just cessation from work but upon something more positive: *physical and mental rejuvenation:* "Six days you shall do your work, but on the seventh day you shall rest, so that your ox and your donkey may have relief, and your homeborn slave and the resident alien may be refreshed" (Exodus 23:12).

The inner religious meaning of sabbath living was elaborated during the period of the deuteronomist reform in which the prophet Jeremiah played an important role. In this development the people are asked to pause and remember the way things used to be, i.e., when they were in slavery.

> *Observe the sabbath day and keep it holy as the Lord your God has commanded you. Remember that you were a slave in the land of Egypt and the Lord your God brought you out from there with a mighty hand and an outstretched arm; therefore the Lord your God commanded you to keep the sabbath day* (Deuteronomy 5:12,15).

Israel now sees rest and sabbath in the light of history. The sabbath is a joyful celebration of redemption and liberation from slavery. In this positive new layer of development, the sabbath's primary emphasis is the *gratitude of a people set free*. The elements of cessation from work, rest and relaxation are carried forward in an encompassing religious celebration expressed both individually and communally.

Ironically, this new emphasis arrives just in time to accompany the people into exile and a new enslavement. That condition is the place for Jeremiah's insight concerning the purpose and value of sabbatical living: *the relationship between sabbath observance and their future happiness.*

> *If you listen to me, says the Lord, and bring in no burden by the gates of this city on the sabbath day, but keep the sabbath day holy and do no work on it, then there shall enter by the gates of this city kings who sit on the throne of David, riding in chariots and on horses, they and their officials, the people of Judah and the inhabitants of Jerusalem; and this city shall be inhabited forever* (Jeremiah 17:24–25).

In a fifth stage, the dimension of *communal worship* is introduced by the priestly group in their prescriptions in Leviticus and Numbers.

> *Six days shall work be done; but the seventh day is a sabbath of complete rest, a holy convocation; you shall do no work; it is a sabbath to the Lord throughout your settlements. These are the appointed festivals of the Lord, the holy convocations, which you shall celebrate at the time appointed for them* (Leviticus 23:3–4).

Numbers 28:10 stipulates the burnt offering for every sabbath, indicating that this is a time to come together to commune with divinity through the ritual of worship.

In this brief overview[10] of the sabbath's development, we see the various facets of meaning which the seventh day holds within itself today: cessation from work, rest and relaxation, communal liturgical celebration as an expression of our thankfulness for God's redemption, and a pledge of the quality of living that awaits us "out of time." The Hebrew scriptures attribute great importance to the sabbath as a time to stop regular activities and bring perspective into one's life by relating it to God. This same idea of refocusing one's values surfaces in the custom of observing a jubilee year every seventh year to provide people with the opportunity to erase their ledger and begin with a clean slate.

This is the origin of the sabbatical year of leave from primary obligations for personal and professional renewal. Since this is available only to a small minority (for most of whom it is everything but a restful time), the general question then becomes: can we, with no substantial time away from our jobs and responsibilities, manage to catch hold of the spirit of sabbath living and integrate it into our lives by recovering the discipline of a weekly sabbath?

The Spirit of Sabbath Living

The first understanding we shall have to revamp is that the seventh day is primarily for the sake of gaining strength for new efforts, since we cannot work continuously. To the biblical mind, the sabbath is a day for the sake of life. We are not beasts of burden, and the sabbath is not for the purpose of enhancing the efficiency of our work on the other days of the week. In short, the sabbath is not for the weekdays; the weekdays are for sake of the sabbath. It is not an interlude to, so much as the climax of, living. The sabbath is the inspirer, the other days the inspired. This is what the other days are for.[11]

Labor is a craft, but genuine rest—the result of an accord of body, mind and spirit—is an art. To attain a degree of excellence in art, one must accept its discipline and abjure slothfulness. Sloth, one of the deadly sins, is laziness at the center while the periphery is a flurry of talk and activity. It is the sin that avoids awareness of our Creator, that deflects the real "work" of learning to be still and know that God is the Sovereign of our lives.

Christians make a gesture at keeping holy the Lord's day by going to church, and then stuff the rest of the day like a small suitcase with projects and movies and study. Of course there are always things to do, to get done. It's not possible for us to accomplish in six days all the work that we have to do. The spirit of sabbath living, however, is to rest on the sabbath as if all our work were done. To rest even from the *thought* of labor. To set apart one day a week for freedom, a day for being with ourselves, independent of external obligations. To declare an armistice day in our economic struggles, a day on which we decline to worship before the idols of productivity and efficiency.

Heschel offers the poetic image of the sabbath as a palace in time[12] which we build. It is made of soul, joy and reticence—the latter, because the splendor of the day is expressed in terms of abstentions. How else express glory in the presence of mystery, of eternity, if not by the silence of abstaining from noisy acts? The sabbath is a mine in which the precious metal of the spirit, its likeness to God, is brought forth and celebrated. This is not a day for *doing*, but for *being*, for giving thanks for all that is and has been freely given. The seventh day is like a palace in time with a room in it for all. It is not a date or a place but an atmosphere. It is a sanctuary which we build, a sanctuary in time, an island harbor in the tempestuous ocean of toil where we may enter and reclaim our dignity. A day of detachment from things, instruments and practical affairs as well as of attachment to the spirit.

The sabbath is not a time for personal anxiety or care, not a time for remembering and confessing one's sins, for fasting or mourning. In the sabbath grace after meals comes the request that "there be no sadness or trouble in the day of our rest."

According to Hasidic tradition, it is a sin to be sad on the sabbath day. It is a day for praise, not for petitions.

A world without the sabbath would be a world without a window in eternity that opens into time. Eternity is not attained by those who barter time for space but by those who know how to fill their time with spirit. The great problem is time rather than space.

The task is how to convert time into eternity rather than how to fill space with buildings, bridges and roads. The solution of the problem lies in study and prayer rather than in geometry and engineering.[13]

Let the Bride Enter In

The ancient rabbis reflected that the act of creation would not be complete unless the six days culminated in the sabbath. They compared it to a king who made a bridal chamber which he plastered, painted and adorned. It lacked only a bride to enter it. The idea of the sabbath as a bride or a queen[14] is not so much a personification of the sabbath as an illustration of God's need for human love, of God's relationship to humankind. Observance of the sabbath is much more than fulfilling a commandment. The sabbath is the presence of God in the world, open to our hearts. It is a divinely established rendezvous, an invitation to consecrate every seventh day to spend just with each other.

About the middle of the third century, Jewish scholars speak of the seventh day not as if referring to elusive and abstract time, but as a living presence. They speak of it as a guest who is coming to see them. And of course a guest who comes to pay a call in friendship must be given an appropriate welcome. Hence it is told of Rabbi Yanni that he donned his robes on the eve of the sabbath and addressed himself to the ethereal guest: "Come, O Bride." The sabbath is a bride, and its celebration is like a wedding. The groom, Israel, is bedecked in its finest garments and does no work on the wedding day.

The reason why the people extended the observance of the sabbath to a part of Saturday night was to show that they do not like to see the departure of the holy guest, that her parting evokes a deep regret. So they detain her, finally accompanying her to the door with song and praise. As for the opening of the sabbath, when all work is brought to a standstill, the candles are lit by the woman of the house. Just as creation began with the word "Let there be light!" so the celebration of the culmination of creation, the sabbath, begins with the kindling of light. And riding on the exquisite symbol of light, the sabbath sends out its presence into the atmosphere of the home. With the soft flicker of candles nodding dreamily to intuitions of eternity, all serenade the bride:

"Come, Beloved, meet the Bride! Let us go and welcome the Sabbath!" And in the synagogue the congregation rises and turns to the west as a sign of welcoming the invisible guest. They all bow their heads in greeting:

Come in peace, crown of God,
Come with joy and cheerfulness,
Amidst the faithful, precious people . . .
Come, Beloved, meet the Bride.

The Church and the Sabbath

The earliest Jewish Christians continued to observe the sabbath and integrated their faith in what God had done in Jesus into that practice. "They devoted themselves to the apostles' teaching and fellowship, to the breaking of bread and the prayers. Day by day, as they spent much time together in the temple, they broke bread at home and ate their food with glad and generous hearts, praising God and having the goodwill of all the people" (Acts 2:42,46–47).

Soon, however, the sabbath observance was called into question and the church decided to shift its observance to Sunday, the day of the Lord's resurrection, and call it "the day of the Lord." This already appears to be the practice in the Book of Revelation, written toward the close of the first century: "I, John . . . was in the spirit on the Lord's day, and I heard behind me a loud voice like a trumpet saying, 'Write in a book what you see and send it to the seven churches' " (1:10–11).

The Christians unfortunately did not carry forward the several layers of sabbath meaning which was their heritage from Judaism. They put the stress upon worship, for example, allowing the emphasis on rest and relaxation to gradually phase out. The emperor Constantine restored it in 321 with "no work on Sundays" legislation, apparently initiated for reasons largely political and economic. The church was slow to back it, but eventually got in line for its own political, as well as pastoral, motives. Not long after, one finds the ecclesiastical authorities putting a religious interpretation on Sundays without work, and using the Mosaic commandment to "keep holy the Lord's day" as a supportive point of reference. Again, however, use of the tradition was piecemeal in its application; this time it is the earliest stage of development in sabbath observance that is stressed: cessation from work.

Generally speaking, Christian developments surrounding the Lord's day throughout history reflect the same kind of patterns that historically characterized Jewish sabbath observance—a tendency to emphasize now one, now another aspect of it, and eventually surround it with rules, regulations, and rituals.[15]

III
CREATIVE BLUEPRINTS FOR SABBATH LIVING

I have developed a walking tour for visitors to downtown Montreal, and one of the first stops is a visit to the Alcan Aluminum international headquarters. All one sees from the street are the stone or brick fronts of four handsome buildings erected in the early part of this century. But when one passes through one of their doors, one enters into a modern, soaring, airy atrium filled with light, sculpture, and colorful banners. It's a marvellous example of integrative architecture. Instead of tearing down the beautiful old structures, the architects found ways to adapt and incorporate them into a new design which capitalizes upon their enduring contribution to the landscape of stately Sherbrooke Street. Much modern knowledge went into the transformation and preservation of the sturdy form, basic materials and aesthetic appeal of the original buildings. The Alcan project serves as a symbol of what we need to do with the Christian sabbath today.

The Lord's day is still a viable structure today, albeit a neglected one, for expressing and confirming the intent of life in the Spirit. But its particular form needs to be reconsidered in the light of our contemporary situation. I am becoming aware of any number of Christian "sabbath architects" who are designing new, creative blueprints for integrating a sabbath rhythm into their lives. One Presbyterian pastor and his wife take their day on Monday since Sunday is a work day for him. They decided to make it a true sabbath and not just a "day off." They didn't have much to follow by way of precedents as neither of them knew anyone in the congregation or beyond who really gave the day to God. They decided to be guided in their design by the two elements which are woven in and out of all the healthy Jewish and Christian emphases historically: praying and playing.

They knew they needed a place and a routine—a sanctuary and a ritual—to support their practice, and chose forest trails for the former and an agreed upon rhythm of silent time and sharing time for the latter. They keep silence in the morning hours, pray together before lunch, and are free to converse through the afternoon and evening. What do they do all day long? Activities designed to restore a sense of the contemplative to their living:

smelling flowers, watching birds and clouds, feeling the weather, reflecting, looking, listening. They keep their sabbath observance in all kinds of weather, whether they feel like it or not. "No other single thing that we have ever done," they say, "comes close to being as creative and deepening in our marriage, in our ministry, and in our faith."

The husband, Eugene, eventually wanted this for his congregation, too. While he couldn't impose a common observance, he recognized that he was in a key position as their pastor to keep their Sundays free from church business and free for worship, free from his concerns and free for their leisure. After several years of this behind-the-scenes "not-doing," he came out in the open with a letter to the congregation entitled "Why Your Pastor Wants You To Keep a Sabbath."

> *One day a week I stand before you and call you to worship God. The conviction behind the act is that time is holy. But how often do you hear anyone say so? More likely you hear, "Time is money." And, as with money, you mostly feel that you don't have enough of it, ever. On occasion, when you have time for which nothing is scheduled, you will "kill time."*
>
> *Odd, isn't it? We have more leisure hours per person as a country than anyone could have guessed a hundred years ago. But we are not leisurely. We are not relaxed. We are anxious. We are in a hurry. The anxiety and the hurry ruin intimacy and sabotage our best intentions in faith, hope, and love—the three actions in which most of us set out to do our best.*
>
> *That is why I as your pastor want you to keep a sabbath. I want you to live well. I want you to live whole and mature, with appreciation and pleasure, experiencing the heights and depths of God's glory in your bodies and your work, your friends and your gardens,*

your minds and your emotions, at the ocean and in the mountains. You can't do that if you are "on the run." You can't do that if you are watching the clock.

Sabbath is the biblical tool for protecting time against desecration. It is the rhythmic setting apart of one day each week for praying and playing—the two activities for which we don't get paid, but which are necessary for a blessed life. A blessed life is what we are biblically promised. A blessed life is not a mere survival life, but a bountiful life. Praying and playing are warp and woof in the bounty.

Keeping a sabbath is simple and easy: we pray and we play, two things we were pretty good at as children, and which we can always pick up again with a little encouragement—if we can only find the time. But we don't have to find the time; it is given to us. A day a week. A sabbath. A day to pray and to play. God's gift. Christian practice orients the first element of the day around the act of worship—praying. This is the great act of freedom in relating to heaven. This is the exercise of our bodies and minds in acts of adoration and commitment, supplication and praise, ventures of forgiving and giving. We explore, enjoy and share it in our assembly for worship. For most of you this praying will start out in our sanctuary each Sunday when I call you to worship God. Simple.

The second element of the day is for playing. This is the great act of freedom in relation to earth. We exercise our bodies and minds in games and walks, in amusement and reading, in visiting and picnicking, in puttering and writing. We take in the colors and shapes, the sounds and smells. We let the creativity of the creation nudge us into creativity. We surprise ourselves by creating a meal, or a conversation, or an appreciation, or

*some laughter that wasn't in our job description. We
have some fun. Easy.*

*So—if it is so simple and easy, why do we find it so
hard? Because the world is in a conspiracy to steal our
sabbath. It is a pickpocket kind of theft (nothing like an
armed robbery) and we aren't aware of it until long after
its occurrence. The "world" is sometimes our friends,
sometimes our families, sometimes our employers—they
want us to work for them, not waste time with God, not
be our original selves. If the world can get rid of the
sabbath, it has us to itself. What it does with us when it
gets us is not very attractive: after a few years of sabbath
breaking we are passive consumers of expensive trash,
and anxious hurriers after fantasy pleasures. We lose our
God and our dignity at about the same time. That is
why I want you to keep a sabbath. Guard the day.
Protect the leisure for praying and playing.*[16]

With his letter, this pastor tried to convey to his people the
secret that lies deep down in living with a sabbath rhythm: the
secret of the reverence and grace that are inherent in time when
one honors it in rhythmic faithfulness through a lifetime of
weeks.

How we keep the day is not biblically prescribed. That we
keep it is commanded. This means there is plenty of space for our
creative architecturing of time. God has given us the broad out-
line. It is for us to write in the details and add color. The best way
to get a sense of the depths and possibilities of living with a
sabbath rhythm is to begin doing it. Only when it is experienced
do we understand first-hand its wisdom and grace.

Half-Sabbaths or Whole-Sabbaths?

In Jesus' own approach to the sabbath, two things are evident. First, he re-emphasizes the importance of genuine sabbath

rest. Second, he reacts negatively to the ritualism and legalism that at times becomes part of sabbath observance and turns it into a burdensome yoke. All his miracles on the sabbath (Luke 6:6–11; 13:10–17; 14:1–6; John 5:1–9; 9:1–41) share a common theme: he wanted to send the message that the sabbath is a celebration of liberation. In Christian faith, Jesus is the liberation for which we long, and his presence as risen Lord is the central reason for our celebration.[17] Thus, intensifying our relationship with him in joy and gratitude should be at the center of our Sunday blueprint. Both playing and praying are essential for good sabbath keeping.

A day given to God that omits one or the other is defective. Half-sabbaths are a speciality of our culture: we've gone to church but haven't played, or gone to the stadium but haven't prayed. There's a story about two fellows who went fishing one Sunday morning which illustrates the mentality. As they were sitting in their boat casting away, one began to think about all the people he knew who were gathering in church that morning. "And here we are, sitting out on the lake fishing," he observed with a tinge of guilt to his partner. "I know what you mean," the other empathized, "but I couldn't have gone to church anyway. My wife is sick."

Often absent from our Sunday activity are the characteristics of sabbath living mentioned in scripture: joy, an awareness of the gifts with which God has blessed us in the present covenant, holistic renewal expressive of our hope for fullness of life, and, flowing from the awareness of our covenant with God as a people, communal worship. But comfort and pleasure are an integral part of the sabbath. It is a day for embodied spirits, and all our faculties should share in its blessing. The sabbath is a delight for body and soul. Is there ever a week when one aspect or another of our lives doesn't need rejuvenation?

We worship our work and work at our play. Sometimes our good ruts are worse than our bad ruts. Distress often arises not from doing bad, nor from failing to act, but, intriguingly, from doing too much good. The endless demands of persons and systems in need overwhelm those who do not possess a clear and shrewd sense of their own limits. We must *choose* not to work (the potential for work being endless) so that other parts of our lives can flourish.

Living with a sabbath rhythm also frees us from the grip of waking up to the deadening feeling of "everydayness." Our utilitarian society seduces us into thinking that everything has to be useful. Last Christmas I noticed how the message had already worked its way down to the children. After tearing off the wrapping and uttering a squeal of delight, the recurring refrain was "Oh I can really *use* this!" The implication is that if it doesn't serve some *useful* purpose, it's not a valued gift.

Celebrating Sunday does not mean merely going to church and staying away from the office. It means living in the presence of God and in some way being useless all day long. It means reading something poetically "wasteful" like a fun novel or book of verse, doing things we wouldn't dream of doing any other day of the week: strolling through an art gallery, enjoying a special museum exhibit, walking in the park, writing a love letter to an appreciated friend.

All these things help us close the door on routine and enter into a playful, festive atmosphere of food, fun and fellowship, rediscovering one another in leisure, laughter and love. The sabbath is the poetry in the prose of the week. Music, art, candles, flowers, picnics, bubblebaths. The seventh day, lived as the window of eternity opening into time, lifts us out of our patterned living, our "good ruts." It is the salt that keeps good self-discipline from rotting.[18]

Our lives require both joy and perseverance. There is a text in Genesis (26:8ff) in which we are told how Isaac and his wife Rebecca went during a time of famine into the land of the Philistines to King Abimelech. Isaac was afraid that the men there would kill him to get the beautiful Rebecca if they knew she was his wife. So, in order to safeguard his life, Isaac presented Rebecca as his sister. But one day King Abimelech looked out his window and saw Isaac "playing" with Rebecca. One translation simply says that he "saw Isaac and Rebecca making love." Others say that Abimelech, "looking out through a window, saw Isaac playing with Rebecca, his wife." Thus King Abimelech recognizes that they are not brother and sister but a wedded pair.

Now "Isaac" means "laughter" in Hebrew, while "Rebecca" means "perseverance." According to the allegorical interpretation, King Abimelech recognizes that laughter and perseverance are wed for life when he sees them enter into "play" together. Earnest and Jest are husband and wife, one flesh. In our efforts to recover and to reintegrate the wisdom of living with a sabbath rhythm, the challenge is to find ways of affirming both work and play without idolatrizing either of them. The only way to do that is to place them both into the broader context of life's meaning and purpose, to see them, not as separate and antithetical elements, but as one flesh, as dynamically intertwined responses to a gracious and caring God. The most uncommon and yet only viable response to the sacred is grave-merriness, laughter and perseverance lying in love together.

Of Rhythm and Complementarity

In his book *Sabbath Time*,[19] Tilden Edwards develops a series of images of sabbath time and work/ministry time which effectively demonstrate that working, playing and praying are all complementary stitches in one seamless garment. The arrows between the sabbath (play-pray) and work columns symbolize their connectedness, reminding us that they do not define a dualistic reality but rather a dialectical one lived out in a rhythmical flow from one to the other. In that rhythmical flow of engagement, withdrawal, return, lies the wisdom of the fourth commandment.

Sabbath Time		*Work Time*
Open surrender	⟷	Confident action
Thank you, Lord	⟷	Lord, have mercy
Letting go	⟷	Engagement/taking on
Relaxation	⟷	Survival/coping/tension
Letting be	⟷	Seeking
Being	⟷	Doing
Mary	⟷	Martha
Contemplative	⟷	Active
Receptive	⟷	Perceptive
Yin	⟷	Yang
Worship	⟷	Science
Intuitive	⟷	Analytical
Background	⟷	Foreground
Open vision	⟷	Concentrated vision
Creature	⟷	Creator
Detachment	⟷	Attachment
Stability/balance	⟷	Movement/thrust
Ultimacy	⟷	Relativity
Appreciation	⟷	Management
Attention	⟷	Intention
Floating	⟷	Swimming
Sailboat	⟷	Motorboat
Integration	⟷	Dispersion
Acceptance	⟷	Judgment
Eternity	⟷	History
Realized	⟷	But not yet fully
Anima	⟷	Animus
Enjoying God	⟷	Working with God
Being known	⟷	Knowing
Root	⟷	Branches
Desert	⟷	City
Simplicity	⟷	Complexity
Quiet prayer	⟷	Active prayer

Retreat	⟵⟶	Pressing forward
Play	⟵⟶	Work
Center	⟵⟶	Border
Home	⟵⟶	Journey
Innocent as doves	⟵⟶	Wise as serpents
Equality	⟵⟶	Hierarchy
Person	⟵⟶	Role
Unity	⟵⟶	Diversity
Humor	⟵⟶	Seriousness
Spontaneity	⟵⟶	Calculation
Vertical	⟵⟶	Horizontal
Slow	⟵⟶	Fast

In Tilden's list, in which I've made some adjustments for our purposes here, we see a graphing out of what John of the Cross meant when he declared that perfect balance is the result of uniting activity with passivity. Each contains the seed of the other.

Preparing to Prepare

There was a time in the Christian understanding of the cycle of the week that Friday was a day of penance. Just as every Sunday is a little Easter, every Friday was a little commemoration of the passion and death of Christ. On this day Christians fasted and made an extra effort to perform some work of charity. In other words, one of the days of the week bore the identity of a "hard" day, a day of the week when we gave particular attention to certain disciplines. Strange as it may seem, some Christians found it easier to ascribe themselves an "easy" day as long as there was a "hard" day in there, too. Having a ritual hard day made embracing a ritual carefree and happy day easier.

The message to be deciphered in this curious complementarity is that, now that Friday has lost its clearly penitential character, it may help us to "greet the bride" on Saturday night if we choose for ourselves one day in the week when we will "carry the cross" of paying the bills, doing the laundry, shopping for groceries, mowing the lawn and setting things right with a neighbor or colleague. The point is to put some clarity into our expectations for the weekend so as to avoid the Sunday afternoon doldrums caused by vague disappointment over another "breather" that failed to refresh. By bedtime Friday night or end-of-breakfast on Saturday morning we should know what we want Saturday to be so that Sunday can hold its promise. If we haven't cleared the decks by Saturday supper of tasks that need to be done, Sunday will inevitably be marred by busy work, anxious fussing, and catch-up jobs.

When our programming toward the useful teams up with our restlessness in the face of a few unassigned hours, the result is usually the erosion of our good intentions for Sunday rest. Naming and bringing to light our hidden expectations for Sunday is half the battle. Identifying Saturday's tasks—or any other day we choose for getting them done—and realistically planning their accomplishment is the other half. One wife and mother who is trying to make the sabbath a living reality for her family has some very clear ideas as to how to go about it.

> **Saturday.** *By sundown Friday, set the work week consciously aside. Use Saturday to ready your home for Sunday. Put the house and yard in order. Wash the car, change the linens, cook something special for Sunday's breakfast or brunch. Husband and wife can help each other with the chores and cooking so that neither has to work without company. Teach the whole family the worthiness of a family meal by including them in the planning and preparation. On Saturday evening, read Sunday's gospel and pray the responsorial psalm together. If there are any customs and rituals that mark the liturgi-*

cal calendar, like making an Advent wreath, cutting out figures for a Jesse tree, or coloring Easter eggs, engage in them as a family. Put the children to bed with greater attention. Save some adult time just for each other.

Sunday. If anyone has new clothes, wear them for the first time on the sabbath. Begin the week with the celebration of the eucharist. Go together as a family if at all possible. Play special "Sunday music" on the stereo while everyone gets ready for church. Don't read the Sunday papers before church. At your Sunday breakfast or brunch, use a special meal prayer that you don't use on other days of the week.

Resolve not to do any unnecessary work. What needs doing (making the beds, setting the table, doing the dishes) can be done by family members together. Play the piano, read a book, go swimming, play ball. Go to a museum, the beach, the zoo, the mountains. Let family members take turns planning a Sunday outing. Whatever you undertake on Sunday, do it in a spirit of mutual understanding and care for one another. Try to do everything without haste or anxiety. Sunday is a day to be fully human and taste of heaven.[20]

An Anglican priest-friend expresses particular concern that our children and young people have an opportunity to experience this different quality of time. Their lives are so often pressured to conform, to achieve, to perform, and they are so easily influenced by our own poor examples. The regular discipline of sabbath time can support their developing sense of community and family, while also witnessing to the joy of life in itself. If you aren't too certain that life is fascinating and delightful, take a walkabout with some children and see through their joyful eyes in your next-sabbath time, or go by yourself for a walk in the world with the eyes you had as a seven-year-old. [21]

Ritual as a Container for the Divine

Mythology expert Joseph Campbell observed that people say what they are seeking is an experience that will give meaning to life. He disagreed: we are seeking an experience of *being alive*. We are seeking experiences that will enable us to feel the rapture of being alive, experiences that will resonate with our inner spiritual intuitions. What we are looking for is a way of living that is open to the mystery present to us, and a way of embodying it in our lives. The experience of eternity right here and now is the function of life. And that is what the sabbath seeks to give us.

Ritual and ceremony is a way for us to engage the inner mystery we seek. It is a creative, poetic act that speaks directly to the heart. When we give form to what is formless, and order to what is chaotic, when we give shape and name and meaning to what is fundamental to our humanness, we have created a ceremony. The conscious action of a ceremony helps us to pay full attention to what we might otherwise think ordinary or routine. The function of ritual is to pitch us out toward Mystery, not back in to where we live all the time. Effective ritual provides a sacred place of creative incubation, a bliss station, a palace in time where we can close the door on routine and touch a Beyond.

In the light of our contemporary cultural circumstances where many people do have to work on Sundays, it seems doubly important to retain the paradigm of time-out-of-time and be creative about the way we protect for ourselves a time to be at leisure, and a time for worship.

We need to create simple day of the Lord ceremonies for use in the home which build upon the Jewish ritual where the mother lights the sabbath candles at sunset to invite and usher in the "sabbath bride," sanctified time. The gesture says that this week is at an end. A new beginning dawns and with it we look backward and forward to see our place in the scheme of things. Our efforts at ritual do not need to be superhuman or artificially pious. They simply need to respond to our need to be touched and transformed.

By doing something, no matter how simple, we proclaim the truth of the Incarnation that these material signs and symbols carry a hidden grace.[22]

The following two ceremonies, for use at the Saturday evening meal, represent attempts in the direction of developing rituals for introducing the Christian day of the Lord's resurrection.

CEREMONY 1

Note: This special rite of blessing would usually be used when there can be a leisurely meal to "open the door" and "greet the bride." The blessing of the light is recited by one of the parents, usually the mother, as the candles on the table are reverently lighted. One or both parents may then bless the children, perhaps with a hand placed on the child's head. Finally one of the parents raises the brim-full cup of wine and recites the blessing of the sabbath. Then the cup is passed for all to share.

The prayers are drawn largely from the traditional sabbath-welcoming meal in a Jewish home.

Welcoming the Sabbath (Blessing of light)
Come, let us welcome the Sabbath,
May its radiance illumine our hearts
as we kindle these tapers.
May the Lord bless us with Sabbath joy.
May the Lord bless us with Sabbath holiness.
May the Lord bless us with Sabbath peace.
(Blessing the children and each other)
May the Lord bless you and keep you.

May the Lord make his face shine upon you
and be kind to you.
May the Lord turn his face toward you
and give you peace.
(Blessing and sharing the cup of wine)
Blessed are you, Lord, God of all creation,
Creator of the fruit of the vine.
Blessed are you, Lord, God of all creation,
you have taught us the way of holiness
through your commandments,
have granted us your favor
and given us your holy Sabbath as an inheritance.
This day is a memorial of creation.
It is a memorial of the breaking of the bonds
of slavery and sin and death.
Blessed are you, O Lord,
you make holy the Sabbath day.[23]

CEREMONY 2

Note: The family stands in prayerful silence around their
table. Two unlighted candles, a plate of bread and a cup of wine
or grape juice are on the table. As yet, the food has not been
placed on the table but waits, prepared, in the kitchen. After a
few moments of silence, the mother of the family begins.

Mother: *Light is the sacrament*
of God's presence among us.
The Lord is our light and our salvation.
We are called to be the children of light,
to be a light unto all nations.
Blessed are you, our Sovereign God,
who has made us lights to one another.

In the spirit of our ancient traditions,
we now light these festive meal candles.
(Candles are lighted)
May our home be made holy, O God, by your light.
May the light of love and truth shine upon us all
as a blessing from you.
May our table and our family
be consecrated by your divine presence
at this meal and at all our family meals. Amen.
(all are seated in silence)

Father: *Come, let us welcome*
this first day of a new week: Sunday.
On this day, our Lord Jesus Christ
rose from the darkness of the tomb.
This meal brings blessings to our hearts
as our workday thoughts and toils are forgotten.
The flames of these holy lights
shine forth to tell us that the Spirit of love
abides within our home.
In that light of love,
all our good fortunes are seen as blessings,
and all our griefs and trials are softened.
As we are gathered together at our table,
God's messenger of peace comes to this table,
turning the hearts of each of us to one another,
and deepening the bonds of friendship
with all those we love.

Mother: *May we praise you, O God,*
with this symbol of joy, our family meal.
Thank you, God,
for the blessings of this past week:
for life and for love,

for our health and for friendship
and for the rewards that have come to us
from our many labors.
From our ancient traditions
that flow from their source
in our holy mother Israel,
we do now bless these our humble gifts
of bread and wine.

(Father takes a piece of bread, holds it up with his right hand
     and says:)
Father: *Blessed are you, God of all creation,*
who gives to us bread
and causes the earth to overflow with good for all.

(Father takes a cup of wine, holds it up with his right hand
     and says:)
Blessed are you, God of all creation,
who from the vine has created the gift of wine.
May it be for us a sign of our love and unity.

     (First, the blessed bread is passed around the table. Each one
breaks off a piece and passes it on to the next person. After the
bread has been passed full circle and consumed, then the cup is
passed. When all have finished this in silence, then the blessing
rite concludes:)

Parent or child: *Blessed be God and blessed be God's holy
     name.*

All toast: *Happy Sunday!*[24]

4

Exercise and Play

EXERCISE AND THE SPIRITUAL LIFE

I'll never forget an experience I had one summer as a seminarian. Most of the staff in the large parish were away, so one priest had to preside and preach at all five of that day's liturgies. He seemed to have as much energy and enthusiasm at the end as at the beginning.

I couldn't help wondering how he did it. When I shared with him how impressed I was at his steady performance, he simply said, "That's why I run faithfully several times a week. It helps me develop the stamina that ministry demands."

That experience showed me how physical fitness could be an expression of responsibility to one's profession. "The last service may have been the fifth one for me," he commented, "but it was the first one for everyone else there. They deserved just as good an effort as those who came to the first service."

The number of Sunday services will reveal that as a Roman Catholic story, but I hope its catholic—universal—application will be recognized. For physical fitness goes beyond responsibility to one's profession or career; it plays a vital role in equipping us for Christian living. We may need no convincing about the value of books, church services, adult ed programs, and prayer for our spiritual lives. But how many would place a health club member-ship, a jump rope, or a good pair of jogging shoes beside their church publications (or bible even!) as indispensable tools for Christian life? If continuing education programs are supposed to fit us for meeting the challenges of gospel living, then one of the best we can undertake will be a program of physical fitness.

Two of the greatest hungers in North America today are the fitness craze and the search for spirituality. The number of people who tune in to the Sunday morning TV evangelists, who go to retreat houses, or who join bible study groups is exceeded only by the jump in memberships at today's fitness clubs and health facili-ties. Yet few people make connections between the two. They don't see that aerobics or swimming or skiing has an important place in their relationship with God.

Christianity has for centuries found itself in the difficult position of trying to affirm the goodness of creation without de-lighting in human bodiliness. Today we are recovering a sense of the seamless totality of our nature as embodied spirits. Our temp-tation is always to give up their unification and to live on two different planes or to restrict ourselves to any one "region," e.g. either a corporeal existence hostile to the spirit, or a spiritual existence filled with disdain for the body. No completely satisfac-tory solution has been found for the fluid relationship of body and spirit in the whole history of human thought. In the philosophy of Plato, the soul is a pure spiritual principle, really distinct from the body and immortal. In Aristotelian philosophy, the soul is united with the body as a form united to matter; its spirituality and its immortality are less evident.

The Semitic thinking of the bible contributes a completely different perspective. The Hebrew scriptures have no special word for the body. The whole person is "flesh" (*basar*), but also soul (*nefes*, i.e., life). The concept signified by *nefes* can be signified by no single word in modern languages. We can only seek the basic meaning and describe it: the human person in his or her total essence is a *nefes*, a psycho-physical totality. The key word is *totality*.

When the two streams of Greek and Semitic thought meet in the Fathers of the Church and Christian philosopy, the more highly developed Greek line of thought, in its Platonic form, dominates.

The Aristotelian concept penetrates later, in the middle ages, and is finally given its Christian form in the teaching of St. Thomas Aquinas.[1]

Muslims share the Jewish and Christian biblical traditions and with them are called "the people of the Book" by the prophet Mohammed.

They have mined certain perspectives from this common scriptural source material that can help Christians recover a holistic attitude proper to their own tradition.

Islam's Harmonizing of the Material and Spiritual Aspects of Life

Islam teaches that all life is essentially a unity because it proceeds from the Divine Oneness. It offers a program of life that seeks complete coordination of the spiritual and the material aspects of human life. In the teachings of Islam, both these aspects are not only reconciled to each other in the sense of leaving no inherent conflict between the bodily and the moral existence, but the fact of their coexistence and actual inseparability is insisted upon as the natural basis of life.

This is the reason for the peculiar form of Islamic prayer in which spiritual concentration and certain bodily movements are coordinated with each other in kneeling, bowing, prostrating, looking right and left. The rationale is simple: human life itself is of such a composition, and we are to approach God through the sum-total of all the faculties God has bestowed upon us.

A further illustration of this attitude can be seen in the

pilgrims' ceremony of walking around the *Ka'bah* or black stone in Mecca. Everyone who enters the Holy City must go seven times around the *Ka'bah*; the observance of this injunction is one of the three most essential points of the pilgrimage. The *Ka'bah* symbolizes the Oneness of God. The bodily movement of the pilgrims represents the activity of human life. The ritual implies that not only our devotional thoughts but also our practical life with all its actions and endeavors must have the idea of God at their center.

The concept of worship in Islam extends beyond the purely devotional practices such as prayer and fasting to embrace the whole of human life. The ideal is that all one's actions, even the seemingly trivial ones, are to be performed with the sense that they constitute a part of God's universal plan. When done with this consciousness, they are considered acts of worship. The permanent worship of God in all the manifold actions of human life is the very meaning of this life. But as long as we divide life into two parts, the spiritual and the material, this purpose remains impossible.

As anyone who has witnessed a group of Muslims kneeling in the corner of an airport lounge and bowing towards Mecca can affirm, Islam has liberated prayer from confinement to specific places.

Islam regards every place, whether it is one's home, one's place of work, or a busy airport terminal, as suitable for worship. So any place is considered appropriate for, and any action performed with the view to carry out the commandments of God is, an expression of worship.

Islamic theory seeks to fuse together spiritual aspirations and bodily desires and to harmonize their directions, thereby creating a comprehensive unity in the universe and in human life. Its aim is to correlate worship to all human activities, bringing them into one path, the path which leads to God. This harmony is not sought at the expense of our physical side, nor at the expense of the spiritual; rather it gives freedom of action to both of them in order to unify their activities and direct them holistically toward goodness and growth. [2]

These themes should hold no strangeness for any Christian who has ever read or listened to St. Paul's letters. "Glorify God in your bodies" (1 Corinthians 6:20). "Pray at all times" (Ephesians 6:18). "Give thanks to God in all circumstances" (1 Thessalonians 5:18). "Present your bodies as a living sacrifice" (Romans 12:1). But we have struggled through the centuries as to how these commands are to be translated into practice. We seem at least in our own time to have clearly rejected the mind/body dualism which characterized Christian life in certain eras. The statement of the former Cardinal Archbishop of Malines-Bruxelles, Leo Suenens, to a scientific Congress convoked in Munich in 1972 by the Olympic organizing committee, said it clearly: "Christian thought, if I may be so bold as to say so, has sided with the human condition. It no longer wants anything to do with the spirituality that sees the body as the prison of the soul. Its concern extends not merely to the soul, but to the human person as a total reality. Christ is not only the life of the soul, but the life of the whole human person. The whole takes first place, rather than the parts. The human person is neither a soul and a body, nor a soul with a duplicate body, but rather inspirited flesh and an enfleshed spirit. One *is* one's body and *is* one's soul, at one and the same time."[3]

As anyone who has improved health and disposition by laboriously sweating along knows, the Jansenistic exaltation of grace but spite for the body is heresy. Christian spirituality challenges us to integrate all aspects of our life into our relationship with God.

We arrive at wholeness by using to the full the stuff of human experience, not by denying it or seeing it as outside the pale of faith. The realm of Christian theology relating to the patterns of behavior which give concrete expression to one's faith is called "spiritual theology" or spirituality. It covers what the Fathers of the Church regarded as mystical theology, ascetic discipline and teaching on prayer. It takes in the relationship between prayer and conduct. That relationship is the focus of this chapter. How do exercise and play relate to Christian life and qualify as potential disciplines for the spiritual life?

Fitness Activities and the Spiritual Life

It is the duty of theology to make us aware of the deepest roots and implications of our activities. Fitness activities are important for the individuals involved and for society. The values reflected in sports make them more than pleasant diversion and recreation. If exercise can help us blow off angry steam, soothe jangled nerves, push along bulky food, teach us to respect and cooperate with others, and smile at the limits with which we discover our bodies are laden, then we can call exercise a faithful friend and should speak more of its holiness, of how it contributes to our spiritual growth.

The human qualities underlying fitness activities are the same as those underlying spiritual life activities. Discipline, dedication, enthusiasm, and perseverance are a few of those human qualities so evident in our play. They are the same ones that will get us out of bed at dawn to meditate, or enable us to protect fifteen minutes a day for the Word of God. The "raw material," i.e., the virtuous quality, is the same. The difference is in its application. Millions of people have the raw material and only apply it in one direction, i.e., physical exercise, when the same basic human virtues at work there could also be bringing them rich spiritual experience.

We noted in chapter one how people usually associate asceticism with fasting and doing penance, but it essentially means the *artful shaping of a material*. The spiritual person is ascetic precisely because the spiritual person is the one who is interested in and dedicated to the artful handling of the world, the artful shaping of one's self, and the artful forming of one's life into something beautiful for God. This artful fashioning of life seldom results from coercion or regimentation. It is best achieved by virtue of spontaneous desire and passionate pursuit—qualities embodied in people's approach to play.

Thus, soccer and basketball and cycling can be disciplines of the spiritual life, too, inasmuch as they help provide one's character and personality with qualities that also lend themselves to the spiritual life ("grace builds on nature"). Through skiing, rock climbing, and white-water canoeing one learns how to deal with and overcome fear and anxiety. Through running, swimming, or rowing long distances one develops endurance and will-power and learns how to deal with boredom. Through golf one can practice intense concentration and subtle control. Team sports can teach us the value of cooperation.

Exercise is an excellent way to bring home to ourselves our inevitable limitations. After years of regular exercise, one finds it relatively easy to live with finitude and ambiguity. My experience with running and swimming is a fascinating study of clocks and rhythms, regularities and unpredictabilities. I never know when I will hit the groove that makes everything flow smoothly and when the workout will be unexpectedly hard. Usually, though, there is a time in between the groans of stretching tight muscles and the panting of a strong finish, a time in the middle in which body and spirit seem to be in harmonious flow. The oxygen filling out the volume of my lungs, the resilience of warmed-up muscles and the sweat that is starting to glisten sing in chorus that this is a good thing to do regularly.

Exercise can be both prayerful and ethically instructive, helping us to see the world more sharply and breathe the air more deeply. Generation by generation, our bodies, properly exercised and our spirits, properly fed, could lead our minds to the sanity necessary for our survival in the face of political disarray, ecological pollution, and the unhappiness of many people around us. We are all simply creatures and our lives are short. The only-begotten Son of God has consecrated our bodies and blood by becoming one of us and opening to us a share in his divine life. This truth, that God so loved us and our world that the Word of God became flesh, can never be sufficiently pondered. Our God chose to become embodied. Surely, life in this inspirited flesh in the balance between the already-now but not-yet-fully of God's reign is the loveliest form of living. Any regular pattern of exercise that breeds affection for the embodied self, mocking it gently while urging it on, cultivates a spirit of human solidarity and compassion. When one has "been there," in however humble a fashion, one can more vigorously applaud the ballerina and the ball-carrier, the master of yoga and the mistress of natural childbirth. Fewer things human are foreign, and all things human become more precious. Jesus the carpenter and Jesus the poet more readily coincide.[4]

Other examples of the constant interchange between bodily activities and spiritual benefits: sports set in motion our mental faculties of attention, observation, analysis, order, judgment, and evaluation. We'll need all of these qualities finely honed if we are to live as Christians and discern gospel values in the midst of a secular society that seems little inclined to recognize God.

Fitness activities will contribute to the building of one's character through self-awareness and self-control, knowledge of one's own limitations, endurance, perseverance in effort, and determination to succeed. No Chrisitan can journey through life without these qualities. They will enable us to get back up on our feet when we have fallen, knowing that we are forgiven, and that we can do nothing without God's help.

In school these activities come under the rubric of "education" because they contribute to our physical and social education, cultivating in us a spirit of mutual assistance, conscience, justice, respect for the other, submission to the rules, cooperation, sharing, and fellowship among people who share the same experience. This sense of teamwork is indispensable in responding to God's call. We are called to come to God *together*, not alone.

All of these points represent links between physical fitness activities and our spiritual lives. Each one of them could be further developed, but I would like to focus on one quality in particular that I believe is the essential link between the world of physical exercise and the world of the spirit: awareness. Its critical importance derives from the fact that experiencing is our fundamental activity. The quality of our lives in fact depends on the quality of our experiencing. And the ability to be *aware* is at the heart of the process of experiencing. Living with greater focus, with a heightened sense of awareness, makes all things new and fresh in our experience.

What does this have to do with our "spirituality," which refers to the movement of God's Spirit in the life of the Christian? Let us begin with the word "spiritual." When people say "spiritual" they mean a great variety of things. Since it comes out of the biblical vocabulary, going back to *spiritus* in Latin and *pneuma* in Greek and *ruach* in Hebrew, we have to ask ourselves what it means in a western context. It means *aliveness*. Spiritual means alive—super-alive, if you want. That you have not yet died is not sufficient proof that you are alive. Aliveness is measured by degrees of *awareness*. And the spiritual work of our time is the task of making people alive, of heightening awareness. The spiritual life is primarily relational, so we are concerned with an awareness of Another, a Presence present to us who communicates with us in many ways. This dynamic initiated by God is most clearly patterned for the Christian in the mystery of the Incarnation in which Jesus as the Word of God reveals this Presence to us in human terms and calls us to enter into a relationship of intimacy and love (John 15:9–17).

The essential connection between spirituality and fitness activity is that exercise makes one alert, mindful, aware—which are precisely the qualities which make every activity become full of presence. To be sure, athletic activity is not the only way to heighten awareness; people do this in many different ways— through music, art, sex, meditation, and so on. My purpose here is simply to speak to how exercise and play do contribute to greater alertness, mindfulness, awareness.

The spiritual life is not a question of *making* us religious, but helping us realize that we already *are* religious in the depths of our being. The work of the spiritual life is to become more *aware* of it. Spirituality does not just bring a set of practices, a booklet of prayers, or a system of doctrine to daily life. It brings an awareness to the people and events of each day that reflects their essential sacredness. There is no special designation of only certain times or kinds of activity as "holy," but an appreciation for the holiness of life and the goodness of creation. The spiritual aspect of existence is not experienced as something to "add on" but is integral to and at the very heart of our lives. The Kingdom of God, in other words, is not a place, but an *experience* of intensity, quality, depth, ecstasy.

Let us briefly examine the relationship of awareness to prayerfulness. People who are in the habit of saying prayers at certain set times often discover that their moments of genuine prayer are precisely at those times when they are not "saying prayers." In fact, they may not even recognize their most prayerful moments as prayer. Others who never say formal prayers are nourished by moments of deep prayerfulness. Yet, they would be surprised to learn they are praying at all.[5]

Suppose, for example, that you are reciting psalms. If all goes well, this may be a truly prayerful experience. But all doesn't always go well. While reciting psalms, you might experience nothing but a struggle against distraction. Half an hour later you are out for a jog on your favorite woodland trail. Now, suddenly the prayerfulness that never came during the prayers overwhelms you. You come alive from within. Your heart expands and embraces those translucent autumn leaves, those explosions of color in the blossoms looking up at you from the grass, those people whom you meet along the trail. Or when you are swimming, there comes a delicious experience of harmony and flow. In your deep being you experience the marvel of bodiliness and the gift-quality of life. As long as this lasts, everything makes sense. Your consciousness is alert and focused. You are communicating with your full self, and your heart experiences a spontaneous rush of gratitude.

Which was the real prayer–the psalms, or your run through the woods or swim?

In reflecting on what makes our prayers prayerful, David Steindl-Rast notes that "sooner or later we discover that prayers are not always prayer. That is a pity. But the other half of that insight is that prayer often happens without any prayers. And that should cheer us up. Especially if we want to do what Scripture tells us to do and 'pray continually' " (Luke 18:1).[6] When the apostle Paul speaks about prayer, he does not speak about prayer as a part of life, but says it is *all* of life. He does not mention prayer as something we should not forget, but claims it is our ongoing concern. He does not exhort his readers to pray once in a while, regularly, or often, but without hesitation admonishes them to pray constantly, unceasingly, without interruption. For Paul, praying is like breathing. "Pray constantly, and for all things give thanks to God, because this is what God expects you to do in Jesus Christ" (1 Thessalonians 5:17–18).

If "praying continually" meant saying prayers uninterruptedly day and night, there is no way we could fulfill that invitation. If, on the other hand, prayer is simply communication with God through a heightened sense of awareness and presence to the Mystery who is present to us in each moment, it can go on continually. In peak moments of awareness this communication will be more intense. At other times it will be low key. Through a prayerful attitude, every activity can and should become prayer.[7]

Those of us who have been saying prayers every day for

many years and who have been trying to make our prayers truly prayerful should have some answer to the question: what is it that makes prayers prayerful? When we try to put into words what the secret might be, words like mindfulness, full alertness, and whole-hearted attention suggest themselves. These are not only the attitudes that make prayer prayerful, but are attitudes required for athletic activity. This is the vital connection that enables me to assert that there are many spontaneous moments of prayer in fitness and sporting activities. On one occasion while alpine skiing in the Canadian Rockies, I took a lift up to the very peak of the mountain and crossed over the top, gliding down into a back bowl. Within seconds I discovered myself completely alone in a vast expanse of space, with the jagged peaks towering above me, no other skier in sight and not a sound to be heard. I stood transfixed for a long while. The Scriptures use the word "theophany" for such moments when the divine is experienced breaking through and transfiguring natural events with a sense of the sacred. When I finally pushed off with my poles, I did so slowly and deliberately, with a sense of one touched by the Holy and visited with awe. Even now, years later, I can recall that experience and those feelings with astonishing clarity. Such spontaneous moments of prayer are certainly evoked more readily in such surroundings, but they can happen anywhere. The ripe fruit of a genuinely prayerful experience is to bring back into the humdrum routine of our daily lives, not just the *thought* of God, but the *awareness* of God's presence. It is primarily a question of refining our inner and outer senses to the presence of the Holy, daily in our midst.

Those participating in fitness activities sometimes tend to assume that the quality of their experience is the result of what they are wearing or the equipment they are using, so they put a lot of emphasis on the externals. They look for better skis, better running shoes, better rackets, better skates, better gloves, better clubs. Although we can alter our performance by changing our equipment and our lives by changing our environment, most significant changes occur when we find effective ways to change our inner landscape.

A regular discipline of physical exercise, in addition to flattening one's stomach and slimming one's hips, can provide foundational experiences for lasting transformation of consciousness. The total involvement of the body and senses all come together to create the precondition for those quality moments that culture calls "mystical." Let us not shy away from that word, for we are all called to mysticism. A mystic is not a special kind of human being; rather, every human being is a special kind of mystic. When the "mental" aspects of fitness activities are given more attention and when the "mystical" elements are allowed to rise from the underground to full awareness, then the transformational elements in the experience of bodily exercise will become more commonly recognized.

Such quality of experience will only surprise those who see the world without benefit of an incarnational spirituality. The constant points of reference must be that we are created in God's own image, and that God has become flesh that we might become like God. No matter how fallen we are, redemption and transformation are readily and presently available. Everything in creation carries the message, most of all this flesh which harbored the Word itself. In the Incarnation, the material world quite literally became the body of God. Ever afterward, we have no grounds on which to dismiss this world as some second-rate practice field for the real life in heaven. The Incarnation states that there is no practice and that nothing is second-rate. Life in this world is the life of God.[8]

The more attuned we become to the flesh God embraced and in which God dwells, exulting in its harmony, strength, and flexibility, learning how to bear its tensions and sufferings gracefully, the more we glorify its Creator, the One who also chose to call it "home."

Why do people in good physical condition have a special aptitude for a rich spiritual experience? Because the dancer or gymnast or crew member knows things through, with, and in his or her enfleshed spirit that pass the rest of us by. For that person has exercised his or her embodied self, while we have lounged and loafed. Our range of humanity, of awareness, is constricted. The potential God gave us is unplumbed.

How could we not know we were supposed to become lithe and well-conditioned? What master craftsman could make such a marvel as the human body and not be disappointed when we allow it to rust?[9]

Where shall we start in cultivating this heightened sense of awareness? It makes good sense to begin with experiences of play and exercise that we take to with spontaneity and that engage us fully. These can be moments of focused awareness which reveal to us what prayer is meant to be. If we could maintain this inner attitude of focused attention, our whole life would become prayerful. The task is to approach not only some but all situations in this attitude of mindfulness. Being "spiritual" is not essentially a question of religious doctrines but of being very alive, very tuned-in and aware of the presence and movement of God's Spirit in creation, in relationships, and within our own bodies, hearts and lives.

The Ultimate Athlete is, in George Leonard's definition, "one who joins body, mind and spirit in the dance of existence; one who explores both inner and outer being; one who surpasses limitations and crosses boundaries in the process of personal and social transformation; one who plays the larger game, the Game of Games, with full awareness, aware of life and death and willing to accept the pain and joy that awareness brings; one who, finally, best serves as model and guide on our evolutionary journey."[10]

This ideal does not exclude anyone because of physical disabilities. In fact, the overweight, sedentary, middle-aged man or woman becomes a hero just by making a first laborious, agonizing circuit of the track. Six months or a year later, many pounds lighter, eyes glowing, aware of new things both without and within, that person may provide a model of the potential for transformation that exists in every one of us.

II
DESIGNING YOUR OWN EXERCISE PROGRAM

All fitness programs focus on the cardio-respiratory system— the heart, lungs and blood vessels. In response to regular activity, the system becomes stronger and more efficient. The heart, for example, pumps oxygen-rich blood to the rest of the body. Like any muscle, the heart can grow stronger and more efficient by progressive "training" in which demand (in this case, oxygen demand) is gradually increased. Fitness refers to how efficiently your body can extract oxygen from the blood and transport it to your muscles during exercise.

Aerobic exercise is the type that progressively places increased demands on the heart, causing it to grow stronger and more efficient. These activities involve steady, continuous motion of the large muscle groups (arms and legs) and place a heavy, continuous energy demand on the heart. Aerobic exercise also increases lung capacity by allowing the lungs to take in more oxygen. The bloodstream carries the oxygen to cells throughout the body, where it breaks down or "burns" stored fuel to create energy. You can think of food stored in the cells as "fuel" and oxygen as the "match" that releases the energy. The more energy you use, the more oxygen you will need to release it. This process of using oxygen to release energy is called aerobic metabolism.

The guidelines of the American College of Sports Medicine (ACSM) are one of the most common standards of reference for designing an aerobic exercise program. It is based on the F-I-T-T principle: *F*requency, *I*ntensity, *T*ime, and *T*ype.

Frequency: exercise 3–5 times a week; do not have more than two days of rest in between periods of exercise.

Intensity: keep your heart rate within your target zone (60–85% of your maximum heart rate).

Maximum heart rate = 220 minus your age.

Multiply maximum heart rate by .60 and .85 to determine your appropriate exercise intensity zone.

Example: 220 − 30 years = 190 maximum heart rate of beats per minute

190 × .60 = 114 beats per minute

190 × .85 = 161 beats per minute

Your target heart rate zone is 114 on the low end and 161 on the high end. To monitor your heart beats per minute during exercise, take a ten second pulse check (for the above figures it should be between 19–27 beats) and multiply by six. To take your pulse, use the ends of your first two fingers and find your pulse either at your carotid artery (at the neck) or at the radial artery (at the wrist). If the pulse rate is less than the low end of the target zone, you aren't exercising intensively enough to improve your fitness level. If the pulse rate is too high, take it a bit easier.[11]

Time: 20–30 minutes of continuous aerobic activity.

Type: any activity that is rhythmical in nature, uses large muscle groups, and can be maintained continuously, such as walking, jogging, swimming, bicycling, dancing, rowing, stair climbing, jumping rope.

A varied exercise program offers the most advantages for good health. Different activities enhance different body systems, e.g., jogging develops endurance, aerobic dancing, flexibility, and weight machines, strength. A variety of activities also helps peak one's interest and anticipation of the exercise period.

The ACSM has found that exercising less than two days a week at less than sixty percent of the maximum heart rate and for less than ten minutes per day is inadequate for developing and maintaining fitness for healthy adults. Fitness, or the positive conditioning response, is *maintained* if you exercise for at least twenty minutes of continuous aerobic activity three days a week. It is *improved* if you exercise five days a week. Research has shown that exercising more than five times a week increases the likelihood of stress-related injuries. But interspersing physical activity throughout the week rather than on three consecutive days can reduce the likelihood of injuries. When people stop exercising completely the fitness benefits gained are quickly dissipated. Within one to two weeks the downhill curve has set in, and within three to eight months all improvements are lost.[12] Beginning an exercise program represents a life-style change. Exercise is a lifetime commitment. Maintaining good cardiovascular fitness requires consistent reinforcement.

When you set fitness and health as a personal priority, you can find ways to fit aerobics into your busy schedule—a walk during the lunch break, riding your bicycle to work, inviting a friend to a workout rather than for drinks.

Phases of a Physical Activity Program

1. *Warm-Up Phase*

— warm-up generates an increase in body temperature that helps prepare the body for overall physical performance.
— specific warm-up concentrates on the portions of the body that will be used in the anticipated exercise, e.g., upper body for swimmers, legs for joggers.
— generally the warm-up consists of low intensity activity for a duration of five to ten minutes.
— warm-up prepares the muscles and joints for exercise and safely raises your pulse toward your target rate.
— the benefits are several: blood flow to the muscles is increased,

as well as body temperature. Muscle tissue becomes more flexible, and cardiovascular response to sudden strenuous exercise is improved.

2. Conditioning Phase

— program should be designed to improve and maintain the five components of fitness: muscular endurance; cardiovascular endurance; muscular strength; muscular flexibility; body composition.
— activities should include both aerobic and strength training.
— benefits of aerobic exercise: improved heart functioning; improved oxygen uptake; increased feeling of well-being; may contribute to the control of blood pressure, cholesterol, weight and stress levels.
— benefits of strength training: increase in muscle strength and endurance; aids in the reduction of body fat by increasing metabolism and calorie utilization; reduces risk of injury; improved physical appearance.

3. Cool-Down Phase

— cool-down has two parts: first, easing out of your aerobic activity with low-intensity exercise; second, some static stretching exercises.
— generally lasts between five to ten minutes.
— promotes the return of the blood to the heart from the extremities and thus prevents potential dizziness.
— gives the body a chance to adjust back to a non-exercising state.
— provides an optimal time to stretch and improve flexibility while the temperature of the muscle tissue is elevated; reduces the chance of developing muscle cramps and soreness.

Understanding How the Body Produces Energy

In order to motivate yourself to give several minutes to warming up and cooling down, it is important to understand how the body produces energy. It has two systems. The first is the *anaerobic* which doesn't require oxygen, and the second is the *aerobic* which does. The anaerobic system is designed for brief, intense bursts of energy. The aerobic system provides most of the energy when you exercise for more than a few minutes. Let's say that Joe and Sally are going to swim some laps in the pool. Sally has been doing some warmup exercises at poolside and in the water waiting for Joe. When he arrives, he jumps right in and takes off. For the first couple of minutes he's fine; his anaerobic system provides him with instant energy, drawn from anaerobic metabolic sources. But the supply here is limited and inefficient, resulting in a build-up of lactic acid in the muscles. Having drawn too heavily on his anaerobic system, Joe pulls up after a couple laps to catch his breath. Meanwhile, Sally goes cruising on by and doesn't stop for half an hour. With her warm-up exercises, she activated her aerobic energy system which brings an increased amount of oxygen-rich blood to her muscles. This system is much more efficient; when it kicks in, there is a steady flow of energy provided.

The cooling down period works similarly. Once the body is heated up, it's like the bulb in a slide projector. After you've been showing slides for a while, it's advisable to turn the light off but keep the fan running to cool the bulb. If you shift immediately to "off" or pull the plug right after the last slide, you'll either blow the bulb or weaken its longevity. When you exercise, coming to a complete stop and sitting down right after finishing hard with your last lap also has negative effects like lactic acid build-up which causes sore and cramping muscles. Coming to a slow gradual stop enables the body to cool down and the heart rate to ease back to normal without any radical drop-off caused by switching suddenly to "off."

Regular activation of the aerobic system causes it to become even more efficient. Golf, bowling, softball, downhill skiing work more off the anaerobic system because the activity they generate is intermittent. Cycling, swimming, jogging, cross-country skiing, soccer, skating, brisk walking activate the aerobic system.

Physical Activity and Body Composition

Research tells us that few North Americans exercise regularly. In fact, according to the United States Public Health Service, approximately six out of ten Americans are sedentary and about three out of ten obese.[13] At best, dieting results are short-lived, and at worst, eating fewer calories does not address the basic cause of weight gain as experienced by the average adult.

As we age, our resting metabolism (the calories our body utilizes at rest) decreases by about one-half percent every year. Because we are burning fewer calories per day to stay alive, some of the previously needed calories are placed into our fat storage areas. The reason we are burning fewer calories to stay alive is that as we age we are also losing about one-half pound of muscle every year. The muscle loss is largely responsible for our slower metabolism because muscle is very active tissue. A pound of muscle requires between 30–50 calories just to maintain itself.[14]

So the real problem behind creeping obesity is our gradual loss of muscle tissue. The good news is that this process is largely preventable and reversible. The muscle lost over the years of disuse can be replaced. More muscle means a higher metabolic rate, thereby putting more calories into use and reducing fat stores. For this reason, the American College of Sports Medicine now recommends two strength or weight training sessions per week to supplement aerobic activity.

One way of doing this is to divide your time in a half hour workout by giving fifteen minutes to aerobic exercise (stationary cycling) and fifteen minutes to strength exercise (nautilus machines). One set of eight to twelve repetitions of eight to ten different exercises that condition the major muscle groups at least two days per week is the recommended minimum.[15] While there is no fountain of youth, sensible strength exercise is the best means for maintaining your muscle mass and metabolic rate through the mid-life years.

Physical activity burns calories. It can increase the resting metabolic rate as much as ten percent and for as long as 24–48 hours after completing the activity.[16] That means that even while relaxing in an easy chair after physical activity the body is burning more calories than usual. To activate your daily routines, take the stairs when possible (or walk a few flights and then take the elevator), park your car at the far end of the parking lot, hand-deliver messages at work rather than picking up the phone, and so on. With a little creativity, you'll find dozens of ways to increase the amount of movement in your daily routines.

The Energy Dividend Takes Time

You probably have known someone who undertook a new program of regular exercise but who felt just the opposite of energized for the first few weeks. A colleague in our office said, "I felt awful. I'd come back to the office or house so sore and tired that all I wanted to do was to curl up and take a nap." In the evenings she'd zonk out in front of the television and nod off an hour earlier than her usual bedtime. She hovered on the brink of giving it up before a month expired.

Anyone who's started an exercise regimen after a sedentary period knows the feeling. Fatigue is one of the reasons for the high dropout rate (from 40–50 percent) among novice exercisers. People who quit, however, have the worst of both worlds: upfront energy drain without any of the long-term energy gain. Yet in study after study, both physiologists and sports psychologists have observed that people who exercise do feel more energetic than people who don't. This holds even for lifelong couch potatoes if they stick to a regular program. The jump in vitality takes two forms: a rise in alertness for a couple of hours after every workout, and an all-around feeling that daily tasks seem easier to do. But it takes some time to feel that overall energy boost— usually a couple of months—because it takes that long for our bodies to undergo the physiological changes that make our energy production more efficient.

One way that exercising changes the body from a jalopy to a BMW is that it increases the number of microscopic energy factories, called mitochondria, in the muscle cells. One study[17] found that the number of these energy factories rose 120 percent in people who completed a 28 week fitness program. Energy is created in these factories through a chemical reaction that begins when your body converts the carbohydrate and fat from food into a sort of chemical fuel called adenosine triphosphate or ATP. The breakdown of ATP releases a burst of energy that serves as the power source for muscular movement.

The bigger and more numerous these energy factories become, the more you tend to burn fat instead of carbohydrate to supply energy to your muscles. The advantage of burning fat is that your body stores much more fat than carbohydrate. Under normal conditions, we have an inexhaustible supply of fat, but our carbohydrate stockpile can be depleted after two hours of heavy exercise. If you're out of shape, your body relies more on carbohydrate for fuel, and so you run out of steam more quickly because the supply being drawn upon is limited.

The more energy factories we have and the more easily they obtain oxygen to produce energy, the more energetic we will feel. The building of those new power plants, however, usually takes a couple of months, during which time one simply has to wait in faith for the increase in vigor to kick in.

Motivation

Most people realize that exercise is good for them and that they would be healthier and feel better if they got some regularly. They even know how to do it. *Actually doing it on a regular basis* is where the breakdown occurs.

The key is to do things you enjoy. If the experience is by and large enjoyable, you'll do it. Or even if you don't particularly enjoy riding your exercycle twenty-five minutes in the evening three times a week, but like the way it makes you look or feel afterwards, then do it for those reasons. If you do it regularly, you will feel better, look better, and may even live longer. Some people say that regular exercisers have difficulty accepting their mortality, that their exertion is aimed at keeping their bodies young and represents a denial of the aging process. Personally, longevity does not motivate me, though I certainly have nothing against it! If I went in for a medical check-up tomorrow and learned I had cancer of the liver and only two months to live, I would not want to change anything about the pattern of regular exercise that has marked my adult years. The reason is not complicated: I simply feel better every time I do it. I have more energy. I sleep better, feel calmer, and can maintain my ideal body weight without worrying about how much I eat. The reward is immediate.

Recent medical evidence indicates that it may be a mistake to exercise just to live longer. Dr. Ralph Paffenbarger of Stanford University sent questionnaires to 16,936 Harvard alumni, aged thirty-five to seventy-four, to determine the influence of exercise on longevity. He found that men who expended 2,000 calories per week exercising lived one to two years longer than sedentary individuals. But when you calculate the time investment involved in exercising each week over the span of an adult life (thirty to seventy-five years old), you realize that you are only lengthening your life by about the same amount of cumulative time that you have spent exercising—about one and a half years.[18] Now if you have enjoyed your exercising, that makes sense. But if you're exercising just to live longer, the strategy is highly questionable.

In another study, Dr. Steven Blair and his colleagues at the Institute for Aerobics Research found that a little exercise goes a long way. Their testing indicated that the mortality rates of those with high levels of exercise were not significantly different from those with moderate levels of exercise. In other words, walking thirty minutes a day reduced premature death almost as much as running thirty to forty miles a week. Conclusion: regular, moderate exercise is enough to provide you with almost all of the health and longevity benefits without most of the stress-related injury risks of more intense exercise. The risk of exercise is in direct proportion to its intensity, so moderate exercise conveys most of the benefits while decreasing the risk. If you *want* to do more because you enjoy it—fine! But do more only if you *want* to, not because you think you *have* to. You don't have to suffer to feel good.[19]

A regular discipline of moderate exercise promises a new perspective on life. Strengthening your physical, mental and emotional stamina changes the quality of your life. You begin to experience life more abundantly.

There's a fine line between giving *of* ourselves and giving *up* ourselves. If our mental and physical health deteriorates, we will be little good to those we seek to serve. Some may simply fail to recognize that their whole life in all its facets—enthusiasm, energy, motivation, spirit—may be negatively affected by poor physical fitness.

It's difficult to genuinely love others, and to invite them to love themselves, if we consistently exempt ourselves from this caring. Taking care of yourself is expressed in the simplest ways: taking time off, getting enough sleep, exercising consistently, eating right. Such simple measures leave one less prone to fatigue, better able to tolerate stress, generally more alert, less tense, and less subject to depression.

III
THE PLAY ELEMENT IN EXERCISE

Exercise will finally be as Christian as the love that it inspires. If it makes us proud or compulsive, it will stand with our spiritual enemies. If it breaks us out of the fears and false sufficiencies that keep the Spirit away, it will stand with our best benefactors. If it frees us from possession by the demons of workaholism, it will be blessed liberation indeed. If it grants us sanctuary into the immunity of carefree play, it will merit the name "holy." The temptation to truly turn our times of exercise into *work*outs and to become *workers* at our play is pervasive in our culture.

Ever since the last quarter of the nineteenth century, games, in the guise of sports, have been taken more and more seriously. The rules became increasingly strict and elaborate. Records were established at a faster rate than anyone ever thought possible. But, with the increasing systematization of sport, something of the pure play quality was inevitably lost; it is lacking in spontaneity, in carelessness. The transformation of sport into a commercial business pushed it further and further away from the play-sphere proper to it.

The history of modern sports shows us play stiffening into seriousness while still being called play. Many examples could be given to support these assertions today, from little league baseball to bantam hockey to college football. Still, other voices have been raised and other movements founded for the preservation or restoration of the play-quality in sports.

The American Alliance for Health, Physical Education, and Recreation, and the national Canadian program ParticipAction have been major forces in developing the "New Physical Education." The goal of the new PE is participation for all. Training starts in the lower grades, with body movements and success-oriented activities designed to help children develop a positive sense of their bodies—the key factor in their eventual self-images. The upper grades are introduced to "lifetime sports," i.e., sports they can participate in for the rest of their lives like sailing, tennis, backpacking, or skiing.

The Essential Difference between Work and Play

There are two poles in all activity: work and play. Work is activity *for* an end; play is activity *as* an end. One assures the resources of enjoyment, the other is enjoyment itself. When a man goes into business, he consents to undergo a certain expenditure of care and labor in order to obtain some ulterior good which is to be his reward. But when a child goes to his or her play, it is by no means to an end; it is itself both end and joy. The moment play becomes wearisome we say, "This is too much like work"— an activity that is kept up, not as being its own joy, but for some ulterior end, or under some pressure. We work because we must, because prudence and responsibility impels. We play because we have in us a fund of life that wants to expend itself.[20]

Play's ability to construct an enclave within the serious world of everyday life causes sociologist Peter Berger to call it a "signal of the transcendent." He does not use "transcendent" in a technical philosophical sense, but literally: play enables us to transcend the normal everyday world by inserting us into the time structure of the playful universe which has the specific quality of offering a taste of eternity.

> *Some little girls are playing hopscotch in the park. They are completely intent in their game, closed to the world outside it, happy in their concentration. Time*

has stood still for them—or, more accurately, it has been collapsed into the movements of the game. The outside world has, for the duration of the game, ceased to exist. And, by implication (since the little girls may not be very conscious of this), pain and death, which are the law of that world, have also ceased to exist. Even the adult observer of this scene, who is perhaps all too conscious of pain and death, is momentarily drawn into the beatific immunity.[21]

It is this curious quality which belongs to all joyful play that explains the liberation and peace of mind such play provides. Faith in God's care further frees one from the burdensome preoccupation of the moment. Knowing that salvation is God's gift, one can "waste time" periodically, closing one's eyes to the piles of unfinished work and allowing the solemn call of duty to fade into the distance. The experience of worry-less freedom knocks out the deadly serious attitude toward life and leaves it lying somewhere amidst the scattered bowling pins or unconscious on the bottom of the swimming pool. We do not always have to be achievers in life.

We can also be a celebrator of what is given. When we lose our capacity for play, we lose our capacity for "useless" presence to the Divine. This capacity is central to prayer which is essentially presence simply open to Presence.

For the Puritans and rationalists, any form of idleness was suspect unless it could be justified in terms of work, either as purifying the mind for more dedicated and disciplined service, or resourcing the body for more of the same. And yet those who have studied the play element in culture—Johan Huizinga, Hugo Rahner, Peter Berger, Robert Neale, David Miller, Jürgen Moltmann—are of one accord that play is connected with no material interest and is valuable for its own sake. There is meaning and value in the experience itself, apart from any significance in relationship to work. Whenever you work, you work for some purpose. If it weren't for that purpose, you'd have better things to do than work. Work and purpose are so closely connected that work comes to an end once your purpose is achieved. You don't continue fixing the car once it is fixed, or washing the clothes once they are clean. But in play, all the emphasis falls on the meaning of your activity. Play needs no purpose. That is why it can go on and on as long as the players find it meaningful.

The experience of play in our lives counterbalances our utilitarian world view. Our thought about the world is that God, of course, created it for a purpose. We are so caught up in purpose that we would feel more comfortable if God shared our preoccupation with work. But God plays. On my way back from India I came through Australia and delighted in the zoos wherever I went. What a playful sense of humor God has! Wombats, kookaburras, wallabies, platypus, dingoes, echidnas, koalas, kangaroos, cassowaries, cockatoos, lyrebirds, emus, fruit bats, frill-necked lizards and brilliantly colored parrots. It's a circus! When we open our eyes and hearts to God's creation, we quickly perceive that we are in courtship with a playful rather than a no-nonsense God.

One valuable contribution of contemporary Christians to society would be the preservation and development of the play element in our lives in general and in our games and sports in particular. Churches should encourage play on all levels as part of their mission of evangelization in contemporary society. If not from the Church, from what quarter can we hope for support in diminishing our idolatrous attachment to work? Allowing the spirit of play to enter into all levels of life is an integral part of the Christian mission to society.

An active fostering of the play element in life is one of the ways Christians are called to witness to the secular society we live in. If Christians are gifted with different values, different perceptions about the quality and value of time, these should be evidenced in the way we use time. Rather than imitating the hectic, overly busy and distracted life-style so common in western society today, Christians might be expected to display a mysterious and attractive difference. If we really believed that our work and careers belong to a larger process of change and redemption, that *we* are not solely responsible for the future of the world, we would be less frenetic and compulsive. We would be friendlier with time and witness to a style of living both more relaxed and more aware. A Christian's attitude toward "useless" time, play time, could be leaven in the dough within a circle of friends.[22]

Exercise and play have definite transformational aspects in which boundaries are crossed, limitations transcended, perceptions gained, and entry is granted into a beatific immunity where the outside world stands still for the duration of the game. We began this chapter with a reminder from Islam to lay unflinching claim to our biblical tradition of the seamless unity of our enfleshed spirits. We end it with a teaching from Zen Buddhism that has strong resonance with what we have said here about the "play-attitude" and the transformational capacity of exercise and games.

The German philosopher Eugen Herrigel spent several years in Japan learning the *Art of Archery*.[23] By the "art" of archery he does not refer to the ability of the sportsperson, which can be more or less controlled by bodily exercises, but an ability whose origin is to be sought in spiritual exercises and whose aim consists in hitting a spiritual goal. Access to the art is only granted to those who are "pure" in heart, untroubled by subsidiary aims.

All of the Japanese arts—ink painting, the tea ceremony, flower arrangement, swordsmanship, and archery—presuppose a spiritual attitude, an attitude which, in its most exalted form, is characteristic of the genre of Buddhism known in Japan as "Zen."

Zen began as a Chinese interpretation of Buddhism. It reached full development in China to be finally adopted by Japan where it is cultivated as a living tradition to this day. The heart of the Zen approach is the experience of the oneness of all things, the wonder of simple "is-ness." Theoretically in Buddhism there is no self and so no barrier to union with nature. In the tea ceremony, archery, or swordsmanship, the ideal is selflessness.

Such activities are but active forms of what the meditator pursues in sitting meditation: to distinguish no more between your self and the world. Distinguishing makes for multiplicity and illusion. The unitive mind represents the height of attainment. [24]

With regard to the art of archery, the bow and arrow are only the instruments of essentially spiritual exercises which enable one to make a decisive leap toward a heightened and more lucid quality of experiencing life. The point is not to accomplish anything outwardly with bow and arrow, but only inwardly, with one's self.

The state described as "spiritual" by the Zen master would provide an excellent description of a genuine "play-attitude." It is a state of mind in which nothing definite is thought, planned, striven for, desired or expected; a state of mind which aims in no particular direction and yet knows itself capable alike of the possible and the impossible; a state which is at bottom purposeless and egoless. But because it is charged with spiritual awareness, it is called "right presence of mind," which means that the mind or spirit is present everywhere, because it is nowhere attached to any particular place. And it can remain present because, even when related to this or that object, it does not cling to it by reflection and thus lose its original mobility. It has a seemingly mystical power because it is free, and it is open to everything because it is empty.

When a pupil risks getting stuck in the mire of his achievement, the master reminds him that all right doing is accomplished only in a state of true selflessness, and that more important than all outward works, however attractive, is the inward work which he has to accomplish if he is to fulfill his vocation as an artist.

The openness to wisdom from the East and the New Physical Education referred to earlier, with its stress upon a sport for everyone, may help return the play-element to sports. There is a growing movement to approach game-playing just for the fun, the challenge, the excitement, and the joy of the play itself. This alone is sufficient incentive for participation. In a culture that is so serious and goal-oriented, these activities provide us with the genuine replenishment of the inner spirit which is the heart of true leisure.

True leisure is a state of mind brought about by an activity freely engaged in and done for its own sake.[25] There is no standard to attain, no victory, only the joy of life experienced in the activity itself—the joy that comes from wholehearted attention to the fullness of this now moment. You run or swim not for a future reward, but for everything that is yours as you do it.[26]

This kind of mindful engagement with the present opens us to wonder and evokes gratitude. Without even noticing it, one slips into the realm of prayer: simple communication with God through a heightened sense of awareness and presence to the Mystery who is present to us in each moment.

5

Prayerful Presence

The disciple was always complaining to his master, "You are hiding the final secret of Zen from me." And he would not accept the master's denials. One day they were walking in the hills when they heard a bird sing.

"Did you hear that bird sing?" said the master.

"Yes," said the disciple.

"Well, now you know that I have hidden nothing from you."[1]

In his book *The Human Adventure*,[2] William McNamara, OCD, presents contemplation as the central human act that puts us perceptively and lovingly in touch with the innermost reality of everything. Precisely because contemplation puts us in touch with the real in personal, passionate presence, it is the key to awe-full existence. He speaks about contemplation as, above all, the loving awareness of God, the in-built capacity of our everyday mind to explore the "inscape" of things, to look into our present reality with loving awareness and see God there.

The first mistake we make is to assume that it is a rare gift for a select few and either to count ourselves out as possible recipients or to nurture a vague hope that maybe someday God will bless us with the grace of contemplation and transform our dull and drab lives. The revelation that this gift has already been given

leaves us incredulous, as exemplified in another of Anthony de
Mello's stories:

"Excuse me," said an ocean fish. "You are older than I, so
can you tell me where to find this thing they call the ocean?"

"The ocean," said the older fish, "is the thing you are in
now."

"Oh, this? But this is water. What I'm seeking is the ocean,"
said the disappointed fish as it swam away to search elsewhere.[3]

As the mythologist Joseph Campbell remarked in a similar
vein, we are standing on a whale fishing for minnows. The one
"given" of the spiritual life is union with God. John of the Cross
explains in what union with God consists. God dwells in every
human being: "In him we live and move and are" (Acts 17:28).
John calls this God's natural presence by which God holds all
things in being. This essential union is meant to become a *conscious* union of love.[4] The spiritual life, then, is the bringing-to-
consciousness of the union we already enjoy. And this growing
awareness of union with God is the graceful result of human
experience deeply participated in and intelligently interpreted in
the light of faith. The adventure of our lives is the discovery that
deep down at the heart of our being we are in direct and immediate contact with the Source of all that is. McNamara's favorite
characterization of contemplative living is "a long, loving look at
the real."

The development of our capacity to savor the mystery of
things below their surface reality is so fundamental to our human
fulfillment that we should think of it more in terms of learning to
walk than learning to fly. It is not a question of seeking after
esoteric "mystical" experiences but rather of an awakened sense of
how the whole joyful and painful adventure of living is in itself
the God experience. Life is not so much a series of problems to be
solved but a mystery to be lived. There is in fact no other way for
us to know God than through the experience of living. By embrac-

ing life and living it with passion, we come to know God the way the lover knows the beloved or the friend knows the friend. In short, we are personally, passionately present to the Mystery present to us.

The focus of this chapter is on ways to cultivate such presence. The human adventure is to become thoroughly and thrillingly engaged in the exploration into our own transcendent inner truth through all the days, weeks, months and years of our lives. In the first part of this chapter we will look at a daily approach to cultivating this sense of presence, in a second part at a weekly or monthly approach, and in a third part at an annual one. We need them all to keep our lives on the rails and moving toward the destination of our hearts' deepest longing.

I
DAILY CULTIVATION OF PRESENCE

Noisy Contemplation

In the early church, people shared the eucharist, listened to the Hebrew scriptures, stories of Jesus, and letters from his disciples. They cared for one another with such striking charity that many new people were attracted to the community. When the age of martyrdom ended with the edict of Milan in 312 and took the pressure off Christians to really live what they professed, some lay Christians decided to keep the pressure on by going off into the desert, beginning what would become the monastic movement. The monastic authors wrote so compellingly of their experience, that their lifestyle and understanding of prayer became the dominant model for imitation. Subsequent ages thus tended to assume that deep prayer required a peaceful physical environment with a minimum of distractions and a detached and serene psychic condition. Contemplative living was not expected from people who lacked the environment and lifestyle (monastic) now commonly judged to be the appropriate one for seeking communion with God.

The explosion of many powerful currents which have nourished lay spirituality in the past twenty-five years—charismatic renewal, bible study groups, directed retreats, meditation and centering prayer, the Liturgy of the Hours—has gone a long way toward balancing the monastic paradigm as the dominant point of reference.

Clearly apparent today are efforts to help ordinary family and working people cultivate contemplative living by using the activity and "noise" of human living as the fuel for their prayer.

One such effort came out of the Quixote Center in Hyattsville, Maryland, under the authorship of William Callahan. Called *Noisy Contemplation*,[5] it adopted a low-cost tabloid format in order to reach more people. As an insightful example of a daily strategy for cultivating personal, passionate presence, it deserves to be set forth again in summary fashion. The starting point is a reflection upon Jesus' own way of praying.

Like every other human being, Jesus sought ways to relieve the pressures and stresses of the demands placed upon him. He went apart to pray and to be alone or to spend some time with friends or disciples. But there is no evidence that he was able to go apart like this each day, or even on most days. Perhaps the writers mentioned it when they did because it was striking enough to be noticeable. Most people can relate to this because the demands of families, work and limited finances put restrictions on extended time apart for them, too. This is a reality of modern living with efforts to help people grow spiritually must come to grips or wither. The environment in which most people spend their day is one of inner and outer noise.

The gospels give us every reason to believe that Jesus' own public life was filled with activity, pressure and tensions, not unlike our own. Did he pray only intermittently, when he had rare moments of peace and quiet or a chance to go apart, or did he pray steadily, in the midst of his daily ministry?

When we look at his encounters with people, what we see is a man who managed to establish strong bonds with people even when the "time" for building relationships was not there, e.g., the Samaritan woman at the well or the repentant thief on the cross.

Jesus seems to have used his senses, his compassion and empathy to contemplate life and the people whom he met. He looked at them, felt their presence, and empathized with their plight with a love that brought deep insight and bonding. He saw people with insight beyond analysis, with a love that cut through considerations of social status and role. He "tuned in" to their present condition and needs and grasped the essential questions they were living. Taking "a long, loving look at the real" was a way of life for him, and may well have been the dynamic which nourished him, the basic way he prayed day after day.

Prayer apart was certainly integral to his ministry and reminds us that, in active, busy lives, it is a blessing to gain some psychic and physical distance from our ordinary living so that we can gain some perspective on it. But he also seemed to practice noisy contemplation, to pray in the midst of his work by contemplating the people and events of his life as he encountered them, drawing nourishment and energy for his own inner life from heart to heart communication with people, or insightful reflection upon yeast, salt, light, weather, grapevines and the like.

The scriptures in fact are full of stories about people who contemplated life as they lived it and who were rewarded with life-giving insight: Mary's response to become a mother; Elizabeth's grasp of what it meant when the child in her womb leaped for joy at Mary's greeting; Simeon and Anna's recognition of the child Jesus in the temple; John the Baptist's encounter with Jesus at the river Jordan. These stories would suggest that our primary source of prayer and faith is the experience which each one of us has of the action of God's Spirit in our lives.

This is not to take away anything from the vital role which religious institutions have in guiding religious belief, or the important contribution made by spiritual directors, silence, leisure, and learning. But it is to say that an adult in faith must trust his or her experience of God in daily life. The experience of living is the soil out of which the movement of prayer most authentically springs. Jesus' gift to us of an Advocate, a Comforter (John 14:16,26) to be with us to guide us makes him far more available to us than when his presence was limited by the ground he could cover or the people he could talk to in an average day in Israel. In other words, ordinary people have the essential resources they need—their life experience and the Holy Spirit present to them in it *all*—to develop an abiding awareness of the Mystery that enfolds their lives. Jesus comes today to the marginalized people in their simple and insecure surroundings, as well as to the middle- and upper-class in their frenetic, scattered, and preoccupied lives.

The actions we repeat every day are an excellent place to begin cultivating our capacity for prayerful living. Family life and friendships are key locations in which to build habits of contemplating people. One person can begin "seeing" the other with an unhurried, loving look. The moment needs no more elaboration than the silent language of an open heart. Partners and friends who habitually greet each other with the eloquence of caring regard soon find themselves reaching out to each other in creative ways that build sharing, love and sensitivity throughout those periods that permit of only momentary interaction. Husbands, wives and friends who grow in this practice will quickly know when they need reconciliation. Our instinct to avert our eyes and refuse our presence when something is amiss will serve as an early cue that alienation is brewing and needs redress.

Parents can develop the habit of contemplating their children when they first greet them in the morning and send them to school. As the children grow up, that loving gaze keeps fresh our appreciation for the years shared and for this human being who remains irreplaceable while always becoming someone new. The empathy engendered by this contemplative living may also help us accept our own aging more gracefully.

Teachers who cultivate the art of contemplating their students as they sit before them working away on an assignment may discover that it helps them love their students and gives them new insights which transform their relationship and help their teaching. Those who work in factories and offices face the special challenge of coping creatively with repetitive tasks and superficial human contact. One friend told me that in her workplace those engaged in sewing garments weren't even *allowed* to talk. Even here, looking at the people when they come in or occasionally glancing at them while they are working can weave moments of prayerful empathy throughout the day.

For those in the helping professions—social workers, clergy, medical professionals, counsellors—such prayerful presence can transform their daily agenda from a series of "cases" into encounters rich with wonder and openness to human beings who bear the image of God. The examples are as multiple as the things people do: flight attendants can contemplate their passengers as they serve them, bus drivers those who get on, store clerks those who present themselves with their purchases. Such moments of open-hearted attentiveness expand to fill the day and our hearts with compassion and kindness. Being personal with people, and experiencing their response, is transformative for the quality of one's day.

We can gradually retrain ourselves to see strangers with the eyes of faith which remind us of the love God has for them and of the gifts with which each one is endowed. Developing the habit of contemplating people is characterized by the same kind of patterns that mark our efforts to integrate any new practice into our lives: some days it hums, and some days it sputters and stalls. We come to accept this in much the same way as we learn to recognize and accept the variation in our energy levels. There are days when following through on our commitments takes more effort than others but we still remain faithful to them. And in that constancy what we call virtue is born: a good action that starts to come naturally. Ignatius Loyola encouraged the members of his order, the Jesuits, to look into their hearts twice a day to review briefly how the day was progressing, to remind themselves of their commitment to follow Jesus, and to encourage themselves to be loving in the hours ahead.

Noisy contemplation is an example of developing a discipline that is suitable to the style of life you are actually living. All the messages of past centuries notwithstanding, going off to the monastery or convent or seminary is not the only way to deepen your relationship with God. Marriage and other close friendships are also a great way of going to God. Helping to bear each other's emotional burdens is a healing, saving process in which two people are ministering the Ultimate Mystery to each other. Being single provides marvellous opportunities for offering hospitable space to others and for supportive presence to a wider circle of friends and families. The point is that, whatever our calling, daily life is the primary field of practice.

Does the practice of noisy contemplation (or any other practice we may have fitted to our lives, like the frequent repetition throughout the day of a prayer phrase) *take the place* of formal, "pure prayer" time? My own conviction is that we still need to commit a certain amount of time each day to just being before the One Who Is in full, loving attention in formal prayer time. Otherwise we get caught up in the pressures of the day and we forget to even focus the intention of occasionally taking a long, loving look at the real. The two have to go together because we need to establish reservoirs of interior silence—and keep them filled—in order to sustain our efforts to contemplate people and events in daily life.

In trying to establish and maintain noisy contemplation and formal prayer time, it is critically important to establish a clear sense of priorities. Time is not our master, but our servant—a gift from God for us to use.

We need to take responsibility for our use of time and structure it so that it reflects our values. We have to recommit day after day to developing the contemplative faculty within us by making the choices that enable us to live with presence. Failure to do so means blaming all the external circumstances, which are just convenient excuses. When that happens, God asks us as God asked Adam in the garden of Eden: "Adam, where are you?" That is a useful phrase to periodically call ourselves from distracted, uncentered living back to personal, passionate presence. To keep us on track, we need a certain period each day, as much of a day as we can get each month, and an even longer period each year— just to keep reminding ourselves of how we want to and should be living.[6]

The Practice of the Presence of God

Nicholas Herman was born in Lorraine, France in the early 1600's. Disturbed by his military experiences during the Thirty Years War, he left the army and decided to devote his life to Christ. He went to Paris and applied for admission as a lay brother at a Carmelite monastery where he became Brother Lawrence of the Resurrection, undertaking menial tasks and serving for the next fifty years in the kitchen and the shoe repair shop. How he was able to turn his despair to peace and happiness through the practice of the presence of God, and how that presence can be achieved, is the theme of his writings—a small collection of conversations, letters, and maxims which has endured for three centuries and which today is more widely read than ever. *The Practice of the Presence of God*[7] has firmly ensconced itself in that enduring body of spiritual works with which Christianity has been blessed over the centuries and acquired the status of a minor spiritual classic. His story is that of a plain, unassuming person beset by the difficulties we all have to endure, struggling to find his way in life, stumbling and falling but managing always to find his feet again. Above all, it is the story of someone who kept firmly in focus, through all his trials, the final goal of life—knowing and loving God. For Lawrence the ultimate goal of every soul is union with God. He believed we can achieve a far greater degree of unity with God in this life than most people think is possible. The way to accomplish this is through practicing the presence of God.[8]

Lawrence's way of doing this was by carrying on a constant conversation with God on all matters great or small and in all circumstances. It was his deep conviction that prayer is not saying prayers but a way of living in which all becomes prayer. It is a great delusion to think that time set aside for prayer should be different from other times; we are equally obliged to be united to God by work in the time assigned to work as by prayer during prayer time. He felt that his work in the kitchen or the shoe shop was no less prayer than his hours in the church; absolutely nothing was outside his intimate relationship with God. And from this relationship he derived a continual sense of joy and a real sense of communion.[9]

In the conversations recorded with him, he states very clearly that in the beginning a persistent effort is needed to form the habit of continually talking with and referring all we do to God, but that with perseverance God's love brings us to it and makes it feel quite natural. We are to act very simply with God and to speak frankly, he counsels, while invoking God's assistance as things occur. He endearingly confesses that, while he would go to chapel when the schedule called for it, such services left him with a profound spiritual dryness and he felt more united to God in his ordinary activities where even the most absorbing work did not divert his consciousness from God's presence. He found that the best way of reaching God was by doing ordinary tasks and came to the conclusion that our sanctification depends not upon changing our works but *in doing for God what we ordinarily do for ourselves.* Neither skill nor knowledge was needed for this, he insists—only a heart determined to devote itself to loving God.[10]

Through this practice he observed that his soul, which up till then was always disturbed, experienced a profound interior peace as if it had found its center. In a letter to a friend, he describes his method in simple and straightforward terms:

> *I keep myself in His presence by simple attentiveness and a loving gaze upon God which I can call the actual presence of God or to put it more clearly, an habitual silent and secret conversation of the soul with God.*[11]

And in a letter to another friend, he elaborates:

> *There is no mode of life in the world more pleasing and more full of delight than continual conversation with God; only those who practice and experience it can understand it. . . . If I were a preacher, I would preach nothing else but the practice of the presence of God; if I were a director I would recommend it to everyone, so necessary and so easy do I believe it to be. . . . Get going on this work; if you do as He wishes, be assured you will soon see the results. . . .*[12]

Noisy contemplation and the practice of the presence of God, two formulas—one contemporary, the other traditional—with essentially the same ingredients and the same desired effect: daily cultivation of our awareness of God's presence.

II
MONTHLY AND WEEKLY CULTIVATION
OF PRESENCE

A *Poustinia Day*

Catherine Kolyschkine was born into a wealthy family in Russia in 1900. Her father was half Polish and a Catholic, and she was raised in that tradition. Yet it was the distinctively Russian incarnation of the gospel that she experienced in her childhood which left a deep mark upon her spirit. At fifteen she married Baron Boris de Hueck. The young couple was soon thrust into the agonies of starvation and civil war following upon the October revolution of 1917. With only the clothes on their backs, they escaped and made their way to England and then to Canada where they arrived penniless in 1920 with a baby son to care for. The Baron's health had been shattered by the war, so Catherine found what work she could as a maid, waitress, laundress and salesclerk to support the family. She first came to know the people of North America by her friendships with the working poor in Toronto, Montreal, and New York.

After several years as a widow, in 1943 she married Eddie Doherty, a famous journalist for the *New York Daily News*. In 1947 they moved to Combermere, a little village 180 miles northeast of Toronto in Ontario. On the first day of their arrival, though facing a future filled with uncertainty, they planted an apple orchard in what seemed to them a wilderness, confident that God could make it bloom. Madonna House was born, and slowly grew into a lay apostolate training center which today has houses in twenty-three countries from which various ministries are exercised. Throughout her life, Catherine de Hueck Doherty found a place of sustenance in the center of her own heart where, she says, "all is silent and where I am immersed in the silence of God."

She called this place her *poustinia,* a secret room where we will be gifted with God's own self if we only go there in faith. In her book by the same name,[13] she unwraps the several layers of the word's meaning.

Poustinia literally means "desert" in Russian, but it connotes much more to Russians than just a geographical place. It means a quiet, solitudinous place into which people enter to encounter in a more focused way the God who dwells within them. It can refer to a place where a hermit lives in silence, solitude and prayer, or to a small room in one's home reserved for prayer and for meditation, or to the quiet "room" in one's own heart. A poustinia can be any place that pilgrims go seeking to enter into the silence of God and listen to God's Word, Christ, in that silence. So in one sense it is a particular place, but in another it is more like a vocation belonging to all Christians by baptism: the vocation to be contemplative. In its essence it is a place within oneself where, as a result of baptism, each of us is invited to acquire a listening heart and to contemplate the presence within of the triune God.

As many citizens of the modern secular city have experienced, deserts and solitudes are not necessarily places but states of mind and heart. These deserts can be found in the midst of the city. So strictly speaking, there is no need for a log cabin in the woods or a cottage in the hills to lead a life of prayer. Prayer is interior. The hut, the log cabin, the chapel is the human heart in which we must learn how to pray. Prayer doesn't need a geographic spot; prayer is a contact of love between God and ourselves, and as the life of Brother Lawrence showed, one can "make love" anywhere.

> *When you are in love with someone, it seems that the face of the beloved is before you when you drive, when you type, when you are taking out insurance, and so on. Somehow or other we can encompass these two realities,*

the face of the beloved and whatever we happen to be doing.[14]

Catherine wanted to make this point very strongly: the first poustinia is within one's heart where one can enter in the wink of an eye, anywhere, anytime. She believed that the poustinia of the heart was the answer for the modern world. The world only knows *about* God, so it can reject, ignore, and be indifferent to God a thousand times a day in the neighbor. But if there were a *personal knowledge* through an experience of God's own revelation to us in the poustinia of our hearts, then God would not be rejected.

But once she had clearly established the preeminence of the poustinia of the heart, she recognized that for many it would take on a definite physical, geographical dimension. Consistent with this, she saw to the construction of several poustinia cabins in the woods and hills surrounding Madonna House and encouraged community members and guests to go away to that "desert place" for one day each month. And to others she said, "If you have a spare room in the house or a large closet, it will do." Then, in letters to the mission houses and others in the growing network of associates, she outlined the reasons why one should go. Among them: To pray for others. To fast. To live in silence. To pray for peace, the missions, and unity among Christians. To learn total surrender to God. To begin to empty yourself, saying, "Here I am, Lord, do with me as you will. Speak, for your servant is listening. I thank you for all you have given me, for all you have taken away from me, for all you have left me."[15]

What to take along? Just the bible, bread and water. The desert is the land of detachment, of living simply. One travels light there, the better to go wherever God wants to lead you. "For 24 hours you are going to be alone with God and the only book that you are going to read is the bible. Don't take any others! If you want to sleep, sleep. If you want to walk, walk. . . . The poustinia is one place where you can relax a little. . . . God knows all about you. Have a little chat, snooze a little, do a little reading, go out and look at the grass and say, 'Gee, how beautiful you made the grass (or snow)' or 'How lovely the rain is.' That's the sort of thing you can do. There's nothing frightening about it. . . . You have said to the Lord, 'I want to take these hours out of my busy life and come to you because I am very tired. The world is not the way you want it, and neither am I. I want to come and rest on your breast as St. John the Beloved. That's why I have come to this place.' "[16]

In my own life, the discipline of a monthly poustinia day has been an anchor, a compass, and a sail. When the throttle is at full go or the waves are bouncing me around, it's an anchor to throw overboard that brings me to a halt and lets me sit quietly in a secluded bay for a while before setting out again. When I've lost my bearings and need orienting, the solitude, silence and prayer are a compass that point me once again in the right direction. When I'm feeling good about life, a day just floating freely about looking at the clouds and enjoying the warmth of the sun represents an open psychic space which serves as a great billowing mainsail for catching the winds of gratitude. Sometimes I spend an overnight and the following day at a retreat house in the city; at other times I leave around 8 a.m. from my house and pass the day just intermittently sitting and walking in the forest of nearby Mount Royal Park. I love the freedom and simplicity of just walking away for a day with a light knapsack bearing only a bible and water bottle. Being single of course makes it easier to do, but some of my married friends have found that, with communication, mutual support and spelling each other, they can do it, too. The restorative magic of the day has to be experienced to be believed.

Because we are so used to cramming every available minute with useful and productive activity, the prospect of an open space of time without any particular agenda can be fairly daunting and disorienting. Some things which I have learned from the Buddhists have proved very helpful in easing me gently into the quiet and settling me down.

Exercises in Mindfulness

The essential Buddhist disciplines are aimed at helping one take hold of one's own consciousness, of becoming more aware of what one is doing. One of my favorite stories in this regard concerns Tenno, a Zen student. No Zen student would presume to teach others until he had lived with his master for at least ten years. Tenno, having completed his ten years of apprenticeship, acquired the rank of teacher. One day he went to visit the master Nan-in. It was a rainy day, so Tenno wore wooden clogs and carried an umbrella. When he walked in, Nan-in greeted him with, "You left your wooden clogs and umbrella on the porch, didn't you? Tell me, did you place your umbrella on the right side of the clogs or the left?" Tenno was embarrassed, for he did not know the answer. He realized he lacked awareness. So he became Nan-in's student and labored for another ten years to acquire constant awareness. [17]

Whenever I mislay my keys or my glasses or fail to put something into my briefcase, I say to myself: "Ten more years!" I think I've accumulated several lifetimes of apprenticeship in the past year alone. But the Buddhist concentration on awareness has to do with more than just remembering things. Mindfulness is the miracle which calls back in a flash our dispersed mind and restores it to one-pointed unity so that we can live each minute of life fully.

Many of the revered teachings in Buddhism take the form of *sutras* ("short, clipped sentences"). The Sutra of Mindfulness says, "When walking, the practitioner must be conscious that he is walking. When sitting, the practitioner must be conscious that he is sitting. When lying down, the practitioner must be conscious that he is lying down. . . . Practicing thus, the practitioner lives in direct and constant mindfulness of the body. . . ."[18]

Awareness of the positions of one's body are not enough, of course. The sutras go on to teach that one must be conscious of each breath, each movement, every thought and feeling, everything which has any relation to ourselves. As one builds up the power of concentration, one discovers an inner calmness and serenity as its fruit. Anxiety, which is usually tied to the future, is shaken off and the mind quieted by focusing upon the present. While relaxation follows, it is only a prelude to the real goal: a tranquil heart and a clear mind. Taking a half hour walk in the park, watching one's breath and maintaining mindfulness, refreshes, restores and eases one gently into a day of encounter with the Mystery shining through all things.

Prayer's essential component is attention. It is the orienting of all the attention of which the soul is capable toward God. This kind of contemplative prayer can be exercised during fixed times of formal prayer, but it can also be exercised at any time in an informal way, like taking a walk in the countryside or in a local park.

The value of awareness exercises, such as watching one's breathing or listening to the sounds or feeling the sun or breeze on one's skin, is that, by literally "bringing us to our senses," they bring us to the present, and thus to Presence. The goal of prayer is not continuously talking with God, but the union of heart and mind with God which results from such continuous conversation. What restores us and unifies our being, bringing us home to where God lives—this, too, is prayer. When we look, listen, taste, smell, and touch with mindfulness, silence overtakes us and we find ourselves filling up with gratitude, the heart of prayer. As a woman paralyzed from the neck down said, "I have all the most beautiful things in the world. I can do all the most beautiful things in the world. I can see. I can hear. I can taste. I can smell. I can feel. I can love!"

Rev. Eido Tai Shimano, a Japanese Zen master who teaches at the Zen Studies Society in New York, shared this story:

> *People often ask me how Buddhists answer the question, 'Does God exist?' The other day I was walking along the river. The wind was blowing. Suddenly I thought, oh! the air really exists! We know that the air is there, but unless the wind blows against our face we are not aware of it. Here in the wind I was suddenly aware, yes, it's really there.*
>
> *And the sun, too. I was aware of the sun, shining through the bare trees. Its warmth, its brightness, and all this completely free, completely gratuitous. Simply there for us to enjoy.*
>
> *And without my knowing it, completely spontaneously, my two hands came together and I realized I was making a deep bow. And it occurred to me that this is all that matters: that we can bow, take a deep bow. Just that. Just that.*[19]

Thus the Buddha responded to his disciples' question: "What difference has being enlightened made in your life?"

"Well, when I eat. I eat. When I look, I look. When I listen, I listen."

"But everybody does that!" they exclaimed.

"If everybody does that," he rejoined, "then everybody is enlightened!"

The fact is, few do that. Few engage in such noisy contemplation and fully enter into the "now" experience. We speak about being "too involved" but in reality we are under- rather than over-involved. Our busyness reflects a condition of being scattered. We need to be slowed by involvement.[20]

In our house, we used to put all the dishes in the dishwasher. It was faster and more efficient and enabled us to get on to other things. But for the past couple of years we've started washing them by hand. There are two ways to wash the dishes. The first is wash the dishes in order to have clean dishes; the second is to wash the dishes in order to wash the dishes.

If while washing the dishes we think only of the newspaper or cup of tea that awaits us, and thus hurry to get the dishes out of the way as if they were a nuisance, then we are not "washing the dishes to wash the dishes." Nor are we apt to savor the miracle of life as we stand at the sink. If we can't wash the dishes, the chances are we won't be able to focus on the cup of tea either. We'll probably drink it absentmindedly as we read the newspaper, keeping an eye on our watch so as not to tune in late for a favorite TV program. So our attention is dispersed in the present and being pulled off into the future. We are incapable of living five minutes of life with one-pointed attention. We need to be slowed by increased involvement with each thing we do. The miracle we discover is that when we do the very next thing we have to do, and do it as though it were the most important thing in the world at that moment, we find at least satisfaction if not delight in it. Even doing the dishes!

The meditation practices in Buddhism and the insights flowing from them can render valuable service in our efforts to live more deliberately and fully. It is not surprising that Buddhists have derived important lessons from meditation. Buddhism started with Siddhartha Gautama's enlightenment experience, which came about as a result of his disciplined and persevering meditation. Whereas Christianity's wellspring experience was the passion, death and resurrection of Jesus, Buddhism's is meditation practice.[21]

One can see the impact of Buddhist meditative exercises in

the traditional rituals of Japan: rock gardens and landscapes, flower arrangements and carefully cultivated miniature trees, elaborate mandalas and haiku poetry which celebrates daily beauties and sorrows in seventeen precise and direct syllables. Everyday commonness is exquisitely veiled with the mist of transcendental inwardness, and the mind penetrates surface struggles and vanities to lay hold of a glimpse of eternity. One Japanese ritual which particularly captures the spirit of contemplative living is the tea ceremony.

In the actual preparation of the tea, the host pays special attention to the fire and the water, but especially to the spoon and the bamboo whisk. The spoon for measuring the powdered tea and the whisk for stirring it both require care and delicacy in order to ensure a perfect balance. When the proper measures of tea and boiled water are poured into the clay cups and stirred with the whisk until exactly right, the visitors lift the cups in both hands, feeling the texture and warmth. They drink the tea, not in one gulp but in small sips, savoring the refreshing liquid. The tea ceremony is a stimulant to meditation: the atmosphere is relaxed, awareness is unhurried, and the conversation is non-argumentative. The purpose of the ritual is to be all there, to be one with the tea, developing attitudes toward existence and nature that ought to permeate one's entire life. As the Zen masters were accustomed to say, "Religion is a most ordinary thing."[22]

A compelling claim of Joan Chittister in her book *Wisdom Distilled from the Daily* is that the foundational vision of the *Rule of St. Benedict* lends itself to secular as well as monastic embodiment. Indeed, the qualities of heart and mind that the *Rule* seeks to promote are precisely those most needed by a wastefully consumerist and exploitative society. Respect for things and reverence for persons—the kitchen vessels treated with the same honor as the altar vessels, the guest greeted as though Christ himself were present—connote attitudes as much at home in the high-rise as in the monastery. Perhaps the attitude most central to the *Rule* as she experiences it is—surprise—*mindfulness:* "Each of us has been given something to keep well: a small garden, a tiny room, a simple apartment, our bodies. That much, surely, we could take care of mindfully."[23] We are geared for spectacular undertakings, but hardly prepared for the demands of the daily. Yet, the everyday, mindfully responded to, provides asceticism enough for most of us, and perhaps our best access to the mystical.

A Zen proverb says: "Before enlightenment, chop wood, carry water; after enlightenment, chop wood, carry water." In other words, our actions may not appear much different externally, but their inner quality has changed because our perceptions have changed.

Walking Meditation

Walking meditation is practicing mindfulness while walking. It is a practice that the Vietnamese Buddhist Zen master Thich Nhat Hanh has popularized for many in the West with his writings and his retreats. Anyone can do it who has some degree of mindfulness and the desire to be serene and joyful. One walks slowly, if possible in some beautiful place. One does not walk in order to arrive, but just to enjoy the walking. The idea is to be in the present moment and to enjoy each step taken. One has therefore to shake off all worries and anxieties, not thinking of the past or of the future, just enjoying the present moment. Though we walk all the time, it is usually more like running toward a finish line.[24]

In walking meditation, each step is peace and joy; that's why we don't have to hurry and why we can wear a pleasant half-smile as we walk. When we walk like that, we print peace and happinesss on the earth with our feet instead of the anxiety and tension carried in heavy, hurried footprints. One might visualize a flower opening in one's footprints as one's light, serene steps touch the ground.

Attention to one's breathing plays an important role in walking meditation. It comes to many as astonishing news that something as simple as attention to breathing has a central part to play in meditation and prayer. It's like a mystery novelist's idea of hiding the diamonds in the goldfish bowl: too obvious to notice. In a Buddhist monastery, everyone learns to use breath as a tool to stop mental dispersion and to develop one's power of concentration.

To master our breath is to be in control of our bodies and minds because our breath is the bridge from our body to our mind. It is the element which reconciles our body and mind and which makes their harmonization possible. Because it is aligned to both, it is the tool which can bring them together in peace and calm. Try it by taking ten minutes to simply observe your breathing. Your thoughts will quiet down like a pond on which hardly a ripple stirs.

To follow your breath and make it calm, try this method.

As you breathe in, count 1 in your mind, and as you breathe out count 1. Breathe in, count 2, breathe out, count 2. Continue up to 10, then return to 1 again. This counting is like a string which attaches your mindfulness to your breath. Breathing consciously is different from breathing unconsciously. When you breathe mindfully, you know that you are breathing. If you take a long breath, you know that you are taking a long breath; when you take a short breath, you know that you are taking a short breath.

In his little book *Walking Meditation*,[25] Nhat Hanh instructs one how to pay attention to breathing and walking at the same time, gradually combining these components with others. You begin by just walking along and breathing normally for a few minutes. Then notice how many steps you take as your lungs fill in and how many steps you take as they empty. In this way your attention includes both breath and steps. You are mindful of both. The link is the counting of your steps as you breathe in (for example: 1-2-3-4) and the counting of your steps as you breathe out (1-2-

3-4). Your half-smile brings calmness and delight to your steps and to your breath. The counting helps to maintain your attention and is an object of attention in itself. After several "practice-walks" you will find that the four elements—the breath, counting, steps, and half-smile—blend together harmoniously and induce a state of equanimity. Mindfulness and peace are the purpose of walking meditation.

Words can be substituted for numbers, e.g. (Breathing in:) "Breathing in I calm my body. (Breathing out:) Breathing out I smile. (Breathing in:) Dwelling in the present moment. (Breathing out:) Knowing it's a wonderful moment." You can design your own phrases, making them equal in length to your breathing pattern. While employing walking meditation on a poustinia day, I oftentimes use a form of the Jesus prayer: "Lord Jesus Christ (in-breath), have mercy on me a sinner (out-breath)." Sometimes you may just want to walk and focus on the miracles all about you, the light filtering down through the trees, the delicate mantle of snow sculpturing every bush and stone, the song of birds or the laughter of children playing in the park. That's fine. The point is to zoom in and focus your attention on whatever you choose to be attentive to. You can't focus on everything simultaneously—your breath, steps, words, half-smile, trees, birds, and children. The focus of your concentration becomes dispersed as the field of your attention widens. If you can enjoy something more by stopping, then stop and sit awhile while you continue to be aware of your breathing.

The practice of walking meditation opens our eyes to the miracles constantly unfolding in the universe about us. But it also helps us to see more clearly the dark side of life: the fear, the greed, the poverty, the suffering. The awareness it cultivates within us enables us to make decisions with greater insight and to respond to people in our daily lives with compassion.

Nhat Hanh suggests that each person should try hard to devote one day a week to the practice of mindfulness. Soon, the effect of that day will begin to penetrate the other days of the week enabling us to live more deliberately each day. Without it, he contends, we lose ourselves quickly in a life full of worry and action.

Whatever day we choose, it is to be entirely our day—not in the sense that we will do only what we want to do, but in the sense of really taking conscious hold of the way we do each thing: calmly, slowly, easefully, without reluctance, and with all our attention. Enjoy and be one with the work; the feeling that it is a nuisance will dissolve if done in mindfulness. If talking is necessary, be attentive to what we say and of the one to whom we're saying it. Let it be the one day of the week where we don't try to combine some other activity with eating, e.g., watching TV or reading the newspaper. Live each activity or encounter by giving it your full attention in the realization that only this actual moment is life. The future doesn't exist yet and the past is already gone. End the day with a slow walk in the fresh night air, following your breath and synchronizing it with your steps by use of prayerful words or counting.[26]

Creative Choices

Some time ago I started combining a weekly mindfulness day with my sabbath observance. So many of the accents of the sabbath day—slowing down, living more deliberately, experiencing gratitude—lined up with a day devoted to mindfulness that it finally dawned on me: "the two are a natural fit!" Taking a walk is an ideal sabbath day activity. The sabbath is less crowded with demands and tasks and hence an arena much more conducive to just calmly living each moment as it comes.

I am more of a "doer," an activist, than a "be-er." From the day of my birth, my parents tell me, my engine had a high idle. My energy level replenishes itself quickly, and I am quite comfortable juggling several projects at once. I tell you this so that you know these exercises in living more deliberately do not come easily for me. There is considerable grinding of gears at times as I attempt to downshift and pass through the day in first or second gear rather than in third or fourth. But the enrichment that I experience along the way is such that there is no argument: this way lies a more truly enjoyable and fulfilling existence. I know what the other way is like, and though I have never officially "burned-out," I have scooted perilously close to the edge any number of times and felt the heat. The conversion process is gradual, but there's no turning back. I'd like to share with you two stories which highlight both the ongoing struggle and the reward.

My community, the Paulist Fathers, has a summer get-away place on the shore of Lake George in upstate New York. It's a large, old, rustic hotel-like structure which sits up on a hill over-looking the lake; down at the water's edge is a marina with more water toys than we know how to use. Then eighteen miles down the lake there is an island named after one of our founders with a bunkhouse on it.

There's no electricity, just coleman lanterns, and a pump that brings in water from the lake. The view down the lake, with the Adirondack mountains rising out of the water on both sides and a sprinkling of other islands in the foreground, is one of the most beautiful I've seen anywhere in the world.

Going to our place at Lake George always presents me with a difficult choice. Staying at the main house near the village offers more options: newspapers, movies, T.V., prepared meals, water skiing, cycling paths, the town.

But my repeated experience is that time on the island is more fulfilling for me—precisely because of its simplicity. The reduced options result in greater focus. I read more, reflect more, and perhaps most important, become quieter and more centered.

One day I simply sat under the pine tree on the point in front of the cabin from morning to late afternoon, focusing first on one sense, and then another . . . the breeze playing around the surface of my skin and on the back of my neck . . . the pine-scented air . . . the song and chatter of birds and the waves lapping on the rocks . . . the dazzling dance of sunlight on water and, of course, the wondrous beauty all up and down the lake. I just sat there and *looked* at things, like flies, ants, ferns, bark, scrub brush. A couple of times I got up and dove in the lake just for the pleasure of the cool water, and then took a life preserver so as to be able to float effortlessly, looking at the sky and trees and the clouds. It was a carnival of the senses, just sitting out there under a pine tree and floating in the water. This kind of day highlights the reward of taking time to simply enter into the joy of being.

My second story took place one fine day in March and highlights the constant struggle to slow down. I belong to a support group of about ten priests who meet once a month in a retreat house in the mountains an hour's drive out of Montreal. We enjoy a meal, pray together, share for a few hours on whatever it is we're living and try to support each other in some aspect of our lives. This time around, such support had to do with getting some exercise. The word went out: bring your skis.

I decided to go up a day early for a combination sabbath-poustinia-mindfulness day. I awoke around 7:30 a.m. and drew the curtains only to discover that the day presented a very special kind of temptation. Some fresh powder snow had fallen during the night, the morning sky was a sparkling metallic blue and the sun glistened upon the sea of diamonds piled up on the ground outside. A perfect day for spring skiing! The day lay before me like a rare jewel for the taking.

I stood at the window processing it all in my mind. Could I integrate this into the spirit of the day? Sure I could. Wasn't this the kind of activity that fulfills the spirit of a sabbath day—something I'd never think of doing any other day of the week? Something frivolous and fun that celebrates the giftedness of life?

I decided to go for it with gusto—but just for the morning, and then return for a quiet afternoon.

I hurried down to the dining room for a quick breakfast, hustled back to my room to get change for the phone booth in order to call and verify that the nearby ski hill had morning-only lift tickets, then scampered back to my room to change clothes. With a yelp for sheer joy at the stunning day, I threw my gear in the car and zoomed off toward St. Sauveur ski station. I started to become aware that I was driving too fast. The morning lift-ticket was good from 8:30 to noon and it was already a quarter to nine. When I looked at the speedometer, I was nonetheless surprised to see that the needle had crept up to 123 kph (77 mph) on a downhill run in the highway. I started to cut back on my speed— but too late. Sitting alongside the highway was a patrol car with its radar on. Hope sprang up within, however, for even as I was slowing down in the right hand lane, another car with a rack of skis on top was passing me in the left hand lane: "Maybe he'll nail him and not me," I thought.

And sure enough, as I passed the patrol car and watched it in my rear view mirror, it pulled out and on went its flashers. But instead of heading into the outside lane to go after the car which had passed me and which was already a considerable way in front of me, he pulled in behind me and signalled me over.

As he was writing me out a speeding ticket, I realized I felt more upset with myself for contravening my own rule than for the breaking the province's speed limit. "Don't hurry. Live deliberately. Awareness is all."

I had rushed around the retreat house getting ready to go, then proceeded to speed down the highway to get to the ski hill as fast as I could. And all in the name of a relaxed day with the Lord, deliberately lived with loving attention. . . .

By the time he returned from his car with a ticket in hand, I had already made up my mind as to what I was going to do. "Thank you, officer," I said, as he looked at me quizzically. "I needed slowing down, and you did it. This ticket is a fine for first of all failing to keep my own code of not hurrying." I started up the car, took the first exit I came to, and *slowly* drove back to the retreat house on a service road. I went up to my room, changed clothes, and went out for a quiet walk in the woods with the Lord, stopping to listen to the birds' early song of spring, to feel the sun warm on my face, to breathe deeply and taste the delicious quality of the air.

There is this saying in the Zen tradition: "However wonderful something may be, it is not as good as doing nothing."

III
ANNUAL CULTIVATION OF PRESENCE

G. K. Chesterton argued that we need more solitude; it's the only way the mind can have a half-holiday, the only way to get any fun out of the facts of life. We accumulate so much baggage as we journey through the course of a year. If we never stop to unpack our luggage, we even lose track of what's in there.[27]

When I set off on my trip to India, my bag was light with a few articles of clothing carefully selected for their serviceability. As I traveled, however, the bag slowly expanded with gifts and mementos, travel literature and books on the Indian culture and religions. At one point it became too heavy to comfortably carry for long distances. When the time came to go into the Himalayas for a course in Buddhist doctrine and meditation practice at the Dalai Lama's colony in Dharamsala, I extracted only what was necessary for that portion of the journey and put it into a knapsack, leaving the larger pack behind at the home of friends to pick up again later. When I came down from the mountains, my knapsack was now bulging with new material. There was no time to sort out the new acquisitions and integrate them into the larger pack as I had to leave immediately for a course in Islam beginning in South India. I just put the small pack on top of the larger one and headed for the train station. I was now carrying a small library on my back and glad to be near the end of the journey.

When I finally reached home and did empty all the contents out of my bag, many little items, wrapped in newsprint and smelling of incense, triggered moments of vivid recollection of the people, sights, sounds, smells and experiences lived in that place. In several cases, I had even forgotten that the object was in my pack. The rigors of travel in India are such that there was seldom time or energy to give to reflective savoring en route. It is only now, in the months following those experiences, that the "unpacking" of them is occurring through reflection and writing.

The best things that happen to us, Chesterton observed, are those we get out of what has already happened. The process of reading my journals and other books I brought back, and the time taken for reflection upon them, are enabling me to grasp more fully the meaning of what I lived in those months. It is like mining the ore that one knows is embedded in the rock but needs extraction. And like mining, it is work, but without the shoveling and the swinging of the pick, there would be much less of value to share.

Each day, each week, each month is filled with a multitude of experiences that need unpacking. This is the real case for solitude—on a monthly basis with a poustinia day, and annually with a retreat of several days taken together. If we are living with any degree of awareness and reflection, within a week or a month there are experiences which beg to be unwrapped and held in the quiet light of reflectivity. But when we just keep traveling through life and putting everything into our pack without ever stopping to savor, digest and assimilate, we become superficial tourists and consumers, like participants in a one-month, ten-country tour of Europe. One of the best pieces of travel advice I ever received (but could not always follow in India) was to leave one free day in the schedule for every five days of programmed travel. The idea behind a weekly sabbath and mindfulness day, a monthly poustinia, and an annual retreat is the same. Without them, we simply pile one experience on top of another and just skim the surface of life, concentrating on mere survival rather than conscious, grateful and deliberate living.

Why are the experiences of rocking a child in silence, of watching a sunset in stillness, of quietly contemplating a work of art so extraordinarily enriching? Because in them both the outward experience and the interior savoring are happening simultaneously. But until we cultivate that capacity within ourselves and realize it on a more daily basis, the existential depth of these experiences can only be retrieved and assimilated into our deepest being through a process of remembering in reflective silence.[28]

This is important not only to extract the gold from the veins which run through our daily living, but also to identify and reject the counterfeit. An elderly confrère with whom I would occasionally enjoy a meal in a restaurant used to say in exiting from one which disappointed him, "Tell me the name of that restaurant again. I don't ever want to forget it." We need to positively recognize and reject many of the negative elements of life that stream toward us each day: exploitive ways of relating, appeals to our baser instincts, abuses of our time. We need to make decisions "not to go there again." Without this careful sifting through the soil and stone of our weeks and months, our consciousness remains a rubble pile of unenlightened experiences and superficial impressions. Knowing one's own mind is necessary for constructive decisions that carry us forward toward truth and authenticity. One day as I was leaving his office, I asked my spiritual director if he was going to watch a particular special on television that night. "I wasn't aware it was on," he said. "I don't watch much television anymore. I realized it was filling my mind with a lot of trivia." That kind of decision is only possible in the first place when there is reflective space in our lives.

The Rhythm of Togetherness and Solitude

When my priests' support group comes together each month, we now spend a half-hour in silent prayer together prior to our life-sharing. Several have observed that, since beginning this practice, the quality of our sharing has improved.

Contemplative tradition has placed much emphasis on the need for silence not only in an individual's life but in the community's life as well. When applied to the family, this would suggest that one of the ways by which couples can allow room for the evolution of growth in their relationships with one another and with God is to balance their together time with some quality "away" time. This was Jesus' rhythm: withdrawal and community. But the withdrawal is never from community or family in the deepest sense, for the time apart sends us back to human relationships with a new freedom. We return to those with whom we live resourced by and in our relationship with God. Having found our balance in that spacious divine center, we are reminded that we are not saved by human interaction but by God. The pressure is off to fulfill every demand that flows from others' neediness. We are mutually freed from expecting too much from one another. Our real hope has shifted from mutually controlling, securing, and self-justifying expectations to a reliance on God's already rich, active presence in and among us, revealing itself in new and surprising ways.[29]

By cultivating an appreciation for how some time in solitude can help enrich their life together, a couple can support each other in reserving three or four days of retreat time on their calendar and in resisting all the reasons that would keep them at home when the time comes to withdraw and go apart. If it is not possible for both to live these days of quiet together at a local retreat house or a friend's available cottage or chalet, one might offer to cover the family responsibility to free the other, an act of love which is later reciprocated so that in the course of the year both have the opportunity for some quality time in silence and solitude.

When such are the circumstances for one's *aloneness*, it is not a question of being *lonely*. There is an important difference between solitude and loneliness. As Brother David Steindl-Rast has insightfully observed, "Aloneness is neutral. Loneliness is aloneness which is cut off from togetherness; solitude is aloneness supported by togetherness. Togetherness without solitude is not truly togetherness, but rather side-by-sideness. We need time and space to find ourselves in solitude before we can give ourselves to one another in true togetherness."[30] The interior silence that comes to birth in solitude, though some might fear it because they are accustomed to always having people and noise about them, is one of the most strengthening and affirming of human experiences. There is nothing more affirming than the experience of God's presence. In it we come to know that we are good, that God created us and loves us. It heals the negative feelings we have about ourselves.[31]

There could be no greater endorsement of the importance of an annual retreat than its presence in the rule of life of all those communities made up of people who have made public professions to take God with utter seriousness. Members of religious communities normally are granted a week's time off each year for prayerful reflection upon their lives. The unfortunate fact is that not all take it. Such is the quicksand effect of our activist lives: once we've got both hands and feet into the work of the apostolate, we find it very difficult to pull ourselves out—even when the community is giving the strongest possible encouragement and willing to cover the expenses.

If we are to witness in today's frenetic marketplaces to the joyful serenity that flows from life in Christ, we need silence and the perspective that flows from it. If we are to be constantly available for service in love, not only physically but by empathy, sympathy, friendship, and understanding, we need silence. If we are able to give ready and generous hospitality, not only of house and food, but of mind, heart and soul, we need silence. When silence is a well from which we regularly drink and at which we meet Jesus, availability to others becomes easier because we recognize his presence in them. And hospitality will be deep and real, for a heart refreshed by that silent rendezvous is a hospice open to all. On one of my annual retreats, Fr. William McNamara said something which continues to be a living, challenging word for me: "Nobody is an intruder and nothing is an interruption." I frequently repeat that to myself when the phone or doorbell rings or someone drops by unannounced. There is undoubtedly more of the Spirit in what spontaneously happens than in my agenda planner for the day. But to *live* that as a conviction of faith, I need those oases of silence where the perspectives of faith can be nurtured.

Henry David Thoreau saw how even our secular existence withers from lack of an interior life. As our inward quiet life fails, "we go more constantly and desperately to the post office," but "the poor fellow who walks away with the greatest number of letters, proud of his extensive correspondence, has not heard from himself this long while. . . . Read not The Times," he concludes, "read The Eternities!"[32] In solitude we find the psychic distance, the perspective from which we can see, in the light of eternity, the created things that trap, worry, and oppress us.

Solitude, however, as reflected in the first part of this chapter relating to noisy contemplation, might well benefit from but does not require a geographical place apart. As Catherine de Hueck Doherty was fond of reminding those who came to Madonna House to spend a few days in a cabin in the woods, "deserts, silence, and solitude are not necessarily places but states of mind and heart." They can be found in the midst of the city and in the little pools of solitude that eddy around the currents of each day. It may be a noon hour taken sitting quietly in a nearby church, or an evening in one's room instead of in front of the television set. The experience such hours bring, if we are disposed to enter them, may be as exultant and as holy as those lived in any desert of the world. For it is the same God who makes all solitudes, deserts and silences holy. [33]

The various disciplines of cultivating presence discussed here all share the same goal: to enable us to experience God in a personal way through deepening our awareness of God's presence in all persons and all creation. Time and effort invested in these practices of the spiritual life open us to the experience of the sacred in the commonplace. Ordinary busyness is transformed into extraordinary grace.

Christ came that we might have life and live it to the full. To enter into life fully is to experience God in risking being open to the joy and the pain, the loves and the losses. Any place is sacred ground because it is potentially a place of encounter with the divine Presence. As we learn to remove the shoes of "being used to it," and come alive to the sacrament of the present moment, we realize, "if not here, where? If not now, when?"[34] Here and now, Ultimate Reality is present to us.

The calling of a Christian is to consciously live in that Presence, becoming more and more aware that we share in the blessedness of resurrection life in our own deep being.

6

Fasting

"Me fast? Are you serious? I don't want to hurt myself!"

If we are honest with ourselves, we may recognize at least a tinge of that reaction in our own response to the idea of fasting. Underneath that reaction lies a confusion between fasting and starvation. The word "fast" derives from *faestan* which in old English means "to abstain." The abstention is voluntary and undertaken for *good* effects. It is life-enhancing. The word starvation comes from the old English *sterofan*, the derivation of the Teutonic verb *sterben*, which means "to die."

Fasting is a positive, freely chosen action that bestows a number of benefits. Starving, in contrast, is usually an involuntary wasting away through the prolonged unavailability of food or inadequate amounts of food. When we fast, we in effect decide that we are going to take our nourishment from the "reserves" we have been storing up in good supply. Starvation begins when the "storage shelves" have been emptied, when the body has consumed its spare resources, craves food, and continues to be deprived.

Think of the last time somebody went on a protest hunger strike. Have you ever noticed that the media doesn't even begin to take note until around the eighteenth to twentieth day? That's because the normal person has about twenty-five days of food reserves in the "cupboard" and until one approaches the end of that supply there is nothing in particular to be alarmed about. I am proposing at most a one-day fast on a regular basis. So relax: you won't die or even become gravely ill! You may, however, discover in it a well-kept secret revealing deep and time-tested wisdom.

What the parents throw away as useless, the children bring back as new-found treasure. What one generation discards, the next generation unearths and enshrines. Today people from all ages and backgrounds are fasting: athletes, musicians, students, teachers, union leaders, clergy, medical professionals, artists, construction workers, designers, writers, photographers, secretaries, actors, bus drivers, and store managers. They're fasting to give their bodies a house-cleaning day, or to give their physical self a rest, a holiday, in much the same way we give our minds a rest after we've been working hard at reading or writing. They're fasting as an aid to self-transcendence, to relieve tension, to sleep better, to sharpen their senses, to quicken their mental processes, to share with the hungry, and to call attention to social issues.

As good and worthwhile and healthy and whatever else all those things might be, we are yet looking for something *more* in fasting: that it be an act of *religion*. Religion, in its root meaning (*re-ligare*), means to re-tie, to reconnect us to God, to bind us again to the Source from whom we came and to whom we are on pilgrimage. Only the Spirit of God can enable the act of fasting to do that for us. In and of itself, like any other external human act, it is ambivalent. In and of itself, as the various reasons for which people fast illustrate, it is religiously an indifferent act. It can even be spiritually *dangerous* in that it can become an achievement of human virtue, a trophy on our mental shelf, a source of spiritual pride. It happened to the pharisees who were "professionally religious" and it can certainly happen to us. The worth of fasting as a religious act lies in the faith and love of which it is the expression. Without such faith and love its meaning lies somewhere else. In these pages, then, fasting means abstention from food and drink (save water and juice) for a specified period of time out of a *religious* motive.

The hinge-pin that makes fasting one thing or the other is my *intention*, which is the doorway for the Spirit of God. If I am open and inviting and willing it, the Spirit can make of my fast a powerful symbol of my own awareness of my creatureliness before my Creator-God. The Spirit can make of my physical hunger a symbol of my soul's deepest yearnings. The Spirit can give me an experience of God's goodness and compassion and stir up within me a deep sense of repentance and desire to change my life. The Spirit can reveal to me the fragmentation of my existence and push me, through fasting, toward true life where "All I want is to know Christ and the life flowing from his resurrection; likewise to know how to share in his sufferings, being formed into the pattern of his death" (Philippians 3:10).

If we undertake this discipline following the Spirit's lead, the Spirit will bring forth fruit in us through fasting. The best test that our fasting is according to the inspiration of the Holy Spirit is the fruit produced. "The fruit of the spirit is love, joy, peace, patience, kindness, generosity, faithfulness, gentleness and self-control" (Galatians 5:22).

I
AN ECUMENICAL AND BIBLICAL SURVEY
OF FASTING PRACTICE

In the Anglican and main-line Protestant churches today, the question of fasting is left to the individual member. Each is to decide for himself or herself whether one will fast and how. In the Anglican Communion, the more important fast days are recommended in the *Book of Common Prayer*. The list includes all Fridays, Lent, certain vigils and the Ember days (observance of penance, thanksgiving and petition for divine blessing on the various seasons). Ember days originated at Rome about the fifth century, probably as replacements for seasonal festivals or agrarian cults. They were observed on a Wednesday, Friday and Saturday four times a year. The *Book of Common Prayer* simply enjoins a special measure of devotion and abstinence on these days, laying down no precise law for their observance, the details of which are left to the discretion of local ecclesiastical authorities.

Martin Luther commended fasting in his *Small Catechism* as a fitting preparation for receiving Holy Communion, and while some Lutherans do urge this, it is left to the devotion of the individual. What this approach highlights is a cultic asceticism that is found not only in Christianity but in many religions. Cultic asceticism touches on abstinence and other acts preparatory to one's participation in the mysteries of divine worship. In the Hebrew scriptures, instances of this are fasting, vigils, sexual abstinence, washings, and the offering of animals.

It is in the Eastern Church that we find the cultic asceticism of fasting more in evidence than anywhere. Days observed by fasting and abstinence have been so numerous at different times that the total has been as high as 180 days in the course of a year. And all of them come as preparatory acts for one's participation in the liturgical mysteries. In addition to the great, or major Lent, three other "Lents" are observed: the Lent of the Holy Apostles (June 16–28), Mary's Lent (August 1–14), and the Lent preceding Christmas (November 15–December 24). In addition to these four extended seasons of fasting, there are the vigils of the Epiphany, St. John Baptist's Day, Holy Cross, and every Wednesday and Friday. Not surprisingly, this regimen, monastic in inspiration, fails to engage the laity.

The Eastern Orthodox churches are laying the groundwork for a Pan-Orthodox Synod for which one of the agenda items is a reform of the fasting laws. Today, such cultic preparation has been relegated to one's individual inspiration, and the church members as a whole do not generally enter into any common cultic preparation in such an ascetical manner. The literature on fasting among Orthodox Christians emphasizes that at all times it is essential to bear in mind "that you are not under the law but under grace" (2 Corinthians 3:6). The rules of fasting, while they need to be taken seriously, are not to be interpreted with dour and pedantic legalism, "for the kingdom of God is not food and drink, but righteousness and peace and joy in the Holy Spirit" (Romans 14:17).

In 1966, the year following the end of the Second Vatican Council, Roman Catholics witnessed a shift in emphasis in a practice by which they were often identified: the Friday abstinence. Western Catholic practice of fasting had degenerated into prescription and lost a clear sense of "the why" of Christian fasting. When the wisdom of the spiritual tradition is no longer understood, the practice ossifies and becomes legalistic. The apostolic constitution of Pope Paul VI, *Poenitemini*, brought a total reorganization of ecclesiastical discipline with regard to fasting and abstinence. Abstinence from meat and meat products, it said, was to be observed on every Friday, and a fast as well as abstinence on Ash Wednesday and Good Friday. On a fast day only one full meal is allowed; two other small meals without meat may be taken according to one's need. The constitution changed the age at which one should begin to observe abstinence from seven to fourteen years, and changed the age at which one ceases to be obliged by the law of fasting to the completion of one's sixtieth year. Most significantly, Pope Paul authorized bishops' conferences to adapt the laws of fasting and abstinence to suit modern conditions and to emphasize prayer and works of charity as substitutes for previous practices of abstinence and fasting.

The American and Canadian bishops lost little time in issuing adaptations, but they were largely misread. In removing the binding character of the Friday obligation, they weren't saying that fasting isn't important anymore. The message behind the seeming sell-out to the modern spirit of convenience and indulgence was that fasting was *so* important that it had to be rescued from the legalism, minimalism and externalism into which it had fallen.

The bishops followed up the pope's document with pastoral statements which recommended that Catholics continue *voluntarily* to observe *some* (note: not necessarily fasting) acts of penance on *all* Fridays of the year. While Friday abstinence from meat was itself not going to be required by law (except during Lent), Fridays were singled out as days on which we should try to give special expression to our everyday call to love by entering into some activities oriented toward others.

The revision of fasting laws in the Roman Catholic Church have been so widely misunderstood or lost from sight that it is worthwhile setting them forth again. The Canadian Conference of Catholic Bishops' liturgical office reiterated the new approach in 1986: "Throughout the year, every Friday is a day of abstinence from meat, obliging all Catholics who are 14 or older. We may substitute special *acts of charity* (such as visiting the sick or aged, helping those in any need, or contributing time or money to a work of charity) or *acts of piety* (taking part in a service of worship with others, praying with our family, or spending some extra time in personal prayer, especially with God's holy word in the scriptures)."[1]

The U.S. Bishops' 1966 Pastoral Statement on Penance and Abstinence develops the "why" of a special Friday observance and the reasons for the broadening of penitential practice to include works of charity and acts of piety.

> *Christ died for our salvation on Friday. Gratefully remembering this, Catholic peoples from time immemorial have set apart Friday for special penitential observance by which they gladly suffer with Christ that they may one day be glorified with him. This is the heart of the tradition of abstinence from meat on Friday where that tradition has been observed.*

Changing circumstances, including economic, dietary, and social elements, have made some of our people feel that the renunciation of the eating of meat is not always and for everyone the most effective means of practicing penance. Meat was once an exceptional form of food; now it is commonplace.

Accordingly, since the spirit of penance primarily suggests that we discipline ourselves in that which we enjoy most, to many in our day abstinence from meat no longer implies penance, while renunciation of other things would be more penitential.

For these and related reasons, the Catholic bishops of the United States, far from downgrading the traditional penitential observance of Friday, and motivated precisely by the desire to give the spirit of penance greater vitality, especially on Fridays, the day that Jesus died, urge our Catholic people henceforth to be guided by the following norms.

Friday itself remains a special day of penitential observance throughout the year, a time when those who seek perfection will be mindful of their personal sins and the sins of humankind which they are called upon to help expiate in union with Christ crucified. Friday should be in each week something of what Lent is in the entire year. For this reason we urge all to prepare for that weekly Easter that comes with each Sunday by freely making of every Friday a day of self-denial and mortification in prayerful remembrance of the passion of Jesus Christ.

Among the works of voluntary self-denial and personal penance which we especially recommend to our people . . . we give first place to abstinence from flesh meat. We do so in the hope that the Catholic community will ordinarily continue to abstain from meat by free choice as formerly we did in obedience to Church law. . . . We shall thus remind ourselves that as Christians, although immersed in the world and sharing its life, we must preserve a saving and necessary difference from the spirit of the world. Our deliberate, personal abstinence from meat, more especially because no longer required by law, will be an outward sign of inward spiritual values that we cherish.

. . . Fridays, please God, will acquire among us other forms of penitential witness which may become as much a part of the devout way of life in the future as Friday abstinence from meat. . . . It would bring great glory to God and good to souls if Fridays found our people doing volunteer work in hospitals, visiting the sick, serving the needs of the aged and the lonely, instructing the young in the faith, participating as Christians in community affairs, and meeting our obligations to our families, our friends, our neighbors, and our community, including our parishes, with a special zeal . . . born of living faith.

. . . Let it be proved by the spirit in which we enter upon prayer and penance, not excluding fast and abstinence freely chosen, that these present decisions and recommendations of this conference of bishops will herald a new birth of loving faith and a more profound penitential conversion, by both of which we become one with Christ, mature sons and daughters of God, and servants of God's people. [2]

Most Catholics who were already adults at the time never caught this broadening of emphasis and still speak today as though something was taken away and nothing positive was put in its place. The bishops in no way intended to de-emphasize the importance of and the need for fasting. Rather, they underlined it in red. But they did it in a way that Roman Catholics haven't been reared to appreciate, i.e., by *removing* the laws of fast and abstinence instead of putting more laws in place. By so doing they challenged us to rediscover the spirit of fasting by freely and responsibly using this spiritual life tool to express our inner conversion of heart. The value of any particular discipline in the spiritual life is related to its ability to enable us to make ourselves more and more aware of God as the deepest reality of our lives. When we have lost the spirit of a practice, lost sight of the reasons and values that undergird it and are engaged only in a mechanical, external compliance, it is perhaps better that it is lost to us for a time so that it can be rediscovered again and embraced once more with feeling and understanding.

Lent itself was in danger of being strangled by the tentacles of legalism. The Mardi Gras pig-out and the Easter Sunday fat-attack symbolized, on one level, an unreal confining of a means of spiritual growth to the six weeks of Lent. But fasting isn't just for Lent—it's for Christian *life!*

The Roman Catholic Church used to stress "the need for" by stipulating the "when," "how long," and "how frequently" of this spiritual life tool. It now chooses just to reaffirm "the need for" and make some recommendations for the "when," leaving the details up to its members. Thus, in their implementation of the 1983 new Code of Canon Law, the Canadian bishops said, "Fridays are penitential days. However, instead of observing the universal law of abstinence from meat on Fridays, Catholics may substitute special acts of charity or piety on this day. The decree of the Episcopal Conference does not specify which particular acts of piety or charity are to be performed on Fridays; this is left to each Catholic to determine."[3]

It asks them to be adults in the faith and to act responsibly, using the disciplines of the spiritual life that fit their needs and situation and that express their inner conversion of heart. Thus, fasting today is an exercise of Christian freedom and individual liberty in response to the movement of the Holy Spirit within. In this we are like the early Christians. But what was true of them is not yet true of us: frequent fasting in liberty was considered *normal*. As we try to recover the spirit of fasting at the heart of our Judaeo-Chrisitan tradition, a brief biblical and patristic survey may be instructive.

Examining Our Roots

In Israel fasts lasted normally from morning until evening (Judges 20:26; 1 Samuel 14:24), except for the prescribed annual fast on *yom kippur*, the Day of Atonement, which continued for twenty-four hours. There are three recognizable categories into which all fasting seemed to fall. The first is as *a sign of mourning*, attested to in the oldest levels of pre-exilic texts (1 Samuel 31:13; 2 Samuel 1:12). The second is as *a preparation for visions* (1 Samuel 28:20–23; Daniel 10:3–9). And the third is as *an act of penance*, occasioned ordinarily by public or private calamity with the hope of deliverance. Penitential fasting also dates from pre-exilic times (Judges 20:26; 2 Samuel 12:16:23) and is characterized by the confession of sins and prayer of petititon (1 Samuel 7:6–8). A special fast of this type is that of *yom kippur* as described in Leviticus 16. The essential note of fasting in the Hebrew Scriptures is humble abasement before the Lord.

The Israelites hoped to receive forgiveness and deliverance as a divine response to their penitential fast, but they were at the same time quite aware that one cannot force God but must simply depend on God's merciful love. The true nature of fasting as an act of worship is expressed well by the prophet Joel: "Return to me with all your heart, with fasting, with weeping and with mourning; rend your hearts and not your clothing" (2:12). Equally important is Deutero-Isaiah's emphasis on justice and charity as a sign of authentic fasting:

> *Is not this the fast that I choose:*
> *to loose the bonds of injustice,*
> *to undo the thongs of the yoke,*
> *to let the oppressed go free*
> *and to break every yoke?*
> *Is it not to share your bread with the hungry,*
> *and bring the homeless poor into your house;*
> *when you see the naked, to cover them . . . ?* (58:6–7).

The Book of Tobit also joins the ideas of almsgiving, prayer, and fasting (12:8–9,13; 14:2,11), as does the Book of Sirach (7:10; 34:31). These passages lead to similar concerns in the New Testament and in the writings of the Church Fathers.[4]

During the time of Jesus, fasting on Mondays and Thursdays was in vogue in Israel. It is generally acknowledged that he and his disciples would have been faithful to the annual observance of *yom kippur* in accordance with Jewish law, but his disciples obviously scandalized some with their infrequent fasting (Mark 2:18). Jesus responded with an image which likened his mission of inaugurating the kingdom of God to a wedding feast: "The wedding guests cannot fast while the bridegroom is with them, can they?" (Mark 2:19). He wanted to emphasize the special, messianic nature of his coming and God's eagerness to reach out in forgiveness and grace. He expressed this message in a variety of ways, including the non-fasting of his disciples. But, "when the day comes that the groom is taken away, then they will fast" (Mark 2:20). In his teaching on fasting, Jesus preferred to talk about attitudes and essential meanings as opposed to specific regulations concerning nature and frequency.

> *And whenever you fast, do not look dismal, like the hypocrites, for they disfigure their faces so as to show others that they are fasting. Truly I tell you, they have had their reward. But when you fast, put oil on your*

*head and wash your face, so that your fasting may be
seen not by others but by your Father who is in secret;
and your Father who sees in secret will reward you* (Matthew 6:16–18).

The accent which comes through these references to the
wedding feast and to looking cheerful is a uniquely Christian
emphasis of joy in fasting. Against the background of Jewish
practice, these teachings do not resonate so much with mourning
or penitence as with preparation for visions—the vision of the
kingdom of heaven! The reign of God is rushing into the world
through the ministry and presence of Jesus, the bridegroom who
has come to establish a mystical marriage with God's people. The
joyous exterior which is to characterize Christian fasting has a
profound meaning which is basic to the Christian faith: Jesus is
bringing new wine. A total transformation is underway. Henceforth, the sign of fasting among his followers is joy and charity.
Fasting is now a recognition of something new that is already set
in motion, though not yet completed: the reign of God in our
midst. The joy that animates Christian fasting is like the joy of
someone who has been told by relatives that he or she has been
handsomely included in their will and, as a matter of fact, can
start drawing upon the inheritance anytime there is need since it's
all going to be given someday anyway.

During this time, the faithful are not idle but wait with busy,
collaborative hands in vigilant preparation for the bridegroom's
return. Fasting is part of this future-oriented waiting until he
comes to make all things full. Because we still struggle to seek first
the kingdom of God, we need disciplines that help us readjust our
priorities and remind us where our real treasure lies. The example of Jesus himself fasting in the desert for forty days (Matthew
4:1–11) portrays his total dependence on God and serves us notice to be wary of fame and fortune as seductive false gods. This
passage (Matthew 4:1–11) should not be taken to mean that he

went totally without food, but that he was in real earnest to know God's will and to sort out the priorities of his life and ministry.

Jesus' sojourn in the desert also lifts up another aspect of his teaching: the linkage between prayer and fasting. Fasting intensifies prayer. You can whip off a prayer with little time or effort or personal investment, but you cannot whip off a fast. We are much more open to God when we combine fasting with prayer. When Jesus healed the epileptic lad whom the disciples had been unable to heal, some ancient manuscripts record that he said, "But this kind does not come out except by prayer and fasting" (Matthew 17:21; Mark 9:29).

The same earnestness is evident in Acts 14:23 when the early Christian communities came to appoint elders, for they were the ones on whom the responsibility fell to carry forward the ministry on behalf of Christ. The prayer and fasting enjoined by Paul and Barnabas are clearly intended to increase the likelihood that the pastors they appointed would be God's choice as well as theirs and the congregation's. Fasting intensifies prayer, opening us wider to God, clarifying our choices. When linked, fasting and prayer slow us down and make us ask what God wants where otherwise we might forge ahead full of ourselves. Jesus intends these practices to be a regular part of the life of faithful disciples "while the bridegroom is away."[5]

Toward the end of the first century the Christians adopted the two Jewish fast days of Monday and Thursday, but transferred them to Wednesday and Friday. Other fasts were also introduced. By the middle of the second century there was a short fast before Easter, and by 250 A.D. it had increased to an entire week, our Holy Week. Finally, during the fifth century, the Lenten fast was extended to forty days, although these were counted differently in various localities. When they fasted, the early Christians, like the Jews, refrained from eating and drinking from sunrise to sundown, taking their one daily meal in the evening.

Fasting Is for Christian Life

One of the most pervasive themes in the New Testament is conversion: the call to fix our hearts more radically upon God as our sustenance.

This is precisely the heart-and-mind-set of fasting. Always when we voluntarily go without food, it is because something else is more important to us. It might be an early departure, slim waistline, or a feeling of physical well-being. But it might also be because I want to say in a very real way, "God, you are number one for me. You are more important to me than life itself, which food symbolizes for me. With this fast I want to send you that message and impress upon myself that you are at the center of my life's meaning."

The focus away from food (and what it symbolizes as one of the goods of existence that we need) to God is deliberate. Yes, these other goods are important. Yes, I need them. But all the needs in my life, if traced down to the deepest core, are rooted in my single greatest need: for fulfillment from the hand of my Creator. From time to time I can forget just which needs in my life are the most important, and my priorities can become all mixed up. Fasting is a discipline for restoring those priorities. And fasting, like a meat cleaver coming down on a butcher's table, cuts through the drift and ambiguity that has crept into my life.

It is a concrete, decisive act that says: "You, Lord, are the still point in my turning world, and please don't let me ever forget it. For you I will upset my routine today of three meals because you are the God I worship, not my routine (which becomes all too important for me sometimes). For you I will give up meeting my friends for lunch today because, even though I need them and like them very much, the love and acceptance I need from them is only a reflection of the love and acceptance I need from you. For you I will live with these hunger pangs today and let them speak to me of my deepest hunger: our hearts are restless, O Lord, until they rest in you."

Meals *are* important in so many ways—as a social event, as a needed break from work, as nutrition—and when we voluntarily forego this as part of the language of our relationship with God it takes on the meaning that we are willing to set aside all else that will interfere with seeking God wholeheartedly. This is the task of Christian living. Fasting is a quintessential Christian discipline because eating symbolizes that which is most essential to us: life and growth. By setting food and drink aside to seek God, we're declaring that God is more important and essential a source of life and growth for us than anything else. It is essentially God's love that creates, sustains and restores us.

> Protect me, O God, for in you I take refuge.
> I say to the Lord, "You are my Lord;
> I have no good apart from you."
> I keep the Lord always before me;
> because he is at my right hand, I shall not be moved.
> Therefore my heart is glad and my soul rejoices;
> my body also rests secure.
> You show me the path of life.
> In your presence there is fullness of joy;
> at your right hand are pleasures forevermore (Psalm 16).

Inspiration from Islam

The setting aside of food and drink as a way of manifesting our conviction that God is more important and essential a source of life and growth for us than anything else is at the heart of the Christian tradition of fasting. But this teaching finds clearer expression in Islam than in Christianity at the level of popular practice. Christians can draw inspiration for their own lives from the Muslims' utter reverence for God as the only Absolute.

Islam literally means commitment and obedience. Etymologically, the root of the word "Islam" is *slm* which means peace. From this comes *aslama*, submitted. *Al-Islam* is religion which brings peace to humanity when it commits itself to God and submits to God's will.

Muslims believe in the prophethood of Adam, Noah, Abraham, Moses, Jesus and Muhammad, and hold that all of them conveyed to humankind the same message from God. Their conviction is that the final revelation came through the prophet Muhammad and is known as Islam—the religion of *all* the prophets, not "Mohammedanism."

Central to the spirituality of Islam is the notion of submission. A Muslim prays five times a day, before sunrise, between mid-day and afternoon, in the afternoon, immediately after sunset and between the time when the twilight is over and just before dawn. It means the Muslim cannot be forgetful of dependence on Allah and derives sustenance and new strength through this remembrance. Islam is a passion against all usurpation. It is the conviction that power, race, state or creed, improperly exalted above God, spell the human wasteland. It is a perpetual warfare against all false absolutes. The Muslim's utterance of faith is, in its negative first half, a constant warning: "There is no god . . ."; but in the positive next words, it is supreme assurance: ". . . except God." Islam understands the world and humankind as set under God, constituted by creation, guided by revelation and summoned to submission. Just as the law from Sinai set Jewry under the claims of the Divine within what they understood as sacred history, so the divine law in Islam makes all life and activity the realm of God's authority and human accountability.

One of the "five pillars" on which Islam is founded is fasting. It is an institution of humanity's responsive awareness of God. "You who believe," says the Qur'an, "fasting has been prescribed for you . . . so that you may do your duty. . . . The month of Ramadan is when the Qur'an was sent down as guidance for humankind, and with explanations for guidance as a Standard. . . . So complete the period and magnify God because He has guided you so that you may be grateful." (The Cow, 2:183ff)

During this lunar month each year (Ramadan), Muslims fast every day from dawn till sunset. During this time, they do not eat, drink, smoke, or engage in sexual intercourse. Some Christians living in the hot climate of India or the Middle East have tried to fast during Ramadan with their Muslim friends to see what it is like. "Try, for just one day in ninety degree heat," a Christian colleague living in India said to me, "to fast as Muslims do for twenty-eight days of Ramadan. From 4:45 a.m. to sundown, take no food, water, or any beverage. Do not even swallow your own saliva. Do not wash your face or bathe during this time. See, through your own experience, what a powerful expression of submission to God this is for hundreds of millions of Muslims who do it together as an expression of God's sovereignty in their lives." The spirit of the fast extends as well to abstention from all evil thoughts, actions and words.

In the evening, after sunset, they break the fast and eat joyfully. The well-to-do can afford to stay up late and sleep in the next morning; but the working class and students are generally in bed before midnight so as to to be up early for work. The month of Ramadan is a time of sharing, of prayer, of return to religious practice, of exercising control over one's appetites. The emphasis is placed upon obedience to God, spiritual purification, charity to the poor, and the bonds of Islamic community. As one Muslim explained, "Ramadan reminds us that we are not on earth to eat, to drink, and to sleep, but to think of God. It's like a debt owed to God. We thank God for all that He has given us. It's a time to set our hearts upon God."

There is a further logic in the communal atmosphere that Ramadan provides. It powerfully reinforces the collective sense of Muslims, providing them with a sort of sacramental sign of oneness and solidarity. It also affords an effective way of strengthening one's sense of identity simply by making occasion for participant adherence. For some, Islam begins in the month of Ramadan, finding its genesis in their lives in a day abstinence and a night meal. In its stark but powerful simplicity, Muslim formulation of faith focuses on the essential: "There is no god but God." The Qur'an asserts that Abraham was the first to proclaim it (Qur'an 6:74–83).

To emphasize God's oneness and transcendence, no proper name is given to God. *Allah* in Arabic is not a proper name at all. It simply means the divinity, i.e., God, and cannot be construed as similar in any way to the proper names of the pagan gods such as Zeus, Jupiter or Baal. To name God would be to place the Divinity in the power of us humans and reduce God to our measure and resemblance.

The experience of entering a mosque brings home the transcendence of God on a visual level. Near the entrance there is a collection of slippers, sandals and shoes. As Moses did at the burning bush (Exodus 3:1–6), shoes must be removed out of respect. Barefoot, one enters. There is nothing on which to focus; no chairs, no pews, only rugs if the mosque is rich, or mats if it is poor. No altar, statues, or paintings. The only piece of furniture is a pulpit. There is no chancel. On one wall there is a sort of niche decorated with some verses of the Qur'an. The niche indicates the direction of Mecca. Just as Christian churches were oriented to the East, Muslims pray turned toward Mecca, their main sacred city. Since God is most great, nothing should represent or be an explicit sign of God's presence.

In the footsteps of Abraham and Muhammad, Muslims think that nothing can be shown which in any sense could be construed as a representation of God. There are not even images of any human being or animal. There is only silence, a few lamps, and the Qur'anic inscriptions. It is not that iconoclasts smashed the statues, leaving empty niches, and removed or burned the paintings as is the case with many of the great churches in England and France; it is simply that they were never there. Representations of living beings could be easily turned into idols and lead to "association" of someone or something with God in divinity.[6]

Fasting at God's Initiative

The relationship between the Islamic emphasis on the "all-ness" of God and the core of Jesus' preaching is clear. The greatest commandment, Jesus said, is to love the Lord your God with your whole heart, with your whole soul and with all your strength. That's the fundamental rationale we have been considering for fasting: to place God more at the center of our lives, to better focus our consciousness upon God with the whole of our being in a prayer that engages our body, mind and spirit. If fasting helps us respond to the greatest commandment there is, can we afford to lose it or to confine it to just a certain season?

Fasting is not just for Ash Wednesday or Good Friday or even the whole of Lent. It is for Christian *life*. Our earlier practice of a fast day each week has much to recommend it.

We would, of course, have to choose weekly and/or seasonal fast days *freely*, because of the value we see in it. There can be no going back to those laws which say we *have* to do it. They will just make us lose the spirit of it all over again. Our fasting must flow out of awareness that "there is no god but God." Our routine, comfort, and the pleasure of eating are not absolutes before which we must bow down in obedience.

What must bow down is our own ego or false self to our deepest and real Self. Fasting that is pleasing to God and not merely an exercise of vanity or mere preservation of temporal life is accompanied by a spirit of humility, repentance, and true sincerity of heart. Fundamentally, fasting represents offering oneself to God in a spirit of openness, readiness, and obedience, inviting the action of the Holy Spirit. Such an impulse must come from God and not be solely of our own planning. Attentiveness to the inner movement of the Spirit is important so that our fasting may be a true, religious act of loving worship and self-surrender. This prevents fasting from becoming a technique taken on solely for health purposes or expanded consciousness or for whatever purpose that could so easily become another idol. Unless we are responding from the heart to an initiative from God, our fasting will be motivated by self-interest. It may look like a dedicated religious act, but the motive of our hearts will be to please ourselves or impress others.

The parable of the pharisee and the tax collector (Luke 18:9–14) is a trenchant critique of those who might "fast twice a week" but who in their arrogance and self-righteousness thank God they are not, like others, "extortioners, unjust, adulterers, or even like this tax collector." Jesus concluded that the tax collector who "would not even lift up his eyes to heaven but beat his breast, saying, 'God, be merciful to me a sinner,' " was justified, while the pharisee was not. Humble confession of sin and supplication before God is much more precious than fasting with pride.

Fasting is not merely renunciation or self-discipline, arduously forged by the human will. Important as virtue is, seeking it too self-consciously can lead to a very subtle but serious error: cultivating virtue as something that depends on my effort alone.

That mode of thinking was tabled as a heresy in 529 at the Council of Orange and called pelagianism, after a British monk named Pelagius, who thought that the human person is in possession of full integrity, even after the Fall. We can accomplish our own salvation by ourselves, according to Pelagius. Adam and Eve gave us a bad example, Jesus a good example. Follow Jesus' good example. That's all there is to it. We need no other support than that of our own freedom and courage. Our discussion in chapter one of synergy, or the interpenetration of God's grace and our freedom, provides the perspective consistent with Christian faith.

The deepest fast, of course, is the fast from sin—rebellion, anger, lust, greed, despair, hardness of heart, egotism, and the worship of a life that leads to spiritual death. It is above all the mind and heart that need to be cleansed by surrendering the illusory foods they love to feed on. But fasting from ordinary food is necessary, too. It keeps us honest, mindful of the bodily nature of the incarnation and the resurrection, mindful of our own bodiliness and of the aim of purity of mind and heart. One of the most favored "words" ever spoken to me about fasting came from Fr. Bob Pelton of the Madonna House Community in Combermere, Ontario.

"I don't think about fasting," he said. "I just do it, the way I pray and sweep the floor and go to bed. The Lord will use it, has already used it, as he uses everything, to show me the glory of his face within my own heart and in the hearts of all my brothers and sisters."

II
THE PRACTICAL ASPECTS OF FASTING

For Jesus, the timing of when to fast is a question of appropriateness: "As long as they have the bridegroom with them, they cannot fast. The days will come when the bridegroom will be taken away from them, then they will fast in those days" (Mark 2:19–20). He linked fasting to immediate circumstances, to felt needs. It is to be an honest reaction, one growing out of real life. Our fasting must likewise flow out of our prayer, our sense of the season, our awareness of what is going on in the life of the Lord as we relive it through the liturgical year and our awareness of what is going on in our own lives. With this approach, the inspiration to fast emerges from an interior sense that *it's time.*

Time to focus our hearts. Time to create a special psychic space within so that the life of Christ's Spirit is intensified within us in Advent. Time to do penance, to make straight the way of the Lord in Lent. Time to open ourselves to a new outpouring of the Spirit at Pentecost. Time to let our whole being overflow with gratitude, as do our harvest bins at the end of summer in autumn's golden days.

Appropriate Times for Fasting

Some times in our own lives when fasting might be an appropriate response:

Times of penance for sinful behavior. As we can seek no exemption from the fact of sin and our participation in it, so from the obligation to penance we can seek no exemption. Forms and seasons of penance vary from time to time and from person to person. But there come moments in our lives when we know that we have failed morally, and we feel an inner desire to express our contrition and desire to begin anew. Sometimes these moments coincide with liturgical seasons where communal and personal acts of penance are called for. Of the many penitential seasons which at one time or another have entered the liturgical calendar of Christians, three have particularly survived to our times: Advent, Lent, and the vigils of certain feasts. Changing customs, especially in connection with preparation for Christmas, have diminished popular appreciation of the Advent season. The anticipatory holiday mood of Christmas serves as a cultural, preemptive attack on the Christian spirit of the Advent season. As a result, this season has unfortunately lost in great measure the role of penitential preparation for Christmas that it once had.

Though no fast before any feastday is imposed any longer, there was a wisdom in our ancestors' observance of "a fast before a feast." There is deeper Christian joy in the great feasts of the liturgical year when we freely undertake, for our own motives and in our own spirit of piety, to prepare for festivals of faith with a day of penitential fasting.

Times of frenetic distraction and psychic clutter. We occasionally need to fast from the numerous distractions of contemporary life with which we are bombarded. But fasting needn't always refer to food. Fasting from electricity and batteries and everything that runs on them may more effectively address our sensory overload and leave us freer to be present to a few savored things that restore our inner equilibrium. Fasting draws us toward simplicity. Whether the impulses we relinquish relate to food, radio, television or stereo, the end result is the same: a braking of our grasping spirit which wants to equate fulfillment with quantity of things consumed. Fasting allows the sufficiency and ease of the moment to emerge.[7] Fasting is one means of pulling ourselves up short before God and letting God search our hearts. As soon as we begin to feel scattered, off-center, or impelled to relentlessly consume, we can turn to God and ask God to show us why our appetite is grasping after ephemeral, surface pleasures.

David's prayer can become our own: "Search me, O God, and know my heart; try me, and know my thoughts. See if there is any wicked way in me, and lead me in the way everlasting" (Psalm 139:23–24). God allows us to get into certain situations which reveal to us whether our hearts are set upon God or intent upon pleasing ourselves. Is God central or are things? What matters most to us? What do we really want?

Times of grief and distress. David's fasting was an honest reaction to the death of Saul and of Jonathan. He did not desire food while the emotions of shock and loss swept over him, so he set aside time for his reactions. He did not try to go on with business as usual, masking his feelings (2 Samuel 1:11–12). Ezra was so disturbed by the sin of his compatriots that he found no better way to express the intensity of his grief and sorrow than this: "He ate no bread and drank no water, for he mourned their transgression . . ." (Ezra 10:6). After he had been knocked off his horse on the road to Damascus, Paul fasted for three days, waiting in total blindness for further direction from the Lord. Such times of complete upheaval, reversal of life purposes or confusion are appropriate times for reaching out firmly through the discipline of fasting, for the still point at the center of our turning world.

Times of fatigue. The recognition that I need a rest can be another moment in the year when fasting is an appropriate response. "Come to me, all you who are heavy burdened, and I will give you rest . . . learn of me and you will find rest for your souls" (Matthew 11:29). I am worn out. I am tired of the sound of my own voice. When someone comes to the door or the phone rings, it feels like an imposition. My mind keeps straying as I am listening to this person. I feel driven. I can't laugh at the mess on my desk; I resent it. It's time to get in touch with myself and to pour out my heart to God. Rest is essential. Fasting makes it a total rest, for *all* of me. In the Mosaic Law, a special day was set aside in which no work was to be done and the people were to fast. The reason? To free the people from daily cares and family responsibilities so that they could deal with their inner lives.

Times of travel. Often when we come to that extended rest time in the year called "vacation" or "holiday" (an old English word harkening back to a time when rest time was a holy time, a holy day), we so plan, control, and package it that it is finished before beginning, dead before having a chance to live. We trek through a pre-determined scene that only amounts to a life-sized version of pictures we looked at even before we left home.

Returning from such a time away, there is an experience of relief: we made it through that potentially unpredictable time without a scratch. We're back, just as we left. No window flew open with a view of God-knows-what unsettling and unpredictable thing. Keeping that window closed was tense and complicated. But we did it. And we're home safe.

Sometimes it can be a wonderful experience to trust that life is basically gracious at its heart and to enter into it as a great dance wherein all the steps are not choreographed ahead of time. A pilgrimage distinguishes itself from an ordinary journey by the fact that it does not follow a laid-out plan or itinerary. Rather, it carries its meaning in itself. The journey from one place to another symbolizes the inner journey, the spiritual quest. If we approach a trip in a pilgrim spirit, entering into it flexibly and waiting on God, expecting unforeseen paths to present themselves, fasting can enter into it very spontaneously. One's train or plane departure time conflicts with meal time, and instead of being chagrined about it, one embraces it as a positive opportunity. Or one is going to take a hike or a bike tour: "What will I take for lunch?" Why take anything? Travelling in the spirit of a pilgrim involves an alertness to the Divine Presence beneath the surface, an openness that is gently expectant, willing to be caught up and pulled into the freshness of divine play.

The point at which our human freedom reaches its peak is when we, having experienced in our daily lives the abundant love of God for us, move freely, spontaneously, and with a spirit of improvisation to return God's love. Thus a person may freely offer to God a day's fasting out of sheer desire to love God. Such a motive represents the quintessential religious act: a desire to return love with love. It is not any hardship or sacrifice involved that is ennobling, but the motive to offer God a free gift out of love.

A fast spontaneously entered into such as this becomes a secret shared between oneself and God, an act of a free spirit, a light-hearted feeling of liberation as one flaunts the convention of eating and locates joy and interest elsewhere. The impulse to make a day in the middle of vacation a fast day can, responded to with the spirit of a pilgrim, be a deeply enjoyable day that has a positive quality about it that is different from all the other days. And no wonder—it harkens back to a time when a holiday was a holy time, a holy day.

Before receiving the Eucharist. My consistent observation is that we have become rather casual about the simple one hour fast prior to mass and communion. Whereas once Catholics felt constrained to precede communion with confession so as to receive "worthily," that is no longer the practice. There seems to be now a clearer sense that the eucharistic bread is food for the hungry rather than reward for the worthy. But given our present cavalier approach to the eucharistic fast, it would seem we're neither worthy nor hungry! Allowing ourselves to feel some physical hunger and thirst prior to receiving communion can put us in closer touch with our spiritual longing for the Bread that comes down from heaven and for the cup of salvation. As anyone knows, prior to a banquet an edge of hunger heightens anticipation. In hunger we touch emptiness; in emptiness, poverty. In our poverty we become grateful, grateful for every piece of bread, every word of love. Gratitude is the heart of eucharistic prayer.

Fasting creates psychic space within. Emptying myself physically is offered as a sign of my desire to have God empty my heart of all that obstructs God from expressing love through me to others. My empty stomach, on a symbolic level, is a creating of space, an invitation for God to come and dwell within, to "fill me up." We literally say with our bodies: "Come. I am making room for you here. The emptiness in my stomach is a sign to you of the space I'm clearing out in my heart." Does fasting bring about what it signifies? One never knows. What we can say is that prayer's effect is in us. Every time we turn toward and reach out for God, we come a little closer by virtue of the intensification of desire within our hearts. The work of "one-ing" is the kind of work the Spirit does in the dark and out of sight. All we can do is dispose ourselves, cultivate the willingness (itself a product of grace) and hope that the Spirit will bring to fulfillment the work begun in us.

Times of intercession. Do we really believe that God hears our prayers and responds? If you were God looking into the hearts of those offering intercessory prayers and one person rattled off some prayer formulas while another went without food and drink, which prayer would you tend to see as the more heartfelt? The next time you say to someone who is desperately looking for a job or seriously ill, "I'll pray for you," consider offering the prayer of a fast day.

Fasting Tips

Fasting, as I have used the word above, refers to abstaining from solid food and to drinking water, vegetable juices and fruit juices only for a time period of one's choosing. Why these certain liquids only? Because we are seeking to quiet and cleanse the self, in all ways, so that we can hear and be more attentive to the One who is present to us and focus more upon this Presence. Drinks like black coffee and non-herbal tea stimulate the central nervous system at a time when we are trying to give the self a rest, a space for focusing upon spiritual realities. Since all fruits and vegetables are plants (herbs), they possess specific medicinal properties. When we drink only water or juices during a fast the effect is much the same as when we wring out a dirty sponge. These liquids facilitate the flushing out of waste materials that keep us running at low-level performance, feeling sluggish, and not very much in the mood to give God joyful praise for the gift of life and health. One should drink at least eight to ten glasses of water and/ or juice on a fast day.

Some of the normal symptoms that this cleansing process is taking place are offensive breath, dark urine, skin eruptions, head-ache, coating on the tongue and elimination of mucus through the nose and air passages. These side-effects are signs of healing; the body is ridding itself of waste materials. This is part of the holistic benefits of fasting. They are signs of inner healing, steps on the way to feeling well, both mentally and physically.

Some people won't have the unpleasant side of these experi-ences at all, even though the purification is going on. The attitude of the one fasting makes a considerable difference. Those who approach it positively, putting their apprehensions and fears behind them as inappropriate, have more agreeable experiences. Should you run into any of those "blessings in disguise," keep the following in mind:

Gnawing in the stomach. Don't be concerned. It's not a "genuine" hunger pang in the sense that your body really *needs* the food nor a distress signal. It's just the alimentary tract accommodating itself to a reduced work load. Deal with it by drinking water more frequently. A glass of water can satisfy what feels like a ravenous appetite.

Coating on the tongue. The tongue is a mirror that reflects the amount of waste matter being eliminated. Normally, we associate bad smells with the process of elimination. That explains why we may have bad breath: the tongue is part of the elimination system. Rinse your mouth with warm water, and gently brush your tongue with a soft toothbrush; then move on to your teeth.

Tiredness, weakness, restless sleep, headache. What's happening here is that when you fast, the waste in your body is being loosened and sent into the circulation system to be discarded. When this is going on, there is an understandable feeling of sluggishness until the waste products are dispelled.

Again, not all people have these experiences to any notable degree. In a conversation with Dr. Stacy Snelling, M.D., a nutritionist and wellness consultant to the Washington, D.C. YMCA, I asked about the symptoms some people experience on a fast day. She said it may be attributable to a low blood sugar level. She recommended a liberal intake of diluted juice throughout the day to help maintain a constant blood sugar level. Diluting the juice with water helps prevent an overload of sugar in the blood and a hypoglycemic response. "Allow for individuals who will have a bad experience with fasting because their blood sugar level is generally low," she said. "But for the majority there should be no problem."

If you suffer from an acute or chronic physical or psychological illness such as cardiac disease, diabetes, manic-depression, if you take presecription drugs, or if you have ever had an eating disorder such as anorexia or bulimia, consult a physician before embarking on even a one-day fast.

There was more genius in the bygone Christian practice of weekly fasting than we realized. The world of science is now coming forward and telling us that such a practice makes a great deal of sense for our physical and mental well-being. When the health of our relationship with God is factored into the equation, the benefits of fasting for our body-spirit make a return (with clear understanding this time) to the practice of a weekly fast day all the more compelling.

How To Start and Stop a Fast

If you are not accustomed to fasting, begin with skipping just one meal, and gradually extend it to two meals up to a twenty-three-hour fast beginning from after supper one day until supper the next day. I suggest this simply because supper is generally the meal that we share with others. Most people can skip breakfast and lunch without drawing attention to themselves. "When you fast, put oil on your head and wash your face so that no one will know you are fasting except your Father who sees all that is done in secret; and your Father, who sees all that is done, will reward you" (Matthew 6:17–18). The real work of prayer and fasting is interior.

This is not meant to make us neurotic about hiding it from everybody when we're going without food. It is simply making us aware that if we aim our actions at pleasing people and impressing them, this is all the benefit we can expect: the esteem of those around us. It is not the exterior actions that others can observe which produce vitality, but the dialogue of heart with Heart, the contact of spirit with Spirit.

In practice this may mean that you go out of the office at noontime and take a walk or spend a quiet half hour in a nearby church, if staying at your desk and working right through is going to make your colleague or secretary start asking questions. There is also a real temptation to turn your normal eating times into increased work time rather than using these free spaces for something like scripture reading or a walk in the park which more directly nurtures the inner spirit. If someone should notice that you're not eating in spite of your efforts to be discreet, simply say "I'll be eating later; my schedule's a little different today." The point is simply not to flaunt it. Start small and build on the effort. Whatever is worth doing is worth doing badly. Once you get into the rhythm of a regular fast day, you won't even think about it. You'll just do it.

A regular rhythm of fasting is important for another reason, too. When we're not accustomed to going without food, doing so can be very preoccupying. But when it becomes part of our lives, we do it the way we "make our bed or sweep the floor," knowing God will use it as God uses everything offered in love.

We live in a society that practically equates "three squares a day" with the preservation of life itself. We live with the mistaken notion that to miss a meal or two would be hazardous to our health and well-being. We don't, however, have as great a problem with overeating. That, we rationalize, allows us to store up reserves for that "emergency situation" when we may have to miss a meal.

What we have yet to understand is that the body tolerates a fast far better than a feast. It has ample resources to nourish itself for surprisingly long periods of time. The process of nutrition continues to take place from the body's "cupboard," and as far as the organs that benefit know, food is still being eaten.

Fasting researchers generally express themselves in favor of shorter, regular fasts over longer fasts infrequently taken. It is better, they say, to try to cleanse the body by a weekly fast-day and an occasional three or four day fast along with a wholesome regular diet, than to try to clean the body with one long fast.[8]

The ancient wisdom from the East concurs with this modern assessment. "Those who eat too much or eat too little, who sleep too much or sleep too little, will not succeed in meditation," Krishna counsels in the *Bhagavad Gita*. "But those who are temperate in eating . . . will . . . learn to withdraw the mind from selfish cravings and absorb it in the Self. Thus they attain the state of union."[9] Buddha later offered the same recommendation of moderation after many years of severe asceticism.[10]

With such moderate, intermittent fasts, the blood is gradually improved, regenerated, and the person is able little by little to dissolve and eliminate toxins and other deposits from the deepest tissues of the body.

Gandhi once said that perhaps more caution and more restraint are necessary in breaking a fast than in keeping it. The rule is simple: begin with little and take even that slowly. After a one day fast, allow for one transitional meal designed rather for its cleansing laxative effect than for its nourishment value, e.g., a raw variety vegetable salad. Lemon juice makes a good dressing. The effect of this salad will be that of a big broom moving right through your intestines. Eating too much too fast can lead to digestive upset. A little bit of food eaten slowly can seem like a great sufficiency. Continue to drink lots of water. There is no need to compensate for the meals you haven't eaten because appetite doesn't accumulate in that manner. Avoid overburdening your digestive system just after giving it a rest.

Throughout this discussion of the various aspects of fasting—historical, theological physiological, practical—I have not labelled certain parts "spiritual" and others "physical."

Continued application of such labels only prolongs the body-and-soul dichotomy and ignores all we have learned about the seamless unity of the human person through the various sciences. In practice what this means is operating from the presumption that what is good for us physiologically is also good for us spiritually, and what is good for us spiritually is also good for us physiologically. There's only one self to which all of these benefits redound. You can discuss different aspects of the human person, but in the end there is only one being which experiences holistically.

Our main objective has been to rediscover the value of fasting as an act of faith, hope and love, a religious act, directed toward God. As such we have talked about fasting as a focus of the heart, as a discipline that clears away the thousand little things that accumulate and clutter the heart and mind. It's like removing the rust and corrosion from a car battery to enable the current to flow more freely. It renews our "contact" with God.

At the same time there is also another dimension of myself that needs the clutter and excess removed: the physiological. It has accumulated mucus, toxins, chemicals and drugs that if unloaded would enable the vital current of life to flow through me much more freely.

The temptation is to label the former concern "spiritual" and the latter as "physical," the one as good for my "soul," the other as good for my "body." But it's all *me*, and therefore it's all related. It is with my *self*, my embodied spirit, that I respond to God. If my digestive system is weighted down, blocked, lethargic, it's going to influence my heart-response to God as regards my experience of the goodness of life. But if I feel that every physical thing is running smoothly, if I feel vitalized and healthy, I will move much more easily to gratitude as the heart of prayer.

One of the definitions of prayer that I learned early in my life was that prayer is the raising of the heart and mind to God. What the eastern religions have made me more aware of is that prayer is not only a matter of mind and heart, but of body, breathing and the whole person. Buddhists would say that if you want to learn meditation you must learn how to eat and how to fast, how to sleep, how to look at things, how to sit, how to breathe and how to relax.

Furthermore, if you make a real commitment to a life of prayer, your life-style will change—not only your eating, sleeping and breathing, but even your clothing. With a commitment to prayer will also come commitment to a simple style of life.

III
FASTING, CHARITY, AND JUSTICE

There are many different disciplines in the Christian treasure chest and each individual must find the ones which are most personally appropriate. The teaching of Jesus and the history of the Church draw our attention to three traditional practices: prayer, fasting, and the sharing of our possessions. The interrelatedness of these three expressions of Christian life cannot be stressed enough. Each is meant to be an aid to the others. *Together* they rightly and harmoniously relate us to God, to others, and to ourselves.

The Interdependence between Fasting, Prayer, and Almsgiving

These three traditional practices are like three poles of a tripod; stability and balance only come when there is support from every direction. The same relationship of interdependence is found in the five pillars of Islam. After the profession of faith come prayer, fasting, and charity (pilgrimage is the fifth). Charity implies that everything entrusted to one belongs ultimately to Allah and therefore anyone in need has a share in it. Each member of society is expected to willingly and gladly help those who are in need; an annual amount is in fact prescribed out of one's income and savings.

The Church Fathers emphasized the relationship between almsgiving, prayer, and fasting, right from the very beginning. In the light of his study[11] of their teaching on these subjects, some excerpts of which are given here, Augustinian Fr. Joseph Wimmer states straightforwardly that a fast is not Christian unless it results in the practice of charity.

St. Justin in his *Dialogue with Trypho* quotes Isaiah 58 and urges the reader to fast and "give your bread generously to those who are hungry" (chapter 15). The *Second Letter of Clement of Rome* states that fasting is more effective than prayer, and that almsgiving is more effective than either of the other two, for "love covers a multitude of sins"(16,4).

Other patristic texts become more explicit and declare fasting a way of obtaining food to give as alms. The *Apology* of Aristides describes the mutual support of Christians as follows: "If there is a poor person among them in need of help, they fast for two or three days and send that person the food which they would have otherwise prepared for themselves" (15,9). In the *Shepherd of Hermas* the reader is exhorted to give the food saved through fasting to a widow, orphan, or someone poor (Similitude V, chapters 1–3). The *Didascalia* portrays Christians as fasting in order to give food to their fellow imprisoned martyrs (V, 1–6). St Augustine's frequent sermons about fasting are almost always in a context of concern for others:

> *Break your bread for those who are hungry, said Isaiah, do not believe that fasting suffices. Fasting chastises you, but it does not refresh the other. Your privations shall bear fruit if you give generously to another. . . . Do you wish your prayer to reach God? Give it two wings, fasting and almsgiving* (Discourse on Psalm 42, section 8).

And in one of his sermons:

> *Increase your almsgiving these days of Lent, as a certain requirement of justice. For what is more just than to turn into mercy that of which you have deprived yourself by abstinence? And what is more unjust than to keep out of avarice or to consume later in luxury that which abstinence has put aside?* (Sermon 210).

St. Leo the Great emphasized the same theme:

> *We enjoin on you this fast and urge you to practice not only abstinence from nourishment but also the works of mercy, so that you may transform into food for the poor that which you have removed from your ordinary table by religious sobriety* (Sermon 189).

We have considered fasting as an act that recognizes the centrality of God's place in our lives, a faith-act that admits there is only One who can fill the deepest hungers of our being, a love-act that says, "You, the Giver of my life, are more important to me than even your gift of life which, symbolized by food, I set aside to focus my heart more clearly on you." When we fast in this spirit, we are already transcending ourselves, already moving beyond *me* as the center of the world.

Involvement with the needs of others—what ministry is all about—costs us many conveniences and preferences. Making room for the needs of others means denying some of our own needs. And fasting, inasmuch as it represents a reordering of some of our priorities, is ministry when the needs of others are taken into account in our "new agenda." We have all witnessed ways in which fasting has been used as an expression of solidarity or protest against some form of violence, exploitation of workers, turning back of immigrants. Those who fast in this context do so in solidarity with the victims of injustice. They fast to question and challenge certain decisions of government and to protect the helpless. Without attention to the situation of others, prayer and fasting tend toward self-centeredness. God has put us together in such a way that we grow in love with God in proportion to our love for others. As a poster I saw once put it: "To know God better, love people more."

The Gospel and Human Justice

Fasting, to be truly Christian, must be characterized by a radical turning of ourselves to God with a corresponding openness to love and serve our neighbor. From this devolves the Christian responsibility to be involved in justice-serving behavior. When we realistically face the problem of hunger in the world we realize that we will not deal effectively with hunger simply through private acts of charity such as giving our lunch money to a beggar on the street corner. It may be possible for us, for example, to feed a hungry family or two near us (something well worth doing), without altering at all the conditions that brought about their hunger. If we really care about hungry people, however, we must eventually ask *why* they are hungry.

They are hungry because they are poor, which means we cannot come to terms with hunger unless we deal with poverty. We are then confronted with some of the harsh realities that explain why some have and others have not. In the end, in order to make lasting gains against hunger, the concern from which charity flows must also give rise to justice.

The Christian tradition has valued (though Christians have not always practiced) simplicity of life and voluntary poverty, a gospel ideal drawn from Jesus himself who had "nowhere to lay his head." It is a life-style expressed daily in the lives of millions of ordinary Christians who have chosen to share what they have with others in response to the Gospel. The transfer of resources involved is relatively limited. The chief value in this lifestyle is spiritual and symbolic—which is not to say it isn't real or valuable. It simply is to recognize that the power behind such commitment consists in lives that are placed more fully at the disposal of God and other people, and that try to keep alive a sense of proportion.

The point to be made here is that going without food for a day a week, and contributing to a good cause the money that you would otherwise have spent on your meals, fails to go to the heart of the problem. It is like swinging at the ball but only nicking a piece of it, as opposed to hitting it squarely. To "hit it squarely," we need to move from the personal to the public realm on this problem. If that move does not happen, the grain that I save by giving up meat three times a week may be sold to feed livestock in a faraway country, or simply not be planted next year by farmers who are worried about low prices. Food will reach hungry people only if government policies see to its proper production and distribution. An adjustment in eating habits without responsible citizenship may prescribe failure and hurt farmers.

To the question, "What can I do besides give?" the World Food Conference held under the UN auspices implicitly told the average citizen: influence government policy. That answer should not discourage giving on the personal, neighborhood, city level; but it tells us that it is necessary to move beyond the adjusted-lifestyle approach if we are really interested in doing something about feeding the hungry. Adopting a more modest life-style can be a powerful witness in the struggle against hunger, if efforts to change public policy accompany it. But we can't afford to stop at the level of life-style. While life-style changes appeal as immediate, personal responses, they can also lull us into a false sense of fulfillment. Cutting down on our food intake, or giving up certain types of food because most of the world's poor cannot afford to eat in the manner of North Americans, may be morally satisfying, but unless it is accompanied by more positive steps, it may do nothing more on the practical level of feeding the hungry than put people out of work.

If, however, I use my lunch hour on a fast day to write a letter that tells my representative in Congress or Parliament what I think of our public policy regarding food distribution and what I want our country to do—that is the kind of response to world hunger that brings together life-style adjustment (my fast) with positive action (my letters—written on time freed-up by my fast) to influence government policy. Our sense of responsibility must become sufficiently deep to encompass both.

The same principle (We Can Deal With Both) applies to the charity-begins-at home argument that says "Shouldn't we eliminate hunger here before we try to solve the problem worldwide?" There's no need to pit domestic hunger against world hunger in an either/or playoff. We can deal with both.

The urgent need is not for churches *as churches* to enter the political fray (although they must take moral stands), but for Christians *as citizens* to exercise their renewed consciences and contact decision-makers. One possible mode of action is to become a voice for the hungry to one's member of government.

A single action by Parliament or Congress, one decision by the President or Prime Minister can multiply—or undo—many times over the effect of all our voluntary contributions derived from fast days. To make an offering in church for world relief is good, but it doesn't go far enough if we leave the big decisions up to political representatives without letting them know what we want.

Our citizenship is our most powerful tool against hunger. Not to exercise it is taken as indifference when policies are being worked out; it leaves leaders free to make decisions by other standards. Hungry people then become victims of political lobbying.

Yes, the problem is enormous. But despair is unbelief. Ordinary people *can* help the nation reach out to a hungry world. To do so we will have to add to our contributions for world relief the offering of our citizenship. In a very real way, the nature of our shared human world does depend on our actions and words. We can destroy it and kin of our own flesh through our failure to inhabit it as justly and responsibly as we should.

What the Lord Asks of You

This is what the Lord asks of you, only this: to act justly, to love tenderly, and to walk humbly with your God (Micah 6:8).

Our churches are not going to *impose* fasting and abstinence upon us today. But true Christian concern will urge us to fast and to use our time, money and energy to touch the minds and hearts of civil leaders so that they become vitally concerned with the realities of poverty and starvation that involve so many. Our experience of God's love, heightened by the clarity of perception that comes from regular fasting, sets us free to care about others. When their need confronts us, we want to know what we can do to help. And if that concern is genuine, we will want the action we take to do more than make us feel good or bring only temporary relief to the people in need. We will want our action to deal with their need as effectively as possible. Dealing effectively with hunger pushes us into the public-policy arena, into questions of social justice.

Our guidelines in that arena are drawn from the values of sacred scripture, the value that God places on human life and the belief that "the earth is the Lord's and the fullness thereof." We affirm the right to food of every man, woman, and child on earth. We want to overcome a situation that flagrantly violates the humanity of the hungry. We want to see those sons and daughters of the same loving God as our own enjoy their full human dignity as God's children.

As believers we do not root our hope in the latest projections of the United Nations or some social scientist's analysis of how things may turn out in fifteen or fifty years. We root our hope in

God and the innate goodness and compassion of those created in God's image. We believe that the future is with God's reign on this earth. We believe that no efforts consistent with this hope are wasted.

Our efforts are signs of the presence of God's Spirit and through them God's work is advanced. The Christian understanding of human nature—flawed, but capable of good under grace—spares us from the disillusionments that make so many of today's crusaders tomorrow's cynics. And our Christian hope gives us staying power long after many others have become disgruntled and gone on to another cause. We remember that to break bread at the Lord's table and to say "Amen" to the Bread of Life is to take responsibility for his Body in all its members and to make a commitment to enable hungry brothers and sisters to break bread, too.

Here is a prayer for use on a regular day of fasting:

All praise be yours, God our Creator,
as we wait in joyful hope
for the full flowering of justice
and the fullness of peace.
All praise for this day.
By our weekly fasting and prayer
cast out the spirit of war,
of fear and mistrust,
and make us grow hungry
for human kindness,
thirsty for solidarity
with all people of your dear earth.
May our prayer, our fasting and our deeds,
done in the name of Jesus,
give you glory and advance your reign
in our hearts and in our world.
Amen.

7

Service

Christianity, rightly understood, has never been a comfortable religion. Anyone who tries to so construe it ignores the beginning of Jesus' life in a stable and the end of it nailed to a cross. The passion cast its shadow over the whole of his public ministry. And over the life of his mother hung the prophecy that one day a sword would pierce her heart. In the liturgical calendar, the Church takes us from the crib on December 25 to the martyrdom of St. Stephen on December 26. Evidently we are not meant to linger very long in the warm and romanticized sentiments of Bethlehem. But our desire to do so is understandable enough: it is easier to rock a cradle than to carry a cross, easier to sing adoring lullabies to a baby than to follow a grown-up from Galilee who asks difficult things of us.

Jesus did not promise his followers happiness and security as the world knows them. The mother of the apostles James and John had to be reminded rather sharply of that when she moved to secure the thrones at Jesus' right and left hands for her sons (Matthew 20:20–23). Anyone who is only concerned to accumulate merits with a view to happiness in the next world—who is, in other words, a Christian only for one's own ends—is not a genuine disciple. When we protest when some trouble comes and act as though this kind of thing isn't supposed to happen (at least to me!), we have not yet begun to understand the gospel of Jesus

Christ. For the real disciple of Jesus there is never any security on either the spiritual or the material plane. None, that is, apart from the insecure security of faith. Whoever would save his or her life will lose it; but whoever is not worried about either losing it or saving it—only in being totally surrendered to the Lord—will find it (Luke 9:24).

Judging from recent surveys[1] on what people think being a Christian means, one might with good reason allege that something has been lost in translation over the centuries. About four out of five North Americans describe themselves as Christians, but the term means many different things to different people. Only about one out of five believes that Christianity has to do with a personal relationship with Jesus Christ. Many more associate it with helping others and being a good person. Some equate it with a general belief in God. Still others say that it has to do with religious practices such as attending church. As always, it's hard for the majority in anything to keep their edge, to avoid taking what they have for granted, to escape becoming bland and lackadaisical. When our "position" seems secure in the standings, we fall off our discipline, soften the hard realities, downplay the importance of commitment and obedience.

Our cultural context of separation of church and state and a pluralist society then becomes a pretext for becoming increasingly private about our faith. It gives us a basis on which to justify our reticence to engage in religious discussion or public advocacy activity based on religious convictions. To the average non-believer, Christians act no differently than anyone else. Our faith appears to be a largely personal preference lacking the power to transform who we are and how we act. The relevance of Christianity for every dimension of our lives is by no means clear for those of another faith or none. In seeking to be followers of Jesus through more than just the words we speak in church, in seeking to give visible witness to the joy, compassion and sense of mission cultivated on Sunday mornings, we need to review some fundamentals.

I

KEY REFERENCE POINTS FOR CHRISTIANS

One day a lawyer put this question to Jesus: "Teacher, which commandment in the law is the greatest?"

Jesus said to him, " 'You shall love the Lord your God with all your heart, and with all your soul, and with all your mind.' This is the greatest and the first commandment. And a second is like it: 'You shall love your neighbor as yourself.' On these two commandments hang all the law and the prophets" (Matthew 22:36–40).

There is a story in Judaism meant to contrast Hillel and Shammai, his rival for rabbinical eminence in the first years of the Common Era. A heathen came to Shammai asking to be accepted as a convert to Judaism, provided that Shammai could teach him the whole of the Torah while he stood on one foot. When Shammai threatened to clout him for his impertinence, he went to Hillel with the same request. Hillel, more flexible in helping people grasp the Torah's essence, responded: "What is hateful to yourself do not to your fellow-man. That is the whole of the Torah and the remainder is but commentary. Go, learn it." Hillel certainly had more to say, but when pushed he was willing to put it all in a nutshell. In the midst of a modern world which has become far too complex for any individual to master, short formulas of faith are a blessing. Hillel was bold enough to consider the golden rule the whole of God's instruction for Israel. As he saw it, the Torah was meant to teach people mutual considerateness—to respond to others' wants and needs as though fulfilling one's own. [2]

Jesus expressed the golden rule in the positive: "In everything do to others as you would have them do to you; for this is the law and the prophets" (Matthew 7:12). Charity as the foundation of the entire covenant is at the heart of his teaching. The God Jesus revealed was certainly less a lawgiver intent on strict justice than a

Lord compassionate and merciful, slow to anger and abounding in kindness. When one read the scriptures and prayed, one was bound to emerge grateful for the largess of God and so inclined to show a similar largess to one's fellow human beings.

This acting out of one's love of God in the instance of one's neighbor is carried forward from the Hebrew scriptures into the Christian scriptures and expressed variously in different books. One of the clearest variations is expressed in James 2:15: "If a brother or sister is naked and lacks daily food, and one of you says to them, 'Go in peace; keep warm and eat your fill,' and yet you do not supply their bodily needs, what is the good of that? So faith by itself, if it has no works, is dead."

Jesus' metaphors and parables, like that of the Good Samaritan, suggested that love of neighbor—which included even one's enemy!—was the key to the nature of God. The community of the apostle and evangelist John brought this insight to full expression, placing this divine love as the foundation and calling of the Christian community. The same emphasis is woven throughout the First Letter of John:

> *How does God's love abide in anyone who has the world's goods and sees a brother or sister in need and yet refuses help? Little children, let us love, not in word or speech, but in truth and action (3:17–18).*
>
> *Those who say, "I love God," and hate their brothers or sisters, are liars; for those who do not love a brother or sister whom they have seen, cannot love God whom they have not seen. The commandment we have from him is this: those who love God must love their brothers and sisters also (4:20–21).*

In applying these biblical precepts to the problems we face today, the Christian is clearly obligated to get personally involved in the search for solutions. The example of Jesus' death suggests that there is no point at which one can say "enough," "this far and no more," or "we will only promote this good if it doesn't interfere with our lives." The image of the Crucified as the key to divine love and liberation implies that no persons, not even the wicked or our enemies, are outside that love. It implies that no persons can be sacrificed. The image of Christ crucified reveals a God suffering the evil and ambiguity of life along with humans. The New Testament does not provide an "answer" to the problem of suffering; it shows rather a compassionate God who is with us in that suffering to support us and to transform us through the experience of it.

The love which is revealed as the essence of God is not a principle that can be demonstrated logically. As John's community testified, "We love, because God first loved us" (1 John 4:19). Our love is in response to a gratuitous act of salvation on God's part. The revelation of God's love for the world serves to critique all our imperfect forms of love, enticing us to look critically at structures which oppress and enslave people. The early Christians did not feel compelled to exalt the uniqueness of their ethical insights—sometimes one gets the (false) impression that Christianity invented love, mercy and compassion—but they did insist that this vision of love was grounded in the very nature of God. Nor are these precepts addressed just to individuals, but to the Christian community as it struggles to learn love and experiences forgiveness. It is not expected that the individual will be asked to do something as difficult as love the enemy or dismantle structures of oppression without the support of a community that loves and aids those whose witness exacts a high price from them.[3]

In the last thirty years, the leadership of that community, the Church, has ever more frequently proclaimed the principles of social justice and has eloquently called us to be disciples of Christ truly concerned with the problems and needs of those near and far. This emphasis has been given high profile in the priorities of the World Council of Churches (WCC) through its program for Justice, Peace, and the Integrity of Creation. The WCC Assemblies meeting in Vancouver, Canada in 1983 and in Canberra, Australia in 1991 have resulted in a renewed focusing of our responsibilities to care for one another and for the creation of which we are a part.[4]

Within that same time frame, Pope John XXIII, the Second Vatican Council, Pope Paul VI, and Pope John Paul II have issued encyclical letters, public statements, and personal pleas that the world family might be formed according to God's plan of harmony, peace and justice.[5] In all the countries through which he has journeyed, Pope John Paul II has constantly called people to become authentic followers of Jesus Christ through lives committed to justice and peace. In an effort to provide a living example of Jesus' own activity, he visits the poor, the powerless, the sick and the sorrowing to show his solidarity with them. The Roman Synod of 1971 said it powerfully in the introduction to its statement "Justice in the World": "Action on behalf of justice and participation in the transformation of the world fully appear to us as a constitutive dimension of the preaching of the Gospel."[6] In short, one cannot be called a good Christian if there is not some direct involvement in working for justice in society.

The Balancing of Prayer and Service

We carry with us into the 1990's the reference points for a Christian spirituality that is better balanced than at any time in this span of thirty-plus years. During the 1950's we were still distinguishing between our sacred actions and our secular ones. Prayer and worship were of course the examples *par excellence* of our sacred acts. The morning offering, a brief prayer by which one consecrated all one's thoughts, words and deeds that day to the Lord, was about as close as our hours of work and service got to participating in the holiness of our times of prayer. The role of the Holy Spirit in transforming all our being and all our actions was never denied, but neither was it brought to the fore.

By the end of the 1960's, however, the common assertion was that service in the world was the most important and holiest act of Christian life. Harvey Cox's *The Secular City* served as the handbook for the times, devoted to showing that the Bible clearly presents action in history for the sake of the reign of God as the most important activity of believers in both the Hebrew and the Christian scriptures. The entire book contained but a few scant paragraphs on the role of prayer in Christian life. The exemplary Christian was no longer the one who spent hours in prayer but the one who was most involved in direct action in society for the furtherance of social justice.[7] People who prayed the rosary did so discreetly, and meditation in any form was fine if you liked that sort of thing, but considered socially irrelevant. Merton seemed to be the only one writing about personal prayer and contemplation; but while his books were inspiring, they didn't tell *you* how to do it. Books like Michel Quoist's *Prayers* and Malcolm Boyd's *Are You Running With Me, Jesus?*—poetic reflections on their daily experience—left less-poetic types feeling as if they could only read someone else's lines in search of some faint reflection of their own experience.

During the 1970's, the pendulum began to swing back toward the center, manifested by a revival of interest in the interior life. The trend continued through the 80's, marked by an abundant harvest of books on topics like mysticism and contemplative prayer, the reprinting in new translations of spiritual classics, and the introduction of a whole line of edited writings never before available to the layperson unequipped for scholarly research.[8] In today's emphasis on holistic spirituality, we recognize our lives as possessing complementary dimensions. Each of them is important and is neglected to the detriment of the whole. The prayer-versus-work and the sacred-versus-secular debates strike immediately false notes. Prayer and service are interconnected, two sides of one coin. Both are done under the influence of the Spirit and mutually support each other. Merton used the image of a spring and a stream to emphasize the unity of the two:

> *Action and contemplation now grow together into one life and one unity. They become two aspects of the same thing. Action is charity looking outward to others, and contemplation is charity drawn inward to its own divine source. Action is the stream, and contemplation is the spring. The spring remains more important than the stream, for the only thing that really matters is for love to spring up inexhaustibly from the infinite abyss of Christ and of God.*[9]

While Merton saw no contradiction between the two and even saw them being potentially fused into one entity, there was no doubt which was primordial: "The trouble is that if prayer itself is not deep, powerful and pure and filled at all times with the spirit of contemplation, Christian action can never reach this high level."[10] But he believed that the highest form of Christian life was sharing the fruits of prayer in action. In this he had the complete accord of Teresa of Avila, whose personal conviction is the more noteworthy because she is one of the greatest mystics in Christian history. In *The Interior Castle* she instructs her Sisters:

> *Here in our religious life the Lord asks of us only two things: love of His Majesty and love of our neighbor. These are what we must work for. . . . The most certain sign, in my opinion, as to whether or not we are observing these two laws is whether we observe well the love of neighbor. We cannot know whether or not we love God, although there are strong indications for recognizing that we do love Him; but we can know whether we love our neighbor. . . . How little (souls) understand the*

> *way by which union is attained; they think the whole
> matter lies in these things (prayer and spiritual de-
> lights). No, Sisters, absolutely not; works are what the
> Lord wants! He desires that if you see a Sister who is sick
> to whom you can bring some relief, you have compassion
> on her and not worry about losing this devotion; and
> that if she is suffering pain, you also feel it; and that, if
> necessary, you fast so that she might eat. . . . If we fail
> in love of neighbor, we are lost.* [11]

In her focus upon concrete, loving acts as the fruit of authentic prayer, Teresa is the rule, not the exception. In the mystics of
the West, the highest forms of divine union impel them to some
sort of active rather than passive life. They are characterized not
merely by the quality of their prayer but also by the intensity of
their activity for God. Evelyn Underhill cites this as the distinction
between Christian and non-Christian mysticism: the Christian
mystics move from the Infinite to the definite. No temperament is
less slothful than theirs; they were energized activists. To be sure,
they began by going apart as a necessary condition of establishing
communion with that Absolute Life which reinforced their own.
A mind distracted by the many cannot apprehend the One. In each
of their lives, one finds something akin to the solitude of the desert.
But once they have established a communion which reorders their
inner lives, they abandoned their solitude and became a medium
for that Life flowing out to others. [12]

Catherine of Siena's poustinia was within her own house.
When she left this solitude, she went out into the city to serve the
poor and sick, attracted and taught disciples, converted sinners,
and began a career of varied and boundless activity which made
her name one of the greatest in the history of the fourteenth
century. Her practical genius, her effective interventions to the
ruling powers of the day, drew their strength and inspiration from
her experiences in prayer. She was the conscious vehicle of "some

power not herself." Similar examples rise quickly to the surface when one opens the lives of Francis of Assisi, Ignatius Loyola, Joan of Arc, Vincent de Paul, John of the Cross, Catherine of Genoa, Bernard of Clairvaux, and Saul of Tarsus. To go alone into the desert and to come back as an ambassador to the world is the unmistakable and repeated pattern.[13] In their prayer they receive a new infusion of vitality, but with it comes the responsibility to take up new and daunting challenges.

Prayer supports service: we could all come up with illustrations of this truth from our own lives, if we but took a few moments to reflect on our experience. The reverse, however, has not always been so obvious.

Service Supports Prayer

This emphasis has received less attention, though it is no less real. Again, as soon as we become reflective about our experience, we recognize its truth. The hospital worker, who assists dying patients finds herself more frequently sitting in quiet at home, prayerfully taking the measure of these verities for her own life. The stockbroker who daily watches the market rise and fall, and with it the fortunes of his clients, begins to cherish more deeply his communion with God in church on Sunday, recognizing it as a treasure which neither rust nor moth can consume. The flight attendant, the train conductor, the bus driver find themselves empathizing with the biblical imagery of a pilgrim people, always on the way, hearts yearning for arrival at a promised land of stability and security. The ordained minister finds himself moved to say things during the homily that were not in his notes, or experiences a flash of insight while counseling someone, and sits reflectively on his bed at night, drawn into a grateful savoring of the Mystery working in his life throughout the day.

Service can be understood as all the activity, in union with the Spirit, that we engage in outside times of formal prayer in order to responsibly collaborate with God's work in the world according to our perceived vocation. What it basically boils down to is the conscientious fulfilling of our daily responsibilities. In the chapter dealing with friendship and family life we described it in terms of availability for service in love. In the chapter on presence, we considered some ways that a noisy job could become an occasion for noisy contemplation. There is no escaping the need to bring our daily work into the conscious embrace of our relationship with God. The arithmetic requires it: this is where we spend the majority of each day. We must not leave it outside the purview of our heart's dialogue with the Mystery present to us everywhere and always. For the majority of the world's Christians, the basic asceticism will be this effort to live the gospel by availability for service in love to those who people the hours of a normal working day. Even when one comes to see service as a support for personal prayer, it is still not giving service its just due in Christian life. Service is a privileged time of union with the Lord, valuable in itself.[14]

People in surprising places are witnessing to this truth. When Thomas Keating, forty years a Cistercian monk, was asked in the context of an ecumenical and interfaith dialogue to speak about the monastic life, he recommended to any Protestants who may be interested in recovering it that they look to Zen and Tibetan monasticism for new models which better integrate an alternating rhythm between solitude and social action. Unlike in the Christian monasteries, Zen monks are not expected to stay in the monastery the rest of their lives. In fact, there is a sort of unwritten rule that says if a Zen Buddhist monk stays in a monastery more than ten years, either he will become an abbot or something is wrong with him. During his time in the monastery he is encouraged to deepen his insight so as to prepare himself to relate more effectively once again to the society around him. Keating questioned whether the structures of monastic life as they now exist in the Christian tradition are the right ones for our

time: "I see a great need for another kind of monastic commitment, one which would be open-ended and temporary. . . . Perpetual enclosure could be replaced by a system that would make
it possible for someone, at a certain period in his or her life, to
serve outside the cloister for a time, or even permanently."[15]

The point for our context is that engagement in the workplace is seen as a valuable place of divine encounter and, at some
point, advancing one's spiritual growth and development *more*
than staying at home or in church. The holiest actions of the day
are those most closely in tune with the Holy Spirit. They might
be service. They might be prayer. We lead but one life under the
Spirit of God.

This perspective situates us precisely at the fulcrum point of
equilibrium. Establishing this balance and then maintaining it in
our lives is a discipline requiring steady monitoring. Most religious traditions, if not most cultures generally, have sensed that a
full human life and mature personality balance contemplation
and action. Buddhism balances morality and ethical action with
meditation and studies of wisdom. Judaism counterpoints the
study of Torah with good deeds and marriage. Hinduism offers
karma yoga (work) as a complement to raja yoga (meditation).
Islam balances prayer five times daily with alms to hoist the
burden from the widow and the orphan.[16]

In Christianity, Mary and Martha have served as symbols of
the need to both listen to the Lord in silence and serve him in
constructive activity. Listen again to Teresa of Avila to her Sisters:
"Believe me, Martha and Mary must join together in order to
show hospitality to the Lord and have Him always present and
not host Him badly by failing to give Him something to eat. How
would Mary, always seated at His feet, provide him with food if
her sister did not help her?"[17] And in another place: ". . . in
order to ascend to the dwelling places we desire, the important
thing is not to think much but to love much. . . . Perhaps we
don't know what love is . . . it doesn't consist in great delight but

in desiring with strong determination to please God in everything. . . ."[18] Invisible love is fatuous. Real love will incarnate
itself in visible expression.

Christianity Is Incarnational

"God is love," proclaims the First Letter of John, but this
love was not invisible. "We declare to you . . . what we have
heard, what we have seen with our eyes, what we have looked at
and touched with our hands . . ." (1:1). The Word of Life who
was with God from the beginning, and who was God, became
flesh and lived among us. Just as Jesus could be known by the
signs he gave, the works he performed, so his followers can be
known by what they do and by how they live. Because of the
Incarnation, the Christian instinct is to treat the world—other
people and nature—with reverence. How we treat those whom
God has already accepted and loves is crucial for the authenticity
of our faith. To abuse creation, not see that water and oil is
sacrament, is to render faith inoperative.

We are not the first generation to work for justice, peace and
the integrity of creation, but in our time the need is more imperative. The ecosystems have never been so despoiled, the planet
never so populous. At the same time, our communication and
technological capabilities send both our awareness of our predica-
ment and our expectations soaring. Our challenge is to ground
our activism in a vision of creation whose deepest sacredness is
the Being-in-Communion of the God who creates, the Savior
who redeems, and the Spirit who makes us whole. The Trinity is
a mystery of relation, and that same relation underlies every
human relationship and concern for the creation as a gift of love
from the Creator.

The Christian is one who lives with others, and who never
monopolizes any good thing, whether material or spiritual, for
his or her own benefit. The Christian is a bearer of an active

concern that each one has access to a life that is always fuller, on earth no less than in heaven. If being in God is essentially a communion of relations, then we who are born of God by water and the Holy Spirit are brought into the mystery of their Trinitarian relationship with each other and with all things. It is for this reason that the Church essentially understands itself as a communion, a *koinonia*, which is symbolized and actualized sacramentally in the eucharistic meal. Here, every participant communes with the Divine and mystically offers himself or herself with Jesus to all the others in the form of *food*.

The Eucharist: Challenge to Action

The renewal of the liturgy following the Second Vatican Council has provided a more vivid and tangible link between the eucharist and the genuine problems that touch people's lives.[19] The eucharistic institution narratives in the New Testament are carried over into the official prayer texts used by the churches at worship: "This is my body which will be given up for you. . . . This is the cup of my blood, the blood of the new and everlasting covenant. It will be shed for you and for all so that sins may be forgiven." Jesus' emphasis on his body being given up for us and his blood being shed or poured out for us is replete with implications for our own sharing in the eucharistic offering. If Christ offers himself equally to each one, it shows us what value each person has in God's eyes. If our eucharistic worship is real, it must heighten our awareness of the dignity of each person. The awareness of that dignity then becomes the deepest motive of our relationship with our neighbor.

When John the Baptist's followers inquire of Jesus whether he is the Messiah, he responds by outlining his ministry in terms of proclaiming the good news of the Father's love and mercy (Luke 7:22). The parable of the Good Samaritan, one of the most transparent Christian summarizations of the whole meaning of the law and the prophets, is another concrete example of this love lived out in practical terms. The mandate with which that story ends, "Go and do likewise" (Luke 10:37), should not be lost upon us as we participate in and try to live the eucharist. Matthew's poignant description of the final judgment of the world ("Lord, when was it that we saw you hungry, naked, a stranger, in prison, sick?") leaves no room for wonderment as to whether God sees us as being in real relationship to one another with definite responsibilities to care for each other (25:31–46).

The liturgy of Holy Thursday drives home the message with particular poignancy. The washing of the disciples' feet is a kind of parable-in-action, a gesture that has a much deeper significance than might at first appear. It is the epitome of the whole life of dedication lived by Jesus as well as a pledge that his legacy is to be one of service. The action of putting himself at the disposal of the disciples is a recapitulation of Jesus' entire life and a foreshadowing of his final act of unconditional self-giving. In that sense, the washing of the disciples' feet points backward to his ministry and forward to the cross.

In the Latin rite, the liturgy appears under the title "The Mass of the Lord's Supper." Yet when the gospel is proclaimed, we do not hear the familiar words of the institution of the eucharist. The other three gospels use those words as the centerpiece of their account of the last supper. The Holy Thursday gospel reading, however, deals only with that one striking incident of the washing of the feet. But that passage carries with it a "last command" similar to Jesus' words over the bread and cup, "Do this in memory of me." When he had washed the feet of his disciples he charged them, "As I have done, so you must do" (John 13:15).

The disciples were able to look back on the events of the passion and death and see the last supper as an act of service that was intimately connected with Jesus' death on the cross. This association was so explicit that the phrase "the service of Jesus" invariably called up the idea of his crucifixion, the ultimate act of putting himself at the disposal of others. Dutch theologian Edward Schillebeeckx points out that in several gospel passages the second coming of Jesus is associated with a heavenly meal, a banquet or a wedding feast. In one of those passages (Luke 12:37), the Lord "girds himself" in order that he might "come and serve them." Apparently he is going to wash the feet of the guests before they share in this banquet. Therefore, service done out of love becomes the final stamp set upon the life of Jesus; further, it is carried over from a historical event to the Lord who is to come. [20]

Jesus does not shield us or mislead us about the cost of discipleship. The requirements are clearly proclaimed: put no one ahead of God, deny yourself, pardon others, take up your cross and follow me (Luke 14:25–27; Mark 8:34–38; Matthew 8:18–22). Those requirements demand the same giving of ourselves, the same pouring out of our energy. Jesus' words become our own: Yes, Lord, this is my body which is given for you all day long in the vocation to which you have called me. This is my blood—my life, my energy—which is daily poured out in service of those you have entrusted to me. Jesus' self-giving does not leave us safe to observe from a distance but calls us to make our lives an extension of his own. The invocation of the Holy Spirit over the elements is not primarily concerned with the bread and wine, but with the transformation of the faithful into authentic members of Christ. The bread and cup are *for us*. One of the prayers for the breaking of the bread uses the words of St. Augustine: "You are the body of Christ and its members; it is your own mystery which lies there on the Lord's table. It is your own mystery which you receive. It is to what you are that you respond 'Amen.'. . . Be what you receive, receive what you are. . . ." Our "Amen" to the body broken for us and the blood poured out for us should effect a gradual transformation in our lives, a surrendering to the Father's will and plan for us.

The most remarkable ecumenical document of our time, *Baptism, Eucharist, and Ministry* (BEM), represents the significant theological convergence between virtually all Christian confessional traditions on these three key areas which essentially establish, express, and order the life of the Church. Particularly noteworthy is the fact that the Faith and Order Commission of the World Council of Churches which produced it includes among its full members theologians of the Roman Catholic and other churches which do not belong to the World Council of Churches itself. One of the sections of the text which has received the most attention and acclaim deals with the eucharist as a communion of the faithful. It brings the integral link between eucharistic sharing and action of behalf of justice and peace to a new level of awareness.

> *The eucharistic celebration demands reconciliation and sharing among all those regarded as brothers and sisters in the one family of God and is a constant challenge in the search for appropriate relationships in social, economic and political life (Matt. 5:23f; 1 Cor. 10:16f; 1 Cor. 11:20–22; Gal. 3:28). All kinds of injustice, racism, separation and lack of freedom are radically challenged when we share in the body and blood of Christ. . . . As participants in the eucharist, therefore, we prove inconsistent if we are not actively participating in this ongoing restoration of the world's situation and the human condition. The eucharist shows us that our behavior is inconsistent in the face of the reconciling presence of God in human history: we are placed under continual judgment by the persistence of unjust relationships of all kinds in our society, the manifold divisions on account of human pride, material interest and power politics and, above all, the obstinacy of unjustifiable confessional oppositions within the body of Christ (par. 20).*
>
> *Solidarity in the eucharistic communion of the body of Christ and responsible care of Christians for one an-*

*other and the world find specific expression in the litur-
gies: in the mutual forgiveness of sins; the sign of peace;
intercession for all; the eating and drinking together; the
taking of the elements to the sick and those in prison or the
celebration of the eucharist with them. All these manifes-
tations of love in the eucharist are directly related to
Christ's own testimony as a servant, in whose ser-
vanthood Christians themselves participate (par. 21).*[21]

Due to the consciousness-raising that has taken place among
us with regard to social justice questions, we now ask ourselves
with regard to the eucharist: What does it mean to eat and drink
at the Lord's table in a world where so many members of that
same body are hungry and thirsty? What does it mean to receive
the broken body of the Lord lovingly into our hands unless we are
engaged to tend to the deeds of the members of that body who are
suffering?

The Most Precious Gift: A Part of Yourself

Anyone who spends some months traveling in India invariably meets people who are on their way to or coming from Calcutta where they have spent some weeks or months, oftentimes
out of their holidays, helping Mother Teresa and the Missionaries
of Charity. They simply arrive on the doorstep of places like
Kalighat, Mother Teresa's Home for the Dying Destitute; Prem
Dan, Home for the Mentally Ill; Shisu Bhavan, Home for Children and Mentally Ill Women; or Titagarh, the Home for Lepers.
Some people freeze on the threshold for a moment or an hour,
wondering what to do next. But what needs to be done becomes
obvious. A hundred people need to be bathed, to be fed, to be
caressed. They need someone simply to be with them.

The nuns don't offer greetings or directions. They don't
have time to give orders or to preach. Volunteers must simply

enter, put on aprons and offer their labor—and more impor-
tantly, themselves. There are no washing machines, no vacuum
cleaners, no clothes dryers. The work is hard because everything
is done by hand. But there is nothing to dull the human contact
between sufferer and comforter. Stripped of walkmans and television sets, there's nothing left to give but a part of oneself.

When we travel, we generally nurture a hope that somehow
we will be changed by our experiences, but we're usually not. We
return with some lingering memories and rolls of photos or slides
which enable us to touch again some of the emotion of peak
moments. But our inner landscape seldom undergoes any significant alteration, and within two weeks of our return we've slid
neatly back onto the tracks of our regular patterns of existence.
This is why the volunteers at Mother Teresa's homes, should you
ever meet one, may "wish you the experience of Calcutta sometime in your life." What they mean is, "I hope you have an
experience of confronting your own limits, weaknesses and
vulnerabilities. I hope you have the opportunity to learn something about courage and love and acceptance. To come face to
face with yourself, and to accept who you are as a human
being—as well as to accept that other person, whose hair you're
stroking or whose hand you're holding, as a human being."

The real challenge is to discover compassion. Compassion
isn't pity. It's a truthful, intimate interaction with another person,
one to one. It's being truly alive with someone. It allows us to
recognize our connection, our essential union with people whose
difference from us seemed at first to be the attraction. With compassion, we recognize ourselves in others. Without it, the world
becomes a museum, a zoo. And the people in it become exhibits
that may interest or excite us, but they remain separate from us
behind glass and bars and cultural moats.[22]

We certainly don't have to go to Calcutta to have an experience that teaches us compassion. Calcutta is simply a dramatic
example of the paradoxes of the spiritual life: it is our friendship

with a mentally handicapped person that heals our own broken-ness, and our volunteer work with the terminally ill that makes us feel most alive. In serving others, the most precious gift is always a part of ourselves. Neither do we have to go far away to be inspired by someone whose life is "all in one place," totally *given* to a cause that transcends herself or himself. If we but look reflectively at our own environment, we will find there people who, in imitation of their Lord and lover, try to promote the well-being of their brothers and sisters at every turn. They have gained union with God by accepting the divine persons into their hearts and abiding with them. Their lives, regardless of their bank ac-count or social status, are a success. The only failure is not to be a saint. They have found the one thing necessary. Regardless even of their natural gifts and talents, they have fought their way, repeatedly picking themselves up or being dragged to their feet again, into the magic circle where all their failures are redeemed, all their dross is turned into gold.

II
TREASURE FROM OTHER RELIGIONS

Thus far we have considered the imperative of service for Christian living, and the importance of balancing action with prayer. Then we looked at the eucharist as a source of both sustenance and challenge in our efforts, and considered how we all have a gift to give which no one can duplicate: ourselves. In the final part of this chapter, we will take a glimpse into other religions—one in particular—to see what insights, wisdom and distinctiveness characterizes their approach to service-related themes like justice, charity and compassion, and to consider what we might be able to appropriate for our own enrichment and that of our particular ministry.

In both Buddhism and Christianity, justice is the hallmark

of authentic religious practice. The Buddhist emphasis on ethical imperatives parallels the Christian stipulation of a radical moral code (to love one's neighbor as oneself). Buddhism pursues a meditational and sapiential practice that gives birth to a lofty morality. The basic precepts against killing, lying, stealing, unchastity, and intoxicants stabilize a practice leading to great selflessness and compassion for others. Christianity may appear more "worldly," more inclined to become politically engaged and to change the environment,[23] but the history of Buddhism in Vietnam, Thailand, Cambodia and Sri Lanka, for example, also provides clear examples of engagement with the political process. Practitioners in both religions draw strength, wisdom and creativity from a contemplative encounter with the Absolute before which Buddhists learn silence from the Buddha. Here their declarations stop; silence represents their *via negativa*, their appropriate response. All descriptions fail before the Transcendent, which they do not deny.[24] The need for equipoise between meditation and action is accented in both religions.

Judaism and Islam tend to think about justice quite practically in charitable terms: giving alms, offering people food, clothing, and shelter. Love of neighbor extends as well to concern for the neighbor's spiritual well-being. The background of Jewish and Islamic charitable activity is a particular understanding of material creation. The goods of the earth come from God and are to be shared equitably among God's children. When they are shared generously, one passes from justice to charity. In the end, all wealth and prosperity will return to their Source, and we will give an accounting of how we have stewarded what was entrusted to us. Helping one another during our sojourn in this life is a normal expression of our inter-relatedness and solidarity as members of one human family under God. Justice plays an important role in Jewish ethics, but the rabbis understood that the letter of the law does not make for the ideal community life. In Jewish perspective, God made life beautiful, good, and satisfying; it is something that should be enjoyed.[25]

The Muslim social code assumes responsibility for the orphans, widows and the poor who slip through the cracks of Arab society. Every Muslim is expected to contribute through a tax amounting to roughly two percent of one's income. "Almsgiving" is by no means limited to the rendering of this tax, but extends as well to helping the ignorant, visiting the sick, sharing one's surplus food and clothing. Regular almsgiving teaches that the goods of the earth are for all its inhabitants; we have a rightful claim on one another. If one sees a brother or sister in need and does not give what help one can, one's claim to love God is bogus. Allah, who has given us freedom sufficient to hold us responsible for helping the needy or not, is watching. Unless one has heeded the cry of the beggars, "Alms for the love of Allah," one will have thin defense on the Day of Judgment. Islam does not preach salvation by faith alone. Only those who *do* the truth come to the light.[26]

Selfless Service

For social activists in every religion, the question of how one avoids personal burnout and discouragement in the face of overwhelming problems is a pertinent one. Here I would like to focus upon a wisdom from which I have derived particular personal benefit: the teaching of the *Bhagavad Gita* with regard to selfless action. The Gita's teachings on ways of salvation for all types of persons has made it Hinduism's most influential text. Its literary context is an extended poem called the *Mahabharata* about a great internecine war that took place in prehistoric times. The *Mahabharata* can be seen as a metaphor for the perennial war between the forces of light and the forces of darkness in every human heart. When one reads that portion of the epic called the

Bhagavad Gita in this perspective, its two main characters, Arjuna, a young warrior, and Krishna, his guru god, become Everyman asking the Lord himself the timeless questions about the meaning of life and our deepest Self, which is divine.

According to *Gita* scholar Eknath Easwaren,[27] the thread running through Krishna's teaching and the essence of the *Gita* can be given in one word: renunciation. Not in the sense of giving up everything one wants out of life, everything one values, but of giving up selfish attachments to material things and to people. Renunciation of selfishness in thought, word and action is a theme that is common to all mystics, East and West alike. Mahatma Gandhi's encapsulation of the Gita's message is *selfless action* inspired by passages like the following:

> *Therefore, Arjuna, you should understand that renunciation and the performance of selfless service are the same. Those who cannot renounce attachment to the results of their work are far from the path* (Chapter 6: 1–2).

This counsel is not given to some ivory-tower philosopher, but to Arjuna, who in the Hindu caste system represents not only military personnel but business people and politicians. The *Gita* counsels the mental discipline of working hard in the world without selfish attachments. Particular attention is to be given to one's motivation, one's state of mind. Work can benefit others and still carry a good measure of ego-involvement. If we don't monitor the inner force behind our actions, we don't fundamentally change or progress. Action without selfish motives purifies the mind; the doer is likely to be less ego-driven later.

> *Performing all actions for my sake, completely absorbed in the Self, and without expectations, fight!—but stay free from the fever of the ego* (3:30).

We have control over our work and actions, but no command over the results. The phrase "renunciation of the fruits of action" appears again and again. Give your best to every undertaking without insisting that the results work out the way you want, or even whether what you do is pleasant or unpleasant.

The Gita's wisdom served me well in the year prior to my sabbatical. The Canadian Centre for Ecumenism depends upon the interest accruing from an endowment fund for about sixty percent of its annual operating budget. For ten years the principle in the endowment remained the same while operating costs steadily rose. The time came when the endowment had to be increased or staff and programs cut. Soliciting money is not what I had in mind in going to work at the Centre, but it was clearly part of my duty at this juncture in the Centre's history. The goal was set at $500,000, but we all knew the timing—a period of ecumenical as well as economical recession—was not propitious. The churches, preoccupied with in-house concerns of dwindling members, funds and personnel, had little energy or resources to put into extramural relationships or the centers that fostered such. The religious communities, who in the fund drive fifteen years ago were the most generous supporters, were now facing reduced income from lack of vocations and were scraping the bottom of the barrel to cover health care costs for an aging personnel.

One night as I was watching a rerun of "Return of the Jedi," there was one exchange in particular that jumped out at me. Yoda, the last remaining Jedi knight, tells Luke Skywalker that his strength comes from the Force within him. Luke asks if he is fully a Jedi now. "No, you lack one thing yet," Yoda responds. "Failure. You must face failure. And face it you will." I immediately related these words to the campaign we were undertaking, and in my reaction to them recognized that my ego was involved. I was feeling uncertainty (I'd never done this before!), dread, and fear of failure.

As we began to knock on the doors of businessmen, bishops, and religious superiors, I kept firmly in front of me the assertions of the *Gita:* the spiritual life is a call to action, but it is a call to selfless action without any attachments to results. You identify what your duty calls for, and if it is to "fight" for survival, then you throw yourself into the din of battle, staying free from the fever of the ego and leaving the question of success or failure to the Lord. The campaign became the framework for a kind of inverted Outward Bound experience of the interior life, a school of purification of the ego (does anyone *like* to go with hat in hand asking for money?), a crucible for a lesson in detachment. And one day, about a year later, a check for $10,000 arrived quietly in the mail and put us over our goal. But it was truly the Spirit's work, using us as instruments to assure the continuation of an important work. The real victory was the inner one.

Each of us has the power to act rightly, but no power to dictate what is to come of what we do. Mahatma Gandhi explains with the authority of his personal experience:

> *By detachment I mean that you must not worry whether the desired result follows from your action or not, so long as your motive is pure, your means correct. Really, it means that things will come right in the end if you take care of the means and leave the rest to Him.*

But "renunciation of fruits," Gandhi warns,

> *in no way means indifference to the result. In regard to every action one must know the result that is expected to follow, the means thereto, and the capacity for it. He who, being thus equipped, is without desire for the result and is yet wholly engrossed in the due fulfillment of the task before him, is said to have renounced the fruits of his action.* [28]

This attitude enables one to live whatever comes—success or failure, praise or blame, victory or defeat—with a peaceful spirit. Nothing can break one's courage or undo one's will; no setback results in burnout and discouragement. Only the person who is at once completely detached and completely dedicated, says Gandhi, is free to enjoy life. Asked to sum up his life in twenty-five words or less, he replied, "I can do it in three: renounce and enjoy!" The person who is selfishly attached to the results of action cannot really enjoy it. When things do not work out, one gets depressed; when they do, one soon becomes anxious about holding on to it. In the *Gita* Krishna describes the kind of disciple dear to him:

> *That devotee who looks upon friend and foe with equal regard, who is not buoyed up by praise nor cast down by blame, alike in heat and cold, pleasure and pain, free from selfish attachments, the same in honor and dishonor, quiet, ever full, in harmony everywhere, firm in faith—such a one is dear to me* (12:18–19).

I have cited Gandhi in conjunction with the *Gita* because perhaps the clearest way to grasp the Gita's counsel is to look at the way it describes those who embody its teachings. For over forty years Gandhi did his best to translate its verses into his daily life.

A Force Born of Truth and Love

In 1908 in South Africa Gandhi deliberately coined the word "satyagraha"[29] and began to use it as the name for the Indian movement. Truth (*satya*) implies love, and firmness (*agraha*) engenders and therefore serves as a synonym for force. The word captures the substance of his idea—firmness for the truth in love—from its conception in South Africa to the final clashes with the British raj during World War II. During that time, satyagraha assumed many forms—marches, fasts, boycotts, civil disobedience. But to Gandhi it always retained the sense of being a life-force, born of the search for truth and a firm adherence to loving non-violence.

However, the search for truth could become contaminated by self-interest. Gandhi's antidote to untruth was the systematic reduction of self-centeredness which he spelled out in a simple tenet: "Reduce yourself to zero." Without the discipline of reducing self-will, the search for truth could lead to self-righteousness, arrogance, and tyranny. Gandhi tried to demonstrate with his own life that the individual who reduces his own self-interest to zero becomes an effective instrument, like the power of light intensified in the laser, for the resolution of conflict at any level. Further, he believed that this power was not confined to a select few, but was available to all who were willing to embrace this discipline aimed at the removal of self-interest.

Gandhi so believed in the moral force represented by one individual truly emptied of self that he contended if a single satyagrahi holds out to the end, victory is certain. Anyone who has experienced first-hand the dizzying variety of religions and languages in India and the seeming impossibility of such a country ever uniting behind the moral example of one man has no need of further evidence. The historic record is there for all to consult: one person emptied of self-interest can become an amazing force in the hand of God. Far from being a doctrine of mass action, satyagraha is fundamentally a private affair that begins within the human heart; it doesn't even require any followers to make itself felt. But its irresistible power is generated only when one is able to rise above the opposing currents of love and hatred, attachment and repulsion. Gandhi did not gloss over the fact that making one's own life a living sermon of one's creed requires tremendous perseverance and continual cleansing of one's mind and heart. He would have been the first to admit that his first opponent was not General Smuts or the South African government. His fiercest campaign was waged in his own consciousness. Out of that struggle emerged the "mahatma," the great soul.

One of my favorite Gandhi stories recounts a mother coming to him to help get her little boy to stop eating sugar; it was doing him harm. Gandhi gave a cryptic reply: "Please come back next week."

The woman left puzzled but dutifully followed the Mahatma's instructions and returned a week later. Gandhi met the boy and after a chat, said, "Please don't eat sugar any more. It's not good for you." Then he gave him a hug and sent him on his way. But the mother, in amazement, asked, "Bapu, why didn't you say that last week when we came? Why did you make me come back again?"

"Because last week," Gandhi said to her smiling, "I too was eating sugar."

One of the things that distinguishes satyagraha from other social action methods which merely attempt to gain self-invested ends is the effort to resolve the underlying sources of conflict, the enmity, the distrust. Satyagraha seeks to resolve conflict by persuading the adversary of the common value of its vision, that *we* have much more to gain in harmony than in discord. The adversary is not an enemy to be conquered, but a participant in the search for a truthful resolution to the conflict. Far from wanting to punish or inflict injury on the opposing party, satyagraha seeks to alter the relationship of conflict to one of esteem and trust, seeking to reach the heart of the other by rendering humanitarian service whenever possible. Imagine what would happen if urban transit workers on strike used their own cars to transport elderly stranded passengers rather than slashed the tires and broke the windows of their grounded buses. Those kind of chivalrous acts leave their potent impress and prepare a suitable atmosphere for a settlement. The satyagrahi knows that the changes asked for will be difficult, so every effort is made to be aware of any hardships caused and to ease those hardships wherever possible.

The supplanting of distrust and ill will with confidence and respect requires the readiness to suffer. But the satyagrahi continues to trust in spite even of frequent betrayals in the belief that the forces of truth are thereby strengthened and victory brought nearer. The actual terms of the resolution of conflict are not the main concern; the establishment of a relationship of trust is. This is the context in which new terms can be arrived at. Non-cooperation is only a means to secure the cooperation of the other. Sympathy, patience, trust, and a willingness to suffer are the satyagrahi's main "weapons" in altering the nature of the relationship from one of animosity to one of respect and confidence. When that point is reached, the tension will be amicably resolved since the adversary is now, in a sense, an ally, and sees that there is something at stake much higher than his own private, vested interests and is moved to subordinate them to a cooperative solution. This "conversion" is the real intent of satyagraha. Its use of strikes, demonstrations and the like are only the tools to bring it about. The acid test is whether, in the end, there is no rancor left behind and the "enemies" have become friends.

When violent means are employed in conflict resolution, bitterness and enmity result and fester, eventually exploding and reversing the conquest. In true satyagraha, no one is conquered; both parties emerge as partners in the solution. Thus the historian Arnold Toynbee remarked at the time of the British troops' departure from India, "Gandhi has not only liberated India. He has also liberated Great Britain." The film footage of the cheering people and the cheering troops tells the tale.

Love and Service in the Home and Workplace

The ideal of selfless service in the *Gita* and its embodiment in Gandhi's life is not meant to be limited to the political realm. It has its applications in the home and workplace as well. The crises that threaten our lives today are not so much political as spiritual, involving personal and social matters of alienation, isolation and increasing polarization. The fact that one of every three marriages today ends in divorce indicates that an increasing number of homes are unable to withstand even the predictable tensions of married life. Gandhi's way, indistinguishable from the teaching and example of Jesus which Gandhi knew well and held in the highest esteem, may offer a breakthrough for those willing to try it: forgive, forbear, support the other person, and when it becomes necessary to resist, do so lovingly and without rancor. In the words of the *Gita:* "When a person responds to the joys and sorrows of others as if they were his own, he has attained the highest state of spiritual union" (6:32).

While relationships at work are less emotionally encumbered than those at home, tension still erupts out of conflicting self-interest wherever people work closely together. As long as individuals sharing the same working environment give their own self-interest top priority, friction will build until it has to be dealt with. The conflicts often devolve from different ways of perceiving and doing things and are frequently fed by petty jealousies and resentments. When an effort is made to bring the parties together in communication, the issues are often cloaked in the language of professional principles, but underneath the surface it is usually a question of two or more dueling egos. As an Indian saying goes,"Everyone thinks his watch has the right time."

The person who can see beyond his or her own opinions and who can rise above self-interest is in a position to view the conflict with some objectivity and to look for common ground. If reasoned appeals fail he or she must be ready to forbear and, with sympathy and patience, work silently and steadily to minimize self-interest in the working environment and to appeal to a broader, unifying purpose. One dedicated satyagrahi, as Gandhi opined, can spread the leavening influence and gradually effect transformation in the environment, enabling work to proceed in cooperation and mutual respect.

The relevance of these teachings, when cast onto the world stage, is only magnified. Dream for a moment and consider what transformations would take place in the world through detachment from more than one's fair share of the world's wealth and goods, from more than one's fair share of influence and power, from the need to dominate others and feel superior to them, from the desire for revenge.

The path charted by the *Gita* begins in the human heart, at home, and gradually spreads to touch friends and colleagues. Gandhi advised his critics to observe the results of his experiments rather than to dissect his theories. Neither does the *Gita* offer a system of philosophy. It is basically practical, a handbook for Self-realization and a guide to action. Gandhi was fond of saying it makes most sense when it is practiced, and that is what he did. The results are there for any to see and, he would remind us, "What is possible for me, is possible for everybody."

When we look at Gandhi, Dorothy Day, Catherine de Hueck Doherty, Oscar Romero, Mother Teresa, Jean Vanier, Desmond Tutu and others like them, we see men and women who yoked all their human passions to the over-riding desire to give and love and serve. And in that unification we see, not the extinction of personality, but its blossoming. This is what it means to be fully human.

John of the Cross wrote that every quality or virtue the Holy Spirit produces in our souls has three distinguishing trademarks: tranquillity, gentleness and strength. In other words, all our actions must be peaceful, gentle and strong. That suggests an immense depth and steadiness which flows from our small action now being part of the work of the Spirit. Fuss and feverishness, anxiety and pessimism are signs of the self-made and self-acting soul. Tranquillity, gentleness and strength carry us through all changes of weather, the varied surfaces of the road, the tensions of family life, the disappointments of our profession, the unexpected intervention of ill fortune or health, and the waning and waxing of consolations in our spiritual lives. Thus there is no tendency to snatch another person's job or dodge dull bits of our own; no frenzied sense of hurry or nervous anxiety about success, no forgetting that God, who is greater than our heart, is greater than this job or project, too. [30]

There is only the ongoing work of "reducing self to zero," allowing God to fill the emptiness, and a firm, faithful refusal to look at that which distracts us from this path. Always looking in that direction and moving in that direction, in spite of weariness, discouragement and roadblocks. Availability for service in love. Selfless action. The journey which will cost not less than everything. But no other path is ultimately worth taking.

8

The Vision of Christian Faith

In his book *The Road Less Travelled*, M. Scott Peck asserted that we only grow spiritually because of challenges, difficulties and problems. "Disciplines" is what he called the means of experiencing these challenges constructively. Disciplines are the basic set of tools we require to solve life's problems; without them we can do nothing. The problem lies not in the complexity of these tools, but in the will to use them. [1]

Over the years, "discipline" has come to be a wonderfully positive and life-giving word for me. I try to avoid the temptation of looking for results and simply live in the trust that God will use my efforts as God uses everything. But even at that, I can't help notice that when I'm faithful to these practices, I have twice the energy and creativity. And when I'm unfaithful to them, I notice that I can only absorb half the stress load. I've come to regard them as pillars that support my roof. When even one of them is out of service—and that's what it really does, render service—some part of my roof (read: life) sags and the leakage spreads inside the walls to cause damage in surprising places.

Many adults today may correctly perceive in one or other discipline for Christian living a call to sacrifice, obedience and selfless service, and judge it to be out of line with their own direction in life. In an era where we are seeking to build our self-esteem and to feel good about ourselves, the commands of Jesus seem like an unappealing prospect or simply seem to ask for too much for people to accept. Today's man or woman may not aggressively challenge or oppose the Christian life-style and belief structure but dismiss it as impractical and unreasonable for to-day's world.

Yet my own experience is that the disciplines for Christian living enhance the quality of my life in every way. The quality of our lives is very much to the point if one believes that the kingdom of God is not so much a place as an experience, and that eternal life is not so much a matter of duration of time as of peace, love, joy and gratitude already commenced here and now though not yet made full. "This is eternal life, that they may know you, the only true God, and Jesus Christ whom you have sent" (John 17:3).

In his television series on "The Power of Myth," Joseph Campbell observed that people say what they are seeking is an experience that will give meaning to life. He disagreed:

> *We are seeking an experience of being alive. We are seeking experiences that will enable us to feel the rapture of being alive, physical experiences that will resonate with our spiritual intuitions. Everyone has the potential to find the place of their rapture. Follow your bliss. What happens when you do? You come to bliss! Don't be afraid. Doors will open.*

We get at different times an intuition of where our joy is. When we get on to it, it's like discovering a rail that's been there all the time waiting for us, and there's a sense of being helped by invisible hands to stay with it. This is the Spirit's doing. We only realize when we look back over a span of years how God has been slowly, almost imperceptibly bringing the various dimensions of our lives—spiritual, physical, intellectual, affective—into har-

mony and balance with one another by leading us to the practice
of this or that discipline.

As we try to integrate new practices into our lives while
maintaining old ones, we feel like a juggler trying to keep several
balls in constant and harmonious flow. We continually lose sight
of one or the other and drop it only to pick it up and start again.
The only thing that really matters is to be on the pilgrimage, to
express our faithful discipleship through the disciplines, to keep
cultivating the garden, confident that "one sows, another waters,
and God gives the growth."

I
THE HEART OF THE GOOD NEWS

"Following my bliss" led me to look for the signs of bliss'
presence in the lives of people of other faiths. When people from
different faiths come together, it should be to listen and to learn
in a dialogue in which people of faith bring their forms of prayer,
their scriptures and their most valued spiritual traditions together
in an act of faithful common witness. Over the centuries Christians have slowly and painfully learned to refer to those who do
not share their faith, not as "pagans" nor as "non-Christians," but
as people with their own identities who profess a belief in sometimes ancient and sophisticated ways of life and practice. The
inter-faith encounter is, just as the words imply, a meeting between people of *faith*. It is an occasion for the Christian to discern and rejoice in the richness of God's self-revelation. When
people come together in this spirit, listening to each other's
prayers, sharing in each other's silence, they are seeking to learn
from the differences, not to bury them.

A spineless relativism which compromises everything that
Christians hold dear is not the only alternative to an aggressive,

literal and triumphalistic proclamation of the Good News. The Catholic tradition has managed to keep alive a different alternative to such exclusivism, based on the expectation that the continuing action of God in Christ, the Word, will be seen speaking in the hearts of all people of faith. Not that such a theology answers all our problems; it is easy for it to become deeply patronising. But at least it recognizes that there is no need to set up an absolute divide between Christianity and other faiths. The way of awareness and appropriation has, in fact, immensely heightened my own appreciation for what is truly distinctive about the Christian proclamation. In inter-faith dialogue, we are learning about ourselves. The encounter with people of other living faiths has made me keenly conscious of where the driving force of Christianity precisely lies.

Ten years ago, I spent a year living with members of different Christian traditions in preparation for my work at the Canadian Centre for Ecumenism. I came back from that year more *catholic* than I had ever been, i.e., rooted in the faith that is everywhere.[2] A decade later, after spending my sabbatical time with Hindus and Buddhists and Muslims, I came back more self-consciously *Christian* than I have ever been. When one grows up in the western world, Christianity is part of the woodwork, and because it is represented on every corner by one church or another, one doesn't derive a sense of its specialness. Consequently many westerners with curious minds run farther afield, looking across the fence at more exotic pastures and easily find something to interest them because we are always enticed by the strange and new.

By entering into those pastures and grazing there awhile, one is better positioned to evaluate and appreciate the quality of the grass there where one was born and raised. Crossing over and grazing in other fields is one way of coming to value the distinctive taste and texture and nutritional value of the clover in our own. Since my return, it is with a newfound sense of joy and gratitude that I rise to preach the gospel of Jesus Christ. "The end of all our journeying," wrote T.S. Eliot in his *Four Quartets*, "is to end up where we began and know the place for the first time."

I am grateful to Islam for its emphasis upon God's greatness and for the priority it accords God's will in all things. What God wills and commands is surely the best thing for the one who submits to God; submission brings peace and wholeness in this present life and in the life to come. I am grateful, too, for Islam's reminder that submission to God is not simply a matter of an individual's response, but means being a part of the community of the *people* of obedience. I find Islam's "seamless garment" approach to religious living inspiring: every corner of life is an area for obedience to God; there is no separation into sacred and secular. And I respect Islamic consistency in desiring that, since God is who God is, God's will should extend over the whole human race. The vision is a compelling one of transforming a wasteland of divided and self-willed humanity, at war with itself and with God, into a garden of blessed orderliness, fruitfulness, divine peace and wholeness.

But in the emphasis upon the otherness of Allah and the unwavering stress upon submission and obedience, I miss the closeness, confidence, and intimacy with the divine witnessed to in Jesus' words, "I call you servants no longer, but friends" (John 15:15). The assertion of the Incarnation, that the Word of God became flesh in the actual existence of a historical person and dwelt among us, becomes all the more dear to me.

I am grateful to Buddhism for its teaching on detachment; its encouragement to mindfulness; its reminder that all things are ultimately unsatisfactory, fleeting, and empty; its high code of ethics and personal responsibility; its spiritual discipline of medita-tion for purifying the mind; its compassion for all living beings; and its commitment to non-violence.

But it does not speak to me of a Creator, Redeemer, and Sanctifier.

It does not tell me of a Savior who, in his love for human-kind, became one of us and freely gave his life in love for us, cancelling out our debt and reconciling us to God's friendship. It does not tell me that God the Sanctifier dwells within our very hearts and has set us free from the burden of the law and from the just punishment due to our wrongs—*free* to serve in loving grati-tude all our days.

And I am grateful to Hinduism for the rich tradition of spiritual wisdom contained in the Vedanta; the deep insight into the nature of God as one which is set forth in the Upanishads; the call of the Bhagavad Gita to do what is right, to enter into the din of battle but to keep my heart peaceful by leaving the results of my efforts to God.

I am grateful for the conviction of God's transcendence in Brahman, God's immanence and presence to my personal self in Atman; grateful for the carefully researched and refined science of yoga as a way of calming the mind and body and preparing me for meditation; grateful for the rich devotional life and faith of the people who are ready to recognize the Formless One manifested in any form and present in all things; grateful for the holy lives of the wandering ascetics and mystics.

But Hinduism's cosmology leaves me imprisoned in circular thinking, karmic rebirth, and the caste system. I must get out of this on my own or eternally come round, strapped to the wheel of karma, paying for my weakness, ignorance, and sinfulness with repeated reincarnations. As I listen to the Orthodox Christian Easter refrain from within this context, its message reaches my heart like the pealing of a great liberty bell: "trampling down death by death (and suffering by suffering), Christ brings freedom and life to those who are in the tomb." That which the Buddhist and Hindu strive for with all their might—a state of freedom from cyclical rebirth and suffering—the Christian joyfully accepts as a free gift of God in Jesus Christ. The heart of the good news is now more clearly focused for me: once you were in bondage, alienated from God, and now you are set free and given a share in the very life of God as sons and daughters.

Without standing within the experience of religions where this glad tidings is simply absent, and seeing the implications reverberate though all other aspects of my life as I projected myself as one living within that worldview, I don't think I would ever have *experienced* in the depth of my being what an incredibly liberating message this gospel brings. I emerge with a sharpened sense of how priceless is the proclamation of the angel to the shepherds at Bethlehem:

> *"Do not be afraid; for see—I am bringing you good news*
> *of great joy for all the people: to you is born this day in*
> *the city of David a Savior, who is the Messiah, the Lord"*
> (Luke 2:10–11).

A Himalayan Festival of Faith

But I was grateful for more than *things*—insights, realizations, broader and deeper understandings of commonalities and differences. I was especially grateful for the *people* through whom these religions become living realities. Face to face with another believer, you not only become aware of your own identity, its riches and its limitations, but you also become aware of another's identity, riches and limitations as his or her reality inspires your own. In these moments of openness to one another, what comes through is a poignant awareness of our mutual humanity. Ken Wilber, a Zen practitioner and leading theorist in transpersonal psychology, tells the story of making a last-ditch effort to stop the spread of his wife's cancer by taking her to a special clinic in Germany for treatments not offered in the United States.

There, while out for a solitary walk one Sunday evening, he realized that his wife was going to die. He came upon a pub in which lively music was playing and a dozen elderly men with rosy cheeks were dancing together in a semi-circle with their arms over each other's shoulders, kicking up their legs in unison in a Zorba-the-Greek type dance.

He sat down at the bar by himself, put his head in his arms and started crying. When he looked up, he discovered that a mug of beer had been placed in front of him. He drank it in one pull, and started crying again. A few of the men danced in his direction and gestured for him to join them. He declined with a gesture. A few beers later, they gestured again, this time tugging at his arm in a friendly way, looking concerned and wanting to help.

Soon he found himself locked arm and shoulder into the semi-circle where, embarrassed and self-conscious, he lost all control over his emotions. Fear, self-pity, panic, laughter, and terror all passed across his face, but the men kept nodding their heads and smiling as if to say, "It's okay, young man, just keep dancing."

In that two hours of dancing and drinking, all his pent-up emotions came to a head and washed through his system and he came to a sort of inner peace about his wife's imminent death.

Afterward, he reflected that he would like to be able to claim that his big illumination experience about accepting his wife's condition and about becoming finally responsible for his own choices to set aside his interests and do everything he could to support her—that it all came from some powerful meditation session with blazing white light and spontaneous insights pouring in a transcendental epiphany. But it happened in a little pub with a bunch of kindly old men whose names he didn't know and whose language he didn't speak.[3]

The experience of human solidarity in the face of life's deep questions provide a peace and reassurance that can only come from the One whom all our hearts seek and who is present to us all in it all.

I was blessed with experiences both of our mutual, human solidarity and of "spontaneous insights flowing from some powerful meditation session." My course in Buddhism at the Himal-ayan Tushita Centre turned out to be the occasion of a "transcen-dental epiphany" and a face-to-face encounter which I will never forget. I had earlier in my sabbatical designated a quiet month as "retreat time"—at Shantivanam ashram in South India. The month passed serenely, without fireworks of the Spirit, though I was looking and hoping for some! Then, in the middle of an intensive course daily involving four hours of lectures on Bud-dhist doctrine, three hours of guided meditation and an hour of group discussion, the Spirit moved strongly within in the form of a palpable thirst for the heart of the gospel of Christ. Unable to contain it, I skipped the afternoon session one day and, taking only my Bible and a canteen of water, climbed higher into the mountains until I found a suitable spot for a few hours of reading.

I began with Paul's Letter to the Romans, then went on to his Letters to the Galatians, Colossians, and Thessalonians. I devoured the words with new eyes, and took the measure of their meaning more deeply than ever before. There, on my isolated perch high in the Himalayas, fireworks of the spirit erupted in a personal festival of faith.

> *When the fullness of time had come, God sent his Son, born of a woman, born under the law, in order to redeem those who were under the law, so that we might receive adoption as children. And because you are children, God has sent the Spirit of his Son into our hearts, cry-ing, "Abba! Father!" So you are no longer a slave but a child, and if a child then also an heir, through God* (Galatians 4:4–7).

What must have been in the mind of God when he watched men drive nails through Jesus's hands and feet and then hoist him up on the cross? From scripture, we can sense what God would have said to us: "I have but one begotten Son, but now—through his death and resurrection—I shall have many adopted sons and daughters (Hebrews 2:10–11). My children, your parents in the flesh, Adam and Eve, turned from me and chose spiritual death. With all their progeny, they shall now have new life! Your inheritance from Adam was isolation from your God. Now, all you who acknowledge my Son shall have a new inheritance as my sons and daughters. You have become co-heirs. You have become co-heirs with him of the eternal heavenly realm (Romans 8:14–17). My love, my wisdom, my patience, my guidance, my healing, my peace are yours, just as they rightfully belong to him.

"You were formerly dominated by guilt from which you had no escape, but through my Son's blood, your guilt has been washed away, and behold, you are made new (Hebrews 9:14; Romans 6:4). You have lived in hopelessness and bondage to sin, fear, and the fleeting pleasures of this world (Ephesians 2:12). You have been slaves to lust, hatred, and anger, but now you have freedom as children of God (Romans 6:17–18; 8:21). My son will rise from the darkness of the tomb and reclaim his rightful position on the throne of heaven. He is the tree of life rejected by Adam and Eve but who now calls you to the tree to eat and receive life" (John 15:1–7; Revelation 2:7).

After twenty years as a member of the Missionary Society of St. Paul the Apostle (more commonly called the Paulists), I felt what I have always imagined missionaries feel: a desire to share my experience of a loving God come near in Jesus, dwelling in fact within our hearts by the Holy Spirit. I wanted to share it simply as a source of joy and meaning and fulfillment in my own life. I wanted others to know and share in this joy, too; to rejoice in what God has done for us through no merit of our own, but by a free gift of love.

In the final days of the course, several opportunities unfolded for wonderfully honest, probing dialogue and witness with others who were involved in the same program. In dialogue, believers must be true to their convictions so that it becomes mutual challenge and proclamation. There is no dialogue that is not mutual proclamation. By the same token, proclamation can only be dialogical. These discussions left no room for any triumphalism, only for humble gratitude for the work of God.

After the final evening session, our meditation instructor came and sat down next to me and started asking me questions about Christianity. She knew very little about it, she said, and had many questions. I was tired and in a mood to go to bed, but felt my energy coming around as we got deeper into discussion. We talked for two hours. Even against my dozen years of experience in national inter-church dialogues in Canada, it was one of the most authentic experiences of dialogue I have ever had.

When you come face to face with another believer, you become aware not only of your own identity and its riches, but also of its limitations, its historical and cultural conditionings. It is an experience that challenges you to growth. Dialogue at this level is neither discussion nor apologetics. It is doxology: thanking and praising God for being so everywhere present and active. Unless this happens at some point genuine dialogue doesn't take place. We're just listening with polite skepticism and incredulity, waiting for the other to stop talking so we can bring the truth. In real dialogue there is always the possibility, when we actually open ourselves to the reality of the other and experience the world as the other sees it, that we may be changed and come out of the experience with our own worldview altered. In this process, conversion from one religion to another is not excluded, provided it is an act of freedom and one's response is to an experienced call of God.

What more frequently happens is that we enter into the outlook of the other and what we experience there transforms our own Christian understanding. We do not, for example, try to read the scriptures of the other as we read our own, but as another set of code words which contribute to an understanding of God.

Through the lectures and meditations and group discussions

I had begun to cross over and stand within the Buddhist worldview, to see its inner logic and coherency. I saw now, through her eyes, how seemingly preposterous the Christian doctrine of the atonement is. "How can one man come and take away everybody's sins—especially the sins of those who haven't even been born yet?" she wanted to know. "Why are so many people born into situations of profound suffering—how do you explain that? For us, it is due to the negative imprints of karma accumulated in previous lives, but if you don't believe in cyclical rebirth, how do you account for this?" We were two people of faith, seeking understanding.

As I did my best to explain to her the Christian doctrine of the atonement and a Christian perspective of suffering, it was as though I were she listening to me explain it, and in that moment I glimpsed what astounding assertions we Christians make. Within myself I experienced the place from which her reaction came; that is, for the first time I *experienced* the question "How could that be?" from within another view of reality.

II
CREDO[4]

One has to choose one's savior in faith, asking again and again what way of life, what modeling of divinity one finds most compelling. There is no unassailable argument from history which, by objective standards, makes Jesus completely unique. So one is free to let a broad range of considerations contribute to one's commitment or non-commitment to Christ. Considerations such as the effect on one's own personal development of Christian liturgy and prayer, and the teachings of Jesus concerning social responsibility. Considerations such as what one finds (e.g., community or the lack thereof) among serious Christian believers; the honesty and love they show or fail to show; the degree to which the Christian saints embody an attractive, holistic humanity.

There is no way to make a detached, academic judgment about something which goes so directly and deeply into the heart of the human project. What is ultimately at stake is a personal option for a way to live and a way to die based on the beauty, coherence and viability of the alternatives offered. In the face of death, evil, suffering, and potential meaninglessness, which way do the brighter and more realistic prospects lie?

Every religion should tread carefully and with humility in claiming a moral superiority. Every living faith constituency has its fair share of saints and sinners. No individuals are necessarily closer to God or human perfection than any other individuals simply because their group feels graced or chosen. What people claim for their faith matters less than what people actually do. And what human beings actually experience and accomplish is, in the final analysis, colored by their perceptions and therefore subjective.

So we are back to faith, "the assurance of things hoped for, the conviction of things not seen" (Hebrews 11:1). It is faith which alone makes possible certain horizons like divine life, immortality, forgiveness of sins, resurrection, friendship with Jesus, love of enemies, joy and peace which surpass the world's understanding. Within the Christian experience, each of these represent deposits of meaning, flowing from the Word of God made flesh in the life and teachings of Jesus of Nazareth, far richer than anything human imagination or reason or love will ever exhaust. I have no desire to stray from this richness, only to more fully appreciate the mystery of it at work in our world.

At the same time as I embrace Jesus wholeheartedly, I have great respect and esteem for other religious leaders like Moses, Mohammed, and Buddha and, in effect, embrace them partially, benefitting from and drawing upon their wisdom, as is amply attested to in these pages. Their adherents find in their legacy a significant salvation. That said, my own personal confession of faith is that the salvation I find in Jesus takes me farther into the mystery of God.

And inasmuch as I find Jesus to be the face of a limitless divine love, I can imagine something Christian at the marrow of everything presenting a divinity compatible with the "Abba" of Jesus. Jesus as the Word spoken by God in self-revelation, and the Spirit, their love who rounds out their perfect mutuality, form the horizon of my religious outlook as a Christian. But the grace of Christ has been poured out for all people and makes its way in many different cultural traditions and forms. My own perspective of faith is that wherever truth and love are pursued, and wherever compassion and service are flourishing, the one whom I name as the Holy Spirit is at work there.

In the scriptures which shape my view of reality, the Word of God appears at the hub of God's actions to make and guide a world. "In the beginning was the Word, and the Word was with God, and the Word was God. All things came into being through him" (John 1:1,3), and "in him, all things hold together" (Colossians 1:17).

To the assertion that the Incarnation of this Word, and his life among us, was the decisive event for the history of all humankind, I say *credo*, I believe.

I believe that in him the gulf between divinity and humanity has been bridged, that he has saved us from sin, brought heaven to earth, incarnated divinity, mediated divine wisdom and life, displayed the love for which all human hearts are longing, and initiated a human community in which he continues to dwell and act through the Holy Spirit. He is for me teacher and lover, Word of God and healer, promise and food. And so I say to him, with Peter, "Lord, to whom can we go? You have the words of eternal life. We have come to believe and know that you are the Holy One of God" (John 6:68–69).

Sixteen years ago I wrote in my ordination invitation: "My

experience is that Christ's life and message confirm my most powerful and hopeful human instincts. I believe that there is in this life a surplus of sense over non-sense, and that in the long run, God's graciousness will triumph." The alignment I sensed then between the human spirit's deepest yearnings and what the Christian faith finds in Jesus has only been reinforced by the intervening years of pastoral experience. The exact junction in this person of flesh and spirit, of the human and the divine, of the mortal and the immortal, of sacramentality and inexhaustible Mystery responds to my understanding of what salvation entails.

Once, and for all people, Christian faith says, God gave the world a pledge of the divine love and showed the divine love to be more powerful than anything that might threaten human existence, including death. Once, and for all, God expressed the divine will to save all human beings and bring them into divine life.

Jesus is the personal place where humanity came to know its vocation to divinization. The love that the Trinity of persons offers in the Christian perspective has parallels in the eastern religions, but certain dimensions of it, like its intimate and incarnational aspects, remain distinctly Christian. In Judaism we find the same divine offer, but Judaism has shied away from claiming divinization. Hinduism, Buddhism, and Islam, along with Judaism, do not speak of divinity actually assuming flesh in the historical existence of a particular person. But they have other gifts to offer which are important for us to receive.

III
GOD'S AMAZING DREAM FOR US

The subjects of these chapters are various means of putting ourselves in a place where God can transform us through love and bring us into intimate communion of life. What ultimately matters is not our ideas, or our experiences or our denying this or doing that. What "matters" is not a method of prayer or a particular style of life. The all-important thing, our unique and ultimate end, is union with God, transformation in God, divinization of our full being. There is ultimately only one failure: the failure to become a saint, to become fully human through the work of God in us. God doesn't think prosaic thoughts, never condones lukewarm dilutions. The message of the Incarnation and redemption is that God had in mind nothing less than that we should be deified, that we should enter profoundly into the inner life of the Trinity in a union beyond human words.

In his *Spiritual Canticle* St. John of the Cross speaks of "a total transformation in the Beloved. . . . The soul thereby becomes divine, becomes God through participation, insofar as is possible in this life. . . . There are two natures in one spirit and love. . . . This union resembles the union of the light of a star or candle with the light of the sun, for what then sheds light is not the star or the candle, but the sun, which has absorbed the other lights into its own. . . . The union wrought between the two natures and the communication of the divine to the human in this state is such that even though neither change their being, both appear to be God."[5]

This is daring terminology. Yet John is careful to avoid any hint of pantheism. There is no fusion as in some eastern religions, no loss of personal identity. This is, in fact, a thoroughly biblical idea. John understands Jesus' prayer at the last supper as referring to this trinitarian transformation:

> *I ask not only on behalf of these, but also on behalf of those who will believe in me through their word, that they may all be one. As you, Father, are in me and I am in you, may they also be in us. . . . The glory that you have given me, I have given them, so that they may be one, as we are one, I in them and you in me, that they*

> *may become completely one, so that the world may know that you have sent me and have loved them even as you have loved me* (John 17:20–23).

This theme is not unique to the evangelist John. A repeated refrain in the letters of St. Paul is that we have become a new creation (Galatians 5:15). "His divine power has given us everything needed for life and godliness," says the apostle Peter, "through the knowledge of him who called us by his own glory and goodness. Thus he has given us . . . his precious and very great promises, so that through them you may . . . *become participants of the divine nature*" (2 Peter 1:4, emphasis mine).

It is these "very great promises" that Teresa of Avila has in mind when she writes:

> *O my Sisters, what nothingness it is, that which we leave! Nor is what we do anything, nor all that we could do for a God who thus wishes to communicate Himself. . . . And if we hope to enjoy this blessing even in this present life, what are we doing? What is causing us to delay? What is enough to make us, even momentarily, stop looking for this Lord as did the bride (in the Song of Songs) in the streets and in the squares?*[6]

John of the Cross, expressing his conviction that absolutely everyone is called to the surpassing joy of union with God, that it is the ordinary development of the life of grace, echoes Teresa's plea to her sisters:

> *O souls, created for these grandeurs and called to them! What are you doing? How are you spending your time?*[7]

Our being filled with God is the reason for everything else in the life of the Church: the structures, the books, the ministries, the sacraments. The eucharist is explicitly aimed at producing eternal life here on earth. "Those who eat my flesh and drink my blood *have* eternal life," Jesus declared (John 6:54). Having this life, and having it to the full, is the reason why he came (John 10:10).

According to the Fathers, everything depends on what happens when a person hears that there is a way to this life. There has to be a *willingness* to plunge in, a willingness for whatever. In a popular story from the early Desert Fathers, Abba Lot says to Abba Joseph: "Father, I fast a little. I pray and I meditate. I live in peace as far as I can. I purify my thoughts. What else can I do?"

And Abba Joseph stood up and stretched his hands toward heaven. His fingers became like ten flames, and he said, "If you want, you can become all fire!"

If you want. . . .

What Do You Really Want?

The key to transformation is desire. We cannot achieve anything on our own. The only thing we can do by ourselves is to say "no" to God. God cannot transform us unless we really want it and allow God to work in us. That is the role of the disciplines: to dispose us, to bring us to the massage table where God's hands can find the points of tension and blockage and begin dissolving them so that the full current of living and loving abundantly can freely flow in us.

We must decide what we really want and bring everything else into line with this desire. We must make up our minds once and for all, renewing the decision countless times daily that we shall let God have everything God wants. We shall trust God, greeting in faith each task or encounter with its joy or pain, seeing and embracing God in it. This kind of surrender is not something to which we can bring ourselves. God must achieve this in us. Whether or not God does depends on the constancy of our desire.[8]

Realizing the promises of Jesus is more than just a possibility. It is an assured *probability* for those who love Jesus and keep his commandments. It is probable rather than certain, not because God does not want it, but because *we may not desire it purely and perseveringly enough.* God makes the offer and awaits our response. What must we do to signal our desire for and acceptance of God's offer? Obey with love.

> As the Father has loved me, so I have loved you; abide in
> my love. If you keep my commandments, you will abide
> in my love, just as I have kept my Father's command-
> ments and abide in his love. I have said these things to
> you so that my joy may be in you, and that your joy
> may be complete (John 15:9–11).

This is the condition upon which the indwelling depends: keeping Jesus' commandments and thus loving him. Here is the unifying principle for the Christian spiritual life directed to union with God. It is a principle with a promise: obedience leads to presence. "They who have my commandments and keep them are those who love me . . . and *I will reveal myself to them*" (John 14:21, emphasis mine). When asked for clarification, Jesus repeated the principle, rephrasing it slightly but without changing it substantially, for the abiding presence of the Revealer and the Revealed, Jesus and his Father, form the core of the revelation.[9]

> Judas (not the Iscariot) said to him, "Lord, how is it that
> you will reveal yourself to us and not to the world?" Jesus
> answered him, "Those who love me will keep my word,
> and my Father will love them, and we will come to them
> and make our home with them" (John 14:22–23).

This is the biblical basis for the constant witness of Christians through the centuries who have testified that fulfillment of this condition—obedience with love—brings a heightened consciousness of union with Jesus and the Father through the indwelling of the Holy Spirit. This is not a direct vision of God, but rather an intimate sense of union through the effects of love, joy and peace culminating in the experience of oneness.[10]

But even this mysterious communion with God which we seek and offer ourselves to is not, in spite of the deep peace it brings, without the pain and tension which must be felt by imperfect human creatures when we stretch toward that incomparable Love in which alone our hearts find fulfillment. Sooner or later, this journey involves sacrifice, struggle and effort because there are two impulses in us which pull in different directions. Their reconciliation is a long and arduous task. This is why the spiritual life requires a definite plan and prayerfully chosen disciplines to serve us on the journey and prevent our getting lost. Spirituality is primarily practical. It looks to action, to love in action. We arrive at union with God through an ongoing series of decisions which open up our minds and hearts to consciousness of the divine presence.

The passwords are habitual constancy, faithfulness, and courage in sticking to the plan, not merely for months but for years. New mental and emotional habits must be formed, and all our interests rearranged around a new center, a practical acceptance of the truth that God alone matters. One cannot push this river and make it arrive sooner, but one can dam it up and divert it indefinitely. Oftentimes we suggest by our behavior that God is less important than the morning newspaper or an evening television program.[11]

Our choice is to be whole and holy or fragmented and mediocre. If we listen to the indwelling Spirit and take up the disciplines which will create the environment and the space in our lives for the Spirit to work, then in God's time and by God's power, transformation, harmony, at-one-ment will be given as dawn is to the night.

A *Thanksgiving Prayer*

When I returned from my sabbatical, a colleague who listened to some of my stories gave me the following "Thanksgiving Prayer After a Deeply Religious Experience."[11] I could not think of a more fitting close.

From the center of my being, I praise you, my Lord and God,
for the beautiful sabbatical experience that you have given me.
This time has enflamed my heart, renewed my dreams,
and enabled me to see with new eyes.
I heard your ancient call
within the words and events of this time now ended;
your call to personal holiness and perfection,
the invitation to prayer and spirituality,
the challenge of the Kingdom and the Church.
As the disciples of your Son were set afire
by your divine Spirit on Pentecost,
this sacred time has encouraged me to greatness
within the scope of my simple life.
I may soon forget the words that were spoken
and the names of those who were involved,
but what has happened has truly shaped my heart.

May the activities of my heart bear witness
in the day to day world to which I return,
to the great grace of what has happened to me.

May this time of spiritual renewal
become part of the fabric of my life;
may it be part of a lifelong enrollment
in the school of prayer.
May I build upon it with daily prayer,
and with the discipline of my spiritual life.

Nourished by prayer, reading, thought and action,
may the seeds of this renewal time
take root and flower forth
in a life-song of glory to you, my Lord and my God.

Amen.

Notes

INTRODUCTION: LET'S GET PRACTICAL

1. Thomas Merton, "Christian Culture Needs Oriental Wisdom," *Catholic World* (May, 1962), p. 79.

2. Thomas Merton, *Seeds of Destruction* (New York: Macmillan, 1967), pp. 187–188.

3. Michael Amaladoss, SJ, "Rationales for Dialogue With World Religions," *Origins*, vol. 19, no. 35 (February 1, 1990), p. 576.

4. Leonard J. Biallas, *World Religions: A Story Approach* (Mystic, CT: Twenty-Third Publications, 1991), pp. 17–31.

5. Thomas Merton, Journal entry for March 3, 1950, in *The Sign of Jonas* (New York: Harcourt, Brace, & Co., 1953), p. 275.

6. Pat Windsor, "Father Thomas Keating Brings Contemplation Out of the Cloister," *St. Anthony Messenger* (February, 1992), p. 16.

1. THE MEANING OF DISCIPLINE
FOR CHRISTIAN LIVING

1. Elaine V. Emeth and Janet Greenhut, MD, *The Wholeness Handbook* (New York: The Continuum Publishing Co., 1991), p. 71.

2. See 1989 *Britannica Book of the Year* (Chicago: Encyclopedia Britannica, 1989), p. 299.

3. Emeth and Greenhut, *The Wholeness Handbook*, p. 81.

4. Teresa of Avila, *The Interior Castle*, trans. Kieran Kavanaugh, O.C.D. and Otilio Rodriguez, O.C.D. (Mahwah, NJ: Paulist, 1979), p. 96.

5. Dallas Willard, *The Spirit of the Disciplines: Understanding How God Changes Lives* (San Francisco: Harper, 1988), pp. 18, 22, 23.

6. *Ibid.*, pp. 32, 36.

7. Thomas Keating, O.C.S.C., *Open Mind, Open Heart* (Amity, New York: Amity House, 1986), p. 72.

8. Teresa of Avila, *Interior Castle*, p. 93.

9. Willard, *The Spirit of the Disciplines*, pp. 234, 235.

10. I am indebted in this section to Maggie Ross' *The Fountain and the Furnace* (Mahwah, N.J.: Paulist, 1987) for its rich development of a theology of kenosis.

11. Richard J. Foster, *Celebration of Discipline* (San Francisco: Harper and Row, 1978), pp. 6–9.

12. Dermot A. Lane, *Christ at the Centre* (Mahwah, NJ: Paulist Press, 1991), pp. 60–62.

13. John of the Cross, "The Ascent of Mount Carmel," Book II, chap. 5, paragraphs 6–8, in *The Collected Works of St. John of the Cross*, trans. Kieran Kavanaugh, O.C.D. and Otilio Rodriguez, O.C.D. (Washington, DC: Institute of Carmelite Studies, 1979), pp. 117–118.

14. Willard, *The Spirit of the Disciplines*, pp. 44–47.

15. David Grandfield, *Heightened Consciousness: The Mystical Difference* (Mahwah, NJ: Paulist, 1991), p. 147.

16. Joseph Cardinal Ratzinger, "Letter to bishops of the Catholic Church on some aspects of Christian meditation," in *L'Osservatore Romano*, 2 January, 1990, pp. 8–10, 12.

17. Ama Samy, S.J., "Can a Christian Practice Zen, Yoga, or TM?" in *Review for Religious*, vol. 50, no. 4 (July/August, 1991), p. 542.

18. Evelyn Underhill, *The Spiritual Life* (London: Mowbray, 1984), pp. 32–35.

2. FRIENDSHIP AND FAMILY LIFE

1. Dean Ornish, M.D., *Program for Reversing Heart Disease* (New York: Random House, 1990), pp. 87–92.

2. Thomas Ryan, C.S.P., "Family Life: A School for Holiness," *Our Family* (vol. 36, no. 8, September, 1985), pp. 26–27.

3. Thomas Ryan, C.S.P., "Father Without Children," *Marriage and Family Living* (Vol. 69, No 9, September, 1987), pp. 12–13.

4. Marguerite Michaels and James Widwerth, "How America Has Run Out of Time," *Time* (April 24, 1989), pp. 58–67.

5. *Ibid.*, p. 58.

6. George Barna, *The Frog in the Kettle: What Christians Need To Know About Life in the Year 2000* (Ventura, Calif: Regal Books, 1990), pp. 69–70.

7. *Ibid.*, pp. 78–79.

8. *Ibid.*, p. 75.

9. See William Hart, *The Art of Living: Vipassana Meditation* (New York: Harper and Row, 1987).

10. *Sutta Nipāta*, II.4, as quoted in *The Art of Living*, p. 125.

11. Anthony de Mello, *The Song of the Bird* (Garden City, NY: Doubleday Image, 1982), p. 94.

12. John of the Cross, "The Spiritual Canticle," stanza 11, par. 10, in *The Collected Works of St. John of the Cross*, Kieran Kavanaugh, O.C.D., and Otilio Rodriguez, O.C.D., translators (Washington, DC: Institute of Carmelite Studies, 1979), p. 451.

13. John of the Cross, "The Ascent of Mount Carmel," Book I chapter 13, par. 11, *ibid.*, pp. 103–104.

14. See Meister Eckhart: *The Essential Sermons, Commentaries, Treatises and Defense*, Edmund Colledge, O.S.A., trans. (Mahwah, NJ: Paulist, 1981), and *Meister Eckhart: Teacher and Preacher*, Bernard McGinn, ed. (Mahwah, NJ: Paulist, 1986).

15. Cyprian Smith, *The Way of Paradox: The Spiritual Life as Taught by Meister Eckhart* (London: Darton, Longman, Todd, 1987), p. 111.

16. See "A Theology of the Paschal Mystery," in *Christ at the Center* (Mahwah, NJ: Paulist, 1991), pp. 103–129.

3. LIVING WITH A SABBATH RHYTHM

1. Gordon Dahl, *Work, Play and Worship in a Leisure-Oriented Society* (Augsburg, 1972), pp. 31ff.

2. George Barna, *The Frog in the Kettle: What Christians Need to Know About Life in the Year 2000* (Ventura, Calif: Regal Books, 1990), pp. 84–87.

3. Martin C. Helldorfer, *The Work Trap* (Whitinsville, MA: Affirmation Books, 1981), pp. 15, 31.

4. James D. Whitehead, "An Asceticism of Time," *Review for Religious* (vol. 39, no. 1, January, 1980), p. 11.

5. *Ibid.*, pp. 12–13.

6. *Ibid.*, p. 4.

7. *Ibid.*, pp. 8–11.

8. Abraham Joshua Heschel, *The Sabbath: Its Meaning for Modern Man* (New York: The Noonday Press, 1951).

9. *Ibid.*, p. 73.

10. Leonard Doohan, *Leisure: A Spiritual Need* (Notre Dame, IN: Ave Maria Press, 1990), pp. 37–44.

11. Heschel, *The Sabbath*, pp. 14, 22.

12. *Ibid.*, pp. 13–24.

13. *Ibid.*, p. 41.

14. *Ibid.*, pp. 53, 54, 60, 68.

15. Doohan, *Leisure: A Spiritual Need*, pp. 48, 49.

16. Eugene H. Peterson, "Confessions of a Former Sabbath Breaker," *Desert Call* (Summer, 1989), pp. 19, 20.

17. Doohan, *Leisure: A Spiritual Need*, p. 47.

18. Monks and Friars of the Nova Nada Community, "A Perfectly Regular Day," *Desert Call* (Winter, 1988), pp. 16–19.

19. Tilden Edwards, *Sabbath Time* (San Francisco, CA: Winston-Seabury, 1984), pp. 41, 42.

20. Gertrude M. Nelson, "Keeping Sunday," *New Catholic World* (March-April, 1987), p. 58.

21. William Derby, "Sabbath Time Rhythm," *Montreal Churchman* (March, 1990), p. 2.

22. Nelson, "Keeping Sunday," pp. 57, 59.

23. Gabe Huck, *Table Prayer* (Chicago: Liturgy Training Publications, 1980), p. 25.

24. Edward Hays, *Prayers for the Domestic Church* (Easton, Kansas: Forest of Peace Books, 1979), pp. 112–113.

4. EXERCISE AND PLAY

1. John L. McKenzie, SJ, *Dictionary of the Bible* (New York: Macmillan, 1965), pp. 836–837.

2. Khursid Ahmad, ed., *Islam: Its Meaning and Its Message* (London: The Islamic Council of Europe, 1975), pp. 123–124.

3. As quoted in Thomas Ryan C.S.P. *Wellness, Spirituality and Sports* (Mahwah, NJ: Paulist, 1986), p. 13.

4. John Carmody, "Exercise," *New Catholic World* (July/August, 1986), pp. 150–151.

5. David Steindl-Rast, O.S.B. *Gratitude, the Heart of Prayer* (Paulist, 1984), p. 40.

6. *Ibid.*, pp. 40–41.

7. *Ibid.*, pp. 39–59.

8. Francis Bauer, O.F.M., *Life in Abundance: A Contemporary Spirituality* (Mahwah NJ: Paulist, 1983), pp. 84–85.

9. John Carmody, *Holistic Spirituality* (Paulist, 1983), pp. 77–78.

10. George Leonard, *The Ultimate Athlete* (Avon, 1974), pp. 287–288.

11. The American College of Sports Medicine also currently uses a different, more complicated calculation method called the Karvonen Equation which takes into account your resting heart rate. To calculate the low end of your target range: training heart rate = [(maximum heart rate − resting heart rate) × (0.60)] + resting heart rate. To calculate the upper end of your target range, multiply by 0.85 instead of by 0.60. If you have known heart disease or are on any heart medications, then these formulae may not be appropriate for you. Consult your physician to help you determine your appropriate heart rates.

12. Dr. Jean Mayer, "Physical Activity," in *Weight Management: A Summary of Current Theory and Practice* (Lifesteps Program, National Dairy Council, 1985), p. 16.

13. Wayne Westcott, M.D., "You *Can* Sell Exercise for Weight Loss," *Fitness Management* (November, 1991), p. 33.

14. *Ibid.*

15. "The Recommended Quality and Quantity of Exercise for Developing and Maintaining Cardiorespiratory and Muscular Fitness in Healthy Adults," The American College of Sports Medicine Exercise Guidelines, 1990, in *Medicine and Science in Sports and Exercise* (April, 1990), p. 53.

16. Mayer, "Physical Activity," p. 13.

17. David Sharp, "The Energy Dividend," in *St. Louis Post-Dispatch*, September 28, 1991, section D, p. 1.

18. Dean Ornish, M.D., *Program for Reversing Heart Disease* (New York: Random House, 1990), pp. 327–328.

19. *Ibid.*, pp. 324, 325, 329.

20. *Horace Bushnell: Sermons*, Conrad Cherry, ed., *Sources of American Spirituality* (Mahwah, NJ: Paulist, 1989), pp. 73–74.

21. Peter Berger, A *Rumor of Angels* (Anchor Books, 1970), p. 59.

22. James D. Whitehead, "An Asceticism of Time," *Review for Religious*, vol. 39, no. 1 (January, 1980), pp. 16–17.

23. Eugen Herrigel, *Art of Archery* (Pantheon Books, 1953).

24. Heinrich Dumoulin, "Spiritualité et mystique bouddhistes," *Bulletin, Secretariatus pro non Christianis* (vol; 18, no. 3, 1971), pp. 151–152.

25. John Neulinger, *To Leisure: An Introduction* (Boston: Allyn and Bacon, Inc., 1981), p. 31.

26. Hans Lenk, "Sport Between Zen and the Self," *Concilium* 205 (October, 1989), p. 130.

5. PRAYERFUL PRESENCE

1. Anthony de Mello, S.J., *The Song of the Bird* (New York: Image Books, 1984), pp. 14–15.

2. William McNamara, O.C.D., *The Human Adventure: The Art of Contemplative Living* (Warwick, NY: Amity House, 1974), chapters one and two.

3. de Mello, *The Song of the Bird*, p. 112.

4. Ruth Burrows, *Ascent to Love: The Spiritual Teaching of St. John of the Cross* (London: Darton, Longman, and Todd, 1987) p. 75.

5. William R. Callahan, *Noisy Contemplation* (Quixote Center, P.O. 5206, Hyattsville, MD, 1983).

6. Tessa Bielecki, O.C.D., "Not Enough Time," in *Speaking of Silence: Christians and Buddhists on the Contemplative Way* (Mahwah, NJ: Paulist, 1991), p. 292.

7. Brother Lawrence of the Resurrection, *The Practice of the Presence of God*, trans. John J. Delaney (Garden City, NY: Image Books, 1977).

8. John J. Delaney, "Introduction," *ibid.*, pp. 26–28.

9. Henri J.M. Nouwen, "Foreword," *ibid.*, p. 12.

10. Brother Lawrence, *ibid.*, pp. 47, 49.

11. *Ibid.*, p. 68.

12. *Ibid.*, p. 60.

13. Catherine de Hueck Doherty, *Poustinia: Christian Spirituality of the East for Western Man* (Notre Dame, IN: Ave Maria Press, 1974).

14. *Ibid.*, p. 74.

15. *Ibid.*, pp. 38, 54, 55, 83.

16. *Ibid.*, pp. 72–73.

17. de Mello, *The Song of the Bird*, p. 20.

18. Thich Nhat Hanh, *The Miracle of Mindfulness* (Boston: Beacon Press, 1975), p. 8.

19. As quoted in David Steindl-Rast, *The Listening Heart* (New York: Crossroad, 1983), p. 83.

20. Martin Helldorfer, *The Work Trap* (Whitinsville, MA: Affirmation Books, 1981), p. 49.

21. Eido Roshi, "Doing Nothing," in *Speaking of Silence*, p. 221.

22. Leonard J. Biallas, *World Religions: A Story Approach* (Mystic, CT: Twenty-Third Publications, 1991), pp. 252–254.

23. Joan Chittister, O.S.B., *Wisdom Distilled From the Daily: Living the Rule of St. Benedict Today* (New York: Harper, San Francisco, 1991), p. 103.

24. Thich Nhat Hanh, *Being Peace* (Berkeley, CA: Parallax Press, 1987), pp. 110, 111.

25. See Thich Nhat Hanh's *Walking Meditation* (Nyack, NY: Fellowship Publications, 1985), for more detailed treatment of different variations.

26. Nhat Hanh, *The Miracle of Mindfulness*, pp. 27–30.

27. As quoted from his book *The Well and the Shadows* in Bob Wild's, "Unpacking: The Case for More Solitude," *Catholic New Times* (September 28, 1986), p. 9.

28. *Ibid.*

29. Tilden Edwards, *Living in the Presence* (New York: Harper, San Francisco, 1987), pp. 75–76.

30. Steindl-Rast, *Listening Heart*, p. 24.

31. Thomas Keating, O.C.S.O., *Open Mind, Open Heart: The Contemplative Dimension of the Gospel* (Amity, NY: Amity House, 1986), p. 66.

32. Henry David Thoreau, *Walden and Other Writings*, ed. Joseph Wood Krutsch (New York: Bantam, 1962), p. 366.

33. de Hueck Doherty, *Poustinia*, pp. 21–22.

34. Steindl-Rast, *Listening Heart*, p. 21.

6. FASTING

1. National Liturgical Office of the Canadian Conference of Catholic Bishops, "Living Lent" (leaflet), 1986.

2. U.S. National Conference of Catholic Bishops, "Pastoral Statement on Penance and Abstinence," November 18, 1966.

3. Canadian Conference of Catholic Bishops' Implementation of the 1983 Code of Canon Law, "Decree no. 8: Fast and Abstinence," May 14, 1985.

4. Joseph F. Wimmer, O.S.A., "When You Fast . . . : A Biblical and Patristic Survey," *New Catholic World* (March/April, 1988), p. 63.

5. Bishop J. Robert Jacobson, in a letter to the Alberta North Synod of the Evangelical Lutheran Church of Canada, April 22, 1987, p. 2.

6. Therese-Anne Druart, "There is no god but God . . ." *New Catholic World* (November/December, 1988), pp. 264–266.

7. Tilden Edwards, *Living in the Presence* (San Francisco: Harper, 1987), pp. 31–32.

8. For more information concerning three-to-five day fasts, see Thomas Ryan, *Fasting Rediscovered: A Guide to Health and Wholeness for Your Body-Spirit* (Mahwah, NJ: Paulist, 1981), pp. 95–97.

9. *The Bhagavad Gita*, Eknath Easwaran, trans. (Berkeley, Cal.: The Blue Mountain Center of Meditation, 1985), chapter 6, vv. 16–18, p. 106.

10. *The Gospel of Buddha*, ed. Paul Carus (Madras, India: Samata Books, 1987), p. 40.

11. Wimmer, "When You Fast . . ." p. 65.

7. SERVICE

1. See George Barna, *The Frog in the Kettle: What Christians Need To Know About Life in the Year 2000* (Ventura, CA: Regal Books, 1990), pp. 111–127.

2. Denise Lardner Carmody and John Tully Carmody, *Peace and Justice in the Scriptures of the World Religions* (Mahwah, NJ: Paulist, 1988), p. 134.

3. Pheme Perkins, *Love Commands in the New Testament* (Mahwah, NJ: Paulist, 1982), pp. 123–125.

4. See *Now Is the Time*, Final Document and other texts from the World Convocation on Justice, Peace and the Integrity of Creation in Seoul, Republic of Korea, 5–12 March, 1990 (JPIC Office, World Council of Churches, PO Box 1200, CH-1211, Geneva 2, Switzerland). See also *Vital Ecumenical Con-*

cerns, ed. Ans J. Van der Bent (Geneva: World Council of Churches, 1986), a compilation of selected official statements from WCC assemblies and Central Committee meetings and regional ecumenical bodies. A good biblical resource is Ulrich Duchrow and Gerhard Liedke, *Shalom: Biblical Perspectives on Creation, Justice and Peace* (Geneva: WCC Publications, 1989).

5. An excellent reference resource is *Proclaiming Justice and Peace. Documents from Rerum Novarum through Centesimus Annus*, eds. Michael Walsh and Brian Davies (Mystic, CT: Twenty-Third Publications, 1991).

6. 1971 Synod statement "Justice in the World," *ibid.*, p. 270.

7. Richard J. Hauser, *In His Spirit: A Guide to Today's Spirituality* (Mahwah, NJ: Paulist, 1982), pp. 102–103.

8. See *The Classics of Western Spirituality* series by Paulist Press.

9. Thomas Merton, *No Man Is an Island* (New York: Doubleday Image, 1955), p. 65.

10. Thomas Merton, *Contemplative Prayer* (New York: Doubleday Image, 1969), p. 115.

11. Teresa of Avila, *The Interior Castle*, trans. Kieran Kavanaugh, O.C.D. and Otilio Rodriguez, O.C.D (Mahwah, NJ: Paulist, 1979), pp. 100–101.

12. Evelyn Underhill, *Mysticism* (New York: New American Library Meridian, 1974), p. 172.

13. *Ibid.*, pp. 173–174.

14. Hauser, *In His Spirit*, p. 111.

15. Thomas Keating, O.C.S.C., "Called into Solitude," in *Speaking of Silence* (Mahwah, NJ: Paulist, 1987), pp. 274–275.

16. Carmody and Carmody, *Peace and Justice*, pp. 168–169.

17. Teresa of Avila, *The Interior Castle*, p. 192.

18. *Ibid.*, p. 70.

19. See Roger Mahoney, "The Eucharist and Social Justice,"

in *The Catholic Faith: A Reader* (Mahwah, NJ: Paulist, 1988), pp. 150–162, to which I am indebted here.

20. James E. Johnston, "Triduum Homilies," *Celebration*, vol. 15, no. 2 (February, 1986), p. 48.

21. *Baptism, Eucharist and Ministry*, Faith and Order Paper no. 111 (Geneva: World Council of Churches, 1982), p. 14.

22. Jim Molnar, "The Gift of Compassion," in *The Montreal Gazette*, Saturday, December 21, 1990, section I, pp. 1, 13.

23. See the discussion between Bro. David Steindl-Rast and Eido Roshi in *Speaking of Silence*, pp. 247–251.

24. Heinrich Doumoulin, "Spiritualité et mystique bouddhistes," *Bulletin, Secretariatus pro non Christianis* (vol. 18, no. 3, 1971), p. 152.

25. Carmody and Carmody, *Peace and Justice*, pp. 127–128.

26. *Ibid.*, pp. 168–172.

27. See his two volume commentary on *The Bhagavad Gita*, translation and introduction by Eknath Easwaran (Tomales, CA: Nilgiri Press, 1985), from which all my citations from the *Gita* are drawn.

28. As quoted in Easwaran's introduction, *ibid.*, p. 35.

29. See Timothy Flinders' appendix, "How Satyagraha Works," in Eknath Easwaran, *Gandhi the Man* (Petalume, CA: Nilgiri Press, 1972), pp. 149–172, of which I offer but a synopsis here. For a fuller exposition, see M.K. Gandhi, *Satyagraha in South Africa* (Greenleaf Books, 1979).

30. Underhill, *The Spiritual Life*, pp. 92–98.

8. THE VISION OF CHRISTIAN FAITH

1. M. Scott Peck, *The Road Less Traveled* (New York: Simon and Schuster, 1978), pp. 15–16.

2. For the stories and learnings of this year, see my *Tales of*

Christian Unity (Mahwah, NJ: Paulist, 1983) and chapter 5 on "Ecumenical Spirituality" in *A Survival Guide for Ecumenically Minded Christians* (Montreal: Novalis/Collegeville, MN: Liturgical Press, 1989).

3. Ken Wilber, *Grace and Grit* (Boston: Shambhala Publications, 1991), pp. 309–311.

4. In these reflections I am much indebted to John Tully Carmody and Denise Lardner Carmody's *Christian Uniqueness and Catholic Spirituality* (Mahwah, NJ: Paulist, 1990).

5. The Spiritual Canticle in *The Collected Works of St. John of the Cross*, trans. Kieran Kavanaugh, O.C.D. and Otilio Rodriguez, O.C.D. (Washington, DC: ICS Publications, 1979), stanza 22, no. 3, p. 497.

6. Teresa of Avila, *The Interior Castle*, trans. Kieran Kavanaugh, O.C.D. and Otilio Rodriguez, O.C.D. (Mahwah, NJ: Paulist, 1974), p. 130.

7. The Spiritual Canticle, *Collected Works*, stanza 39, no. 7, p. 559.

8. Ruth Burrows, *Ascent to Love: The Spiritual Teaching of St. John of the Cross* (London: Darton, Longman and Todd, 1987), p. 111.

9. David Granfield, *Heightened Consciousness: The Mystical Difference* (Mahwah, NJ: Paulist, 1991), pp. 148–149.

10. *Ibid.*, pp. 160–163.

11. Evelyn Underhill, *The Spiritual Life* (London: Mowbrays, 1990), pp. 122–123.

12. Edward Hays, *Prayers for the Domestic Church* (Topeka, KS: Hall Directory, Inc., 1979), p. 45, slightly adapted here.